VULNERABILITY TO PSYCHOSIS

VULNERABILITY TO PSYCHOSIS

A Psychoanalytic Study of the Nature and Therapy of the Psychotic State

Franco De Masi

KARNAC

Originally published 2006 in Italian as: *Vulnerabilità alla Psicosi* by Raffaello Cortina Editore, Milan.

First published in English in 2009 by
Karnac Books Ltd
118 Finchley Road, London NW3 5HT

British Library Cataloguing in Publication Data

A C.I.P. for this book is available from the British Library

ISBN: 978 1 85575 504 8

Translated by Philip Slotkin and others

Edited, designed and produced by The Studio Publishing Services Ltd,
www.publishingservicesuk.co.uk
e-mail: studio@publishingservicesuk.co.uk

www.karnacbooks.com

CONTENTS

*To my patients, who probably do not know
how much I have learnt from them.*

ACKNOWLEDGEMENTS

The Preface, Introduction, and Chapters One to Three were origi-
nally translated in draft form by the late Malcolm Garfield. Chap-
ters Four to Seven, Ten, and Twelve to Fifteen were translated by
Philip Slotkin. The original translator of Chapter Eight is unknown.
The first version of Chapter Eleven was translated by Harriet
Graham. A previous version of Chapter Nine, translated by Mary
Rubik, appeared in *Shared Experience: The Psychoanalytic Dialogue*,
L. Nissim Momigliano and A. Robutti (Eds.), published by Karnac
(1992). Earlier versions of Chapters Four, Five, Six, Eight, and
Eleven were published in the *International Journal of Psychoanalysis*.
All previously translated material has been edited by Philip Slotkin.
The permission of the relevant copyright holders to use this mater-
ial is gratefully acknowledged.

ABOUT THE AUTHOR

Franco De Masi is a training analyst of the Italian Psychoanalytical Society and former President of the Centro Milanese di Psicoanalisi and Secretary of the Training Institute of Milan. He is a medical doctor and a psychiatrist who has worked for many years in psychiatric hospitals. For the past thirty years he has been working as a full time psychoanalyst in Milan. He has published several papers in the *International Journal of Psychoanalysis* and in the *Rivista Italiana di Psicoanalisi*.

His main interests have been focused on the theoretical and technical psychoanalytical issues related to severely ill or psychotic patients. He has published five papers on this topic in the *International Journal of Psychoanalysis*. Some of these papers were reprinted in important international reviews and translated into Spanish, French, German, Portuguese and Romanian.

In addition, in the past few years he has published *Sadomasochistic Perversion: The Object and Theories* (Karnac, 2003), and *Making Death Thinkable: A Psychoanalytical Contribution to the Problem of the Transience of Life* (Free Association, 2004), as well as editing *Herbert Rosenfeld at Work: Italian Seminars* (Karnac, 2001).

PREFACE

"Since then analysts have never relaxed their efforts to come
to an understanding of the psychoses . . . they have managed, now in this place and now in that, to get a glimpse
beyond the wall. . . . It is true that in this sphere all our
knowledge is not yet converted into therapeutic power; but
the mere theoretical gain is not to be despised, and we may
be content to wait for its practical application"

(Freud, 1925d, pp. 60–61).

The title of this book might seem a little puzzling at first sight, since
the clinical term *psychosis* includes different disorders of varying
kinds and degrees of gravity. The two nosographic entities traditionally assigned to this category are manic–depressive psychosis
and schizophrenia.

In this volume, I use the term *psychotic state* to denote a pathological condition other than manic-depressive psychosis, whose
aetiology and pathogenesis were amply illustrated by Freud and
Abraham, and which allows the patient intervals in which he[1] can
function more or less as he did prior to its onset. The psychotic

state, on the other hand, accompanied as it is by delusions and hallucinations, has different origins and an outcome that can be described as "healing with a defect". As discussed more fully later, the psychotic nucleus, split off from consciousness, is present in attenuated form and continues to threaten the patient even in phases of apparent reintegration.

This book postulates that the trigger of the psychotic condition is located in the basic processes which structure the first emotional relations. Their early and prolonged distortion lays the foundations for an altered perception of internal psychic reality, which is dissociated and replaced by a fantasy world. From this viewpoint, it might appear that psychosis is no different from other forms of mental suffering whose roots can be traced back to infancy. However, this is not the case. The difference lies in the specific form of its development and the fact that the course of the disease involves intense pressure towards destruction of the emotional functions and cognitive processes.

In this volume I shall attempt to present some of the reasons why patients succumb to the attraction of a course doomed to result in the permanent derangement of their minds.

In its early days, psychoanalysis was hailed as a possible treatment for psychosis. Though Freud remained uncertain whether psychotic patients were analysable, he nevertheless encouraged and supported Abraham and Ferenczi, who had committed themselves to the treatment of this pathology. In Berlin in the 1920s, a group of analysts led by Abraham founded the Psychoanalytic Policlinic, which applied the psychoanalytic method to the treatment of a large number mental conditions, including psychotic disorders. Melanie Klein was among those working at the Policlinic, offering her services free of charge, and her experience with severely ill children led to important insights for the treatment of psychosis.

As we know, the hopes placed at that time in the treatment of psychosis gradually diminished, as clinical experience proved extremely arduous. A psychoanalyst who opts to work with psychotic patients cannot expect to sleep soundly at night, for such treatment calls for intense concentration, great skill, and much experience. The course of the illness is unpredictable, and the analyst is well aware of not yet possessing the appropriate tools for the job. After all, in treating a psychotic patient, we cannot refer to our personal analysis or to professional experience with other patients. We find ourselves in totally uncharted territory.

That is one reason why the treatment of such patients is rarely dealt with in the scientific debate or discussed among analysts, and why clinical contributions on this matter sometimes appear to avoid the fundamental issues.

In this book, I shall attempt to convey my ideas on the nature and analytic therapy of the psychotic state, ideas that have matured over the many years of my clinical practice. At the start of my career, when I worked in psychiatric institutions, it seemed to me that psychosis could be treated with medication and therapeutic interviews, but that its therapy was riven with uncertainty. I sometimes could not understand why a given patient had recovered from a psychotic crisis, or else I would be forced to accept that even a patient who had apparently been "cured" might suddenly need to be readmitted owing to an inexplicable relapse. A new attack might also take place after suspension of pharmacological therapy, even though the dose had been so small that it seemingly had no effect on the patient's psychic equilibrium. The suspension of drug treatment, which had manifestly been a highly effective means of warding off the disorder, prompted a new episode of decompensation.

After ceasing to work in the psychiatric unit twenty-five years ago and devoting myself entirely to the psychoanalytic profession, I hesitated a long time before taking on a psychotic patient or one who had had a psychotic episode. Despite my experience at university and in hospitals, my study of the psychoanalytic literature and my attendance at conferences, I felt helpless in the consulting room. It was, therefore, with great caution that I decided to undertake the analytic treatment of a psychotic patient. Even now, I believe that it is inadvisable to have more than one psychotic patient in treatment at a time.

My aim in this book is to contribute to our understanding of the specific difficulties encountered in the analytic treatment of psychosis. I hope that, by demonstrating the strengths and limits of our therapeutic capacity, this volume may go some way towards explaining the complex nature of the disease and open up new perspectives on this mysterious investigative field.

Some parts of this book have previously been published in the *International Journal of Psychoanalysis* and subsequently reproduced in other international psychoanalytic journals. The volume also brings together and highlights the extraordinary contributions to our knowledge of psychotic disorders made by a number of authors, and pays tribute to the many colleagues who came before us. It is they who first ventured to explore these most arduous regions of psychoanalysis, which await the arrival of further minds capable of taking up the challenge of what is still unknown.

FOREWORD

Franco De Masi is well known for his psychoanalytic work with patients suffering psychotic illnesses. In this book, De Masi addresses the human vulnerability to psychosis, but the modest title of his book belies the depth of its investigations and conclusions. De Masi invites the reader into a thoughtful, systematic exploration of many aspects of the complex problems associated with psychotic illness: its ontogenesis and the emotional crises that lead to the dominance of psychotic thinking, the function of psychosis with regard to reality, its eruption or progression (depending upon the type of psychosis involved) and, crucially, the difficult and painstaking task of treatment. This latter theme is explored in considerable detail by De Masi, and is perhaps the most telling message of this book. Example after example of his engagement with patients illuminates his central objective, the gradual disinvestment by the patient of psychic energy allocated to ostensibly protective, but ultimately self-destructive, psychotic constructions and a reinvestment in neurotic or more normal psychic reality: a world the patient largely has had to forsake under the sway of delusion.

We are all vulnerable to psychotic anxieties. This does not mean, of course, that we all become psychotic. In those individuals who, for constitutional, environmental, psychogenic, or other reasons, or a combination of these reasons, succumb to the tyranny of psychotic thinking, a special kind of catastrophe has occurred, and De Masi sets out to delineate the nature of the crisis and how he has approached it in his work. Although psychosis is a uniquely devastating experience that requires highly specialized help, there is a value to De Masi's contribution in that it demonstrates with clarity and down-to-earth honesty that there are no short cuts to treating psychotic illnesses. Delusional thinking and psychotic structures are complex and they infiltrate and dominate the mind with tenacity. It takes time, care, and enormous patience to unpick the webs so carefully spun in the deluded mind.

De Masi's realism is refreshing. Today, regrettably, we live in a tantalizing age of seemingly quick-fix solutions that impact on most aspects of life. The area of mental illness is not immune from this trend towards superficiality; throughout the western world we see "fast-food psychiatry" being deployed in hospitals where patients with psychosis are being treated. These patients may be offered examination or interview followed by pharmacological relief and thereafter swift discharge, with "the community" being charged with the care of their complex illness and their psychological and emotional needs. Too often, little or no attempt is made to understand the meaning of the patient's psychotic illness as it pertains to the individual's life course, its psychological origins, its emotional conflicts, and its dynamic and expressive forms. As a consequence, many patients remain unnecessarily impaired through a failure to be able to talk about their experiences in sufficient depth. This matter is made worse, and is more serious for future patients, as psychiatrists and other mental health workers are today less likely than in the past to be taught about these complex clinical facts and to know how to discuss them with patients. This can lead to "treatments" that amount to, at worst, little more than behavioural management tactics rather than serious, lasting therapeutic interventions designed to alleviate suffering and permit the development of insight and self-knowledge, thereby facilitating a gradual, progressive shift from psychotic ideation towards enduring, non-psychotic thinking. At best, the patient may be fortunate enough to receive sensitive pharmacological help and find a psychiatrist or psychoanalyst like De Masi, or a psychotherapist, or a nurse, who takes the necessary time to explore the condition with the patient. Sadly, this opportunity is becoming all too rare, and is often denied according to spurious arguments that such forms of engagement are uneconomical.

It is not as though psychiatry does not already possess the knowledge needed to offer patients an enduring, substantive improvement to their condition. Since Freud, psychoanalysts have amassed an impressive and growing understanding in depth of psychotic states and the mental processes that give rise to them (cf. Abraham, Fromm-Reichmann, Arieti, Pao, Searles, Bion, Ogden, Freeman, Segal, Rosenfeld, Rey, Jackson, and many others). Improvements in pharmacological treatments have been, despite their limitations, impressive in their effects and, judiciously applied, can reduce distress to a point where the patient may well become emotionally and intellectually available for engagement in a discussion around the meaning of his or her illness. Why do we not provide patients with such an integrated approach to their treatment, one that combines all these proven branches of know-ledge? It is as though western mental health services seem no longer able to face up to the size of the task and to provide com-mensurate care. Our postmodern world reifies speed, gratification, and efficiency. We tend to idealize the *chimaera* of rapid cure, even though the treatment of serious illnesses can take a great deal of time and effort by everyone involved, above all the patient. Because treatment of psychosis can be painfully slow and take a number of years, rather than weeks or months, a curious irony emerges from the post-modern fad of quick-fix thinking. The "magical" efficacy of high-speed treatments bears at times an odd resemblance to the instantaneous quality of delusional thinking in psychosis, which delivers omnipotent, all-purpose "solutions" to the patient's psy-chological difficulties. The danger in adopting a comparatively shallow outlook to the treatment of psychosis is that patients can be wittingly or unwittingly deceived into believing that their devas-tating condition is being taken as seriously as possible, when it is not. They are implicitly promised progress that cannot be delivered because we, the clinicians involved, have failed to address the psy-chotic state in sufficient depth. In so doing, we may even place patients at further risk of illness, marginalization, and stigmatiza-tion as a consequence of a treatment philosophy that is in part rooted in hopelessness, or else is justified on the grounds of "economic realism" while being purveyed as curative and comprehensive. This is an ethical dilemma that no one in the mental health arena can afford to ignore.

De Masi helps us to understand how things do not have to be this way in our approach to understanding and treating psychotic states. He does this without recourse to politics or the sociology of medicine, but through the painstaking elucidation of his patients' difficulties via the psychoanalytic work he undertakes with them. An experienced psychiatrist and psychoanalyst with many years' experience working in mental hospitals, De Masi understands the multi-disciplinary nature of the care needed by a patient with psychosis, but he emphasizes in *Vulnerability to Psychosis* the central and indispensable role of personal understanding by the clinician of the nature and meaning of the patient's particular illness and the lasting healing quality that this hard-won knowledge may provide. He conveys this method of understanding patients in a number of ways, the most important of which, in my view, is an observation that constitutes the heart of an attempt to help a person suffering from psychosis. This observation is that the nature and structure of mental processes that give rise to the earliest emotional relations of the life of the infant is the crucible from which the distortions of thinking in psychosis emerge. Unlike in neurosis, which also has its origins in early emotional relations, psychotic states are characterized by precocious and prolonged distortions of emotional and mental experiences which have the effect of altering the subject's perceptions of psychic reality to a point where a fantasy configuration of the world prevails over a more realistic grasp of subjective and objective circumstances. Once this fantasy configuration holds sway over the personality through the media of hallucination and delusion, psychosis's unique impact on the mind of the sufferer takes hold. This comprises an intensification of processes that seek to destroy normal emotional functioning, object-seeking impulses, and rational cognition, and which, if left unchecked, can dominate the mind of the patient, destroying the individual's humanity. De Masi provides a road map for dealing with this progressive violence to the patient's mind.

He begins by outlining various psychoanalytic models of psychosis from Freud onwards, including the work of Abraham,

Fenichel, Federn, Klein, Hartmann, Pao, Fairbairn, Winnicott, Bion, Lacan, and Aulagnier. This in itself is a helpful teaching chapter, tracing as it does the evolution of analytic understanding of psychosis over a century. Psychosis is seen in all these contributions as a primal malfunction deriving from early emotional difficulties in primary relationships and one that damages the symbolizing capacity of the ego. De Masi discusses processes of symbolization, mentalization and the constructions of pathological fantasies as they bear upon the emergence of delusion structures that displace reality. He then differentiates the primitive from the pathological and interrogates the confusion inherent in the longstanding idea that adult psychotic phenomena reflect childhood ideation, as though infants are "normally psychotic":

> I believe that the analogy between the primitive state and psychosis is unsustainable, since the psychotic state is very different from a child's fantasy life. Whereas psychosis is a subversion of thought that leads to the disintegration of the mind, the magic world of the infant is open to the unknown and makes for the construction of a personal meaning to be assigned to that world. In a word, the psyche of a normal child is vastly different from that of a psychotic adult. [p. 7]

Pursuing a more complex model, he addresses three different levels of distortion of reality that culminate in delusional structures: conscious, unconscious, and, finally, the delusion itself. He proposes that, notwithstanding the deployment of primitive defences in psychosis, there occurs the creation of psychopathological structures at various levels of mental functioning that have the effect of massively altering the perception of reality. These may be maintained in place by a variety of means—narcissism, perversion etc. The passage to psychosis is a type of journey into a progressively deepening, bizarre world that is self-generated and solipsistic. De Masi then proceeds to discuss the role of the unconscious in psychosis from a variety of perspectives, including by providing an overview of how major psychoanalytic thinkers have understood the role of the unconscious in psychosis. He sets out his understanding of the dynamic versus the emotional unconscious and how these bear on the evolution of delusional thought. The crucial role of the superego is discussed along with the pressures that lead to hallucination formation, including in analysis, and useful clinical examples are employed throughout to illustrate the ideas proposed.

Many of the problems associated with the analytic treatment of psychotic states are examined in this book. Temporary recovery, relapse and the return of psychosis, difficulties for the patient in maintaining equilibrium, and the power of the "primary delusional nucleus" are all discussed in ways that the clinician will find helpful technically as well as conceptually. In particular, the multiple vicissitudes of transference that are encountered in psychosis are looked at not least from the perspective of theory of technique, which will provide any serious clinician with insight into the pitfalls that treating psychosis entails. The relationship between intuitive and delusional thought is scrutinized, as is the distinction between the dream as a thought and the dream as a delusion, and the role of trauma in the aetiology of psychosis (other "points of entry" into psychosis are also identified in the book). One of the most interesting chapters looks at the progressive colonization of the patient's personality, sense of self, and, ultimately, identity under the progressive sway of delusional thinking. De Masi manages to convey with clarity the inexorable logic and power of growing delusions and how they can infiltrate almost every aspect of subjectivity, leading to pervasive disorientation and dehumanization.

This is a relatively small book, but one that is large in scope and substantial in content. It provides the clinician with important perspectives on the origins and development of delusions in psychosis and offers a new perspective regarding the radical differences between delusional and normal or neurotic thought, and how these differences come about. It moves our thinking forward in an area that has too often been neglected, and for this we need to be grateful.

Paul Williams
Belfast
March 2009

Introduction

"... analysis doesn't always come to an end in a tidy way—
all neatly parcelled up with a bow on top—but that it goes
on after the physical contact has finished, and ... perhaps
some of the most vital work is done then"

(Frances Tustin, from an interview with
Virginia Hunter [Hunter, 1994, p. 103])

In the preface to *Schizophrenic Disorders*, Pao (1979) points out that, in attempting the treatment of a psychotic patient, we must be prepared at any moment to accept the most painful disappointment a therapist can face: the breaking off of the treatment. Those concerned should therefore try to explain why working with such patients proves to be so frustrating, difficult, and indeed, often impossible. One obvious reason for such failures is that, notwithstanding decades of study and research, we still know very little about the nature of this disorder: all attempts, whether or not psychoanalytic, to treat psychosis are subject to similar difficulties. The psychotic state is still a mysterious world that no discipline has so far been able to explain convincingly.

Since we know virtually nothing about the origins of the emotions and the formation of thought (the unconscious operations which enable us to perceive psychic reality and relate to our fellows), we are also ignorant of the nature and specificity of the psychotic pathology in which these two functions are altered. It is, therefore, doubtful whether psychoanalytic theory today is in a position to explain psychosis, or even to come close to an adequate explanation. As psychoanalysts, we have not yet reached levels of depth and precision in either the theoretical or the clinical field that would enable us fully to comprehend other states of mental suffering. The theoretical hypotheses we use in our clinical work with neurotic patients concern mental attitudes and equilibria that are constant in time. They are totally different from the catastrophic changes and mental fragmentation observed in the psychotic process. For example, which specific mental states should we take as our reference when, during psychosis, the mind implodes and no longer contains thoughts?

When treating these patients, we meet with unknown difficulties of a kind never encountered in the treatment of other pathologies. To facilitate the understanding of such difficulties, I have deliberately chosen not to discuss the different clinical forms of the disease; this subject has been amply tackled by the psychiatric manuals which illustrate the various scenarios, from isolated delusional episodes to the development of full-blown schizophrenia. Rather, I have decided to concentrate on how psychotics enter into the delusional state and how they may emerge from it, in order to highlight the specific nature and qualities of psychotic transformation. Focusing on a restricted clinical area in fact leads to more fruitful observation.

In initial psychotic situations—those most often encountered by psychoanalysts—there are two main clinical configurations. The most frequent is when the patient has already had an attack, been hospitalized, received medication, and entered analysis in an attempt to overcome the condition. The second is that of a latent psychosis, concealed behind neurotic or borderline symptoms, which may develop into out-and-out psychosis in the course of analysis. In either case, we should not underestimate the enormous power of the psychotic nucleus, whether it has already exploded or is yet to do so.

The traditional advice is to work on psychotic states in the inter-vals between crises. This indication is to be found in the work of Abraham (1916) and concerns the treatment of patients suffering from manic-depressive psychosis. Abraham recommends working with patients in periods when they are well because, during an attack, patients are not in a position to understand the nature of their psychopathological state. They find it extremely hard to co-operate with the psychoanalyst because they lack the mental instru-ments for understanding psychic reality. That is the specific difficulty in the way of the treatment of psychotic states. The delu-sional imagination underlying the psychotic state prevents the use of intuitive thought, which enables us to understand and integrate psychic experiences.

A psychotic has *revelations* rather than thoughts about things; his mental state is analogous to that of a mystic who comes into con-tact with the divine. The study of mystical experience is useful for understanding the psychotic transformation: whereas the asceti-cism of the mystic permits a return to the normal state, psychosis goes beyond the mystical experience and a return to normality is far from easy.

None the less, even in lucid intervals when the capacity for thought has seemingly been restored, the psychotic matrix is still active and tends to recur. Even when not clinically manifest, delu-sion can re-emerge at any time.

One of the aims of analytic treatment is to help patients recover normal emotional–intuitive functioning (which, in fact, is never completely lost), thus enabling them to register and understand their own psychic reality and that of others. It should, however, be added that the onset of the delusional state is frequently preceded by signs or communications that are often understood only in ret-rospect. In this connection, I recall a supervision seminar held by Herbert Rosenfeld in Milan about twenty-five years ago. The ana-lyst presenting the case reported a dream in which the patient was surrounded by a swarm of bees that threatened him from all sides. The patient had no associations and the analyst remained silent. In the course of the supervision, the analyst also reported that during the session he was overcome with sleepiness, which prevented him from being mentally active. After the session, the patient had a psy-chotic episode and was admitted to hospital. Rosenfeld maintained in the seminar that through the dream the patient had described the psychotic episode that was about to engulf him (the swarm of bees trying to attack his head) and that the analyst could have understood the communication and made use of it. With hindsight, one can say that the patient had projected on to the analyst the same hypnotic state which the psychosis induced in him and that this projection was so powerful that it clouded the analyst's usual perception.

In analysis, we can often allow for the psychotic development, provided that we can understand the patient's communication. When, on the other hand, a psychotic crisis is already in progress, it is far more difficult to contain it. Psychosis projects itself into the patient's mind and invades his entire perceptual apparatus (the swarm of bees), turning him into an unwitting actor in a plot that overwhelms him with events that take place outside his awareness and independently of his will.

As I shall attempt to show in this volume, it is not possible to work analytically with a psychotic patient unless one has a specific theoretical approach to this mental state. My principal contention is that, alongside the dynamic unconscious, there exist mental processes that belong to the broader area of the *non-conscious*.

The classical conflict situations described by Freud concern the dynamic unconscious, in which love-related or aggressive wishes are repressed. The repressed wish continues to act unconsciously in conflict with other agencies and produces anxiety. Besides the dynamic unconscious, there exist other functions of which we are unaware and which *are unknowable*. For instance, we are unaware of the thought function: we can be conscious of the final result of thought, but we cannot know *how* we formulate our thoughts.

In my view, psychosis is the result of a disorder of the basal functions that belong not to the dynamic, but to the *emotional* unconscious. Distortion of the emotional processes occurring other than on the level of awareness, which predisposes to psychosis, takes place to varying degrees in other mental conditions, too, but only in psychosis is it extensive enough to trigger irreversible changes. I believe that the psychotic experience originates from a desperate perception of powerlessness, which from infancy on tends to impel the patient towards the subversion of the organizing functions of thought and affects. I postulate that the psychotic

solution is a successful attempt at destruction of the mental apparatus by means of an acquired ability to alter the organs of perception and thought, thus compromising the sense of reality and
transforming personal identity. In this way, psychosis annihilates
human relations and destroys the sense of awareness of self, of the
body and of the mind.

We may hypothesize that, at the very beginning of mental life,
something potentially self-destructive insinuates itself into the
areas devoted to the development of the capacity to think and to
perceive emotions. Many psychoanalytic studies have shown the
importance of the earliest affective responses of the baby's human
care-givers: in order to develop, the child needs the other's mind in
order to contain and confer meaning on his lived experience. A
child who grows up in an environment that does not provide adequate emotional responses cannot have the fundamental experiences necessary for understanding his relationship with the world
that surrounds him, and will consequently be unable to confer
meaning on his life.

If we listen to our patient analytically, it will be possible to discover the sometimes traumatic affective factors and experiences
that triggered the psychotic state, and to trace them back to the
infantile situation, which has never been worked through, that
underlies the patient's vulnerability to illness. The entry into the
psychotic state shows that the potentially vulnerable patient has
embarked on a course in which mental growth and development
are impossible. This is why the clinical onset of the disorder is preceded long in advance by the radical emotional break with psychic
reality.

Besides the distorted emotional response of adults, a fundamental step towards illness is taken when the child withdraws his
link with and interest in the world of human relations. To describe
the psychotic patient's isolation, Freud uses the term *autoerotism*,
which denotes a pathological process that he regards as a repetition
of a primitive form of development in which the newborn lives in
a state of withdrawal into the body. The term *autoerotism*, therefore,
describes both psychotic withdrawal and the objectless phase of
human development: i.e., the primitive phase when the child seemingly concentrates on his own bodily sensations and is ignorant
of the world around him. Freud's insight remains useful for

understanding certain aspects of the psychotic state, for example, when a patient, having totally detached himself from emotional reality, withdraws into his body and produces perceptions *ex novo*. Hallucinations originate in the body and are stimulated by bodily sensations.

Both in my personal experience and in supervision, I bear in mind that, in order successfully to analyse patients who have had a psychotic episode, particular attention must be paid to understanding the transformation that has taken place. Normally, patients try to disregard the catastrophic experience they have undergone by playing it down or dissociating themselves from it. Thus, they attempt a possible "cure" as if the psychosis had never occurred.

Clinical experience shows that the psychotic nucleus, though silent, tends to weave its web again and to crop up continually within the analytic process. The analyst must ask himself why the patient was compelled to embark on the path of psychotic transformation and must be aware of the circumstances that may cause it to recur. I believe that, in treating a patient who has had a breakdown, the analyst should trace the reasons for the attack back to the childhood situation which was never worked through and which underlay the patient's *vulnerability* to the psychotic solution.

The necessary condition for recovery from a psychotic breakdown and for ensuring that it does not occur again is a relationship with a therapist capable of understanding the specific nature of the psychotic process (how often do our patients tell us that we cannot understand them because we treat them only as neurotics!), as well as the establishment of a good situation of dependence. Anyone working with psychotic patients is well aware of the need for a different kind of analytic listening from that used with neurotic patients.

The approach advocated in this book does not entail changes in analytic technique in terms of the mental setting or the organizational structure of the treatment. Rather, it emphasizes the specificity of certain aspects of therapy and seeks to identify what must be analysed first and foremost. In the analytic treatment of the psychotic process, the transference as it is traditionally thought of—as a new edition of the past or as a projection of objects from the patient's internal world on to the analyst—has relatively little importance. What may instead arise is a psychotic transference or a transference psychosis. Although certainly not desirable, these two eventualities help us understand psychotic functioning and must be allowed for and adequately worked through.

While fully respecting the psychoanalytic method, my approach also takes account of the *biological basis* of psychosis and the complex relationship between the mind and the brain. Many psychiatric and neuroscientific studies have drawn attention to biological alterations in the brain occurring in the psychotic state. In my view, rather than a biological basis for psychosis, we should speak of *biological mediation* of the mental disorder: I contend that psychosis is a biopsychological transformational experience, a *psychosomatic disorder* in which the "mind" is capable of producing changes in its biological substrate. (The conception of psychosis as a psychosomatic disorder was advanced by Silvano Arieti (1955), albeit in different terms from mine. In his opinion, a psychotic patient's prolonged anxieties constitute stressors that can give rise to complex and profound organic changes.) The psychotic state is the equivalent of a self-induced drugged condition, through which the mind produces biochemical alterations in the soma (the brain). These changes in turn affect the perceptual apparatus, making it increasingly difficult to master or transform the disorder. That is why there is no alternative to the use of drugs to alleviate psychotic symptoms and to enlisting the help of psychiatric colleagues at certain particularly critical moments in the analysis of psychotic patients.

Psychosis clearly shows that, when the capacity for thought and emotional relations is built on insecure foundations, it is liable to destruction. In the past, the condition would frequently become chronic or worsen precisely because the importance of the therapeutic relationship was not realized and pharmacological treatments did not exist. While the use of psychopharmaceuticals does not bring about a real change in the psychopathological structure, it undoubtedly alleviates symptoms and controls the more devastating aspects of the illness. It is usual nowadays for patients who have had, or are at risk of, a psychotic episode to have already started drug therapy before entering analysis. When this is not the case, it is advisable to refer the patient to a psychiatric colleague with a grasp of the significance of the analytic experience. It will otherwise be far more difficult to do this later if and when a crisis occurs. In that case, the patient will strenuously resist recourse to a specialist, whom he sees as an outsider, and will feel abandoned by the analyst.

I am convinced that it is *mental and emotional facts that trigger the psychotic state*, which in turn gives rise to the observed biochemical changes. Psychoanalytic intervention proves indispensable for transforming the psychic and emotional factors that contribute to the causation of the biochemical changes. In this sense, psycho-analysis or analytically oriented psychotherapy not only constitutes an alternative and a supplement to medication, but also potentially offers patients a real way out of their pathology.

Only the concerted efforts of a great many psychoanalysts can, I believe, ensure the future further development of the psychoana-lytic theory of the psychoses. In my opinion, fresh progress will depend on the possibility of acquiring in-depth knowledge of the functioning of the areas of the mind responsible for thinking, dreaming, and the planning of our lives: that is, the areas severely damaged in the course of the psychotic state. Our research should also not shun comparison with that of other disciplines—especially the neurosciences—in which the non-conscious operations of the mind that underlie our psychic functioning are explored.

Note

1. Translator's note. For convenience the masculine form is used through-out this translation for both sexes.

The fantastic is generally speaking what carries a person into the infinite in such a way that it only leads him away from himself and thus prevents him from coming back to himself. When emotion becomes fantastic in this way, the self is simply more and more volatilized. [Søren Kierkegaard, 1849, p. 61]

If you ask me what psychoanalysis can do about psychosis, I must give you two contrasting answers: one is that psychoanalysis can really do little, and the other that it can and must do a great deal. [Paul C. Racamier, 1994]

CHAPTER ONE

Some psychoanalytic models of psychosis

"Analysts have to admit that where quantitatively massive upheavals of the personality are concerned, such as in the psychoses, the purely psychological methods by themselves are inadequate and the organic and chemical means have the advantage over them"

(A. Freud, 1968, p. 131)

The analytic model

Biological models postulate that psychosis stems from a genetic vulnerability that is expressed in structural or biochemical alterations of the central nervous system. By investigating the symptoms—manifestations of underlying organic changes—we can seek out and identify the biological defect that lies upstream of them.

According to psychological models, on the other hand, the symptoms are the expression of a psychic dynamic whose origins can be traced back to the patient's current or childhood relationships. The psychoanalytic view is that the reasons for mental disorders are unconscious; thus, psychoanalytic investigation is based on a general theory of psychopathology and follows an eminently individual path. Psychoanalytic theory itself stems from in-depth study of a small number of individual clinical cases, which, however, allowed the development of general theories of mental functioning. Based as it is on clinical experience, psychoanalysis proceeds through theories that are open to modification in time, with new paradigms replacing and supplementing earlier ones. In this respect, it is no different from other disciplines whose theories are subject to verification and change.

Although psychoanalytic theories may change, the method itself remains the same. The analyst thereby reconstructs the patient's infantile history and relationships with significant figures, identifies primal traumas, and seeks to understand the dynamics of the patient's mental suffering, starting from the first emotional experiences. It is, therefore, important, in the case of psychosis, for the psychoanalyst to have a valid theory for understanding the genesis and particularity of that state—a theory that accounts for the patient's vulnerability and differentiates it qualitatively from other psychopathological conditions.

The encounter between psychoanalysis and psychosis occurred very early on: many analytic intuitions stemmed from the observation of psychotic states or were used to explain them. For example, the theories of primary narcissism, autoerotism, and withdrawal of libido from the outside world owe their existence to the study of psychotic processes. Many characteristics of the unconscious, such as the primary process, timelessness, and the absence of contradiction, closely resemble those of psychosis, understood as an invasion of the ego by the unconscious. The idea of hallucinatory wish fulfilment in children is also based on this analogy.

In his description of the unconscious processes that underlie dream production, Freud uses psychotic phenomenology as his model. In *An Outline of Psycho-Analysis* (1940a [1938], p. 172), he writes that a dream is nothing but a minor psychosis that occurs every night: "A dream, then, is a psychosis, with all the absurdities, delusions and illusions of a psychosis . . . an alteration of mental life [that] can be undone and can give place to the normal function".

The earliest psychoanalytic theories linked psychological disorders to corresponding phases of infant development. According to such theories, mental disease corresponded to primitive modes of psychic functioning and there was an equivalence between the primitive and the pathological. Psychosis, too, was included in this hypothesis: Freud's view was that psychosis coincided with an autoerotic withdrawal and a regression to forms of primitive development.

Melanie Klein (1946) also believed that the impulses and anxieties underlying states of schizophrenic persecution corresponded to primitive functioning dominated by sadism and the death drive. In her opinion, the disposition to psychosis depended on primitive impulses and anxieties that were normally transformed in the course of infantile development. If this did not happen, the psychotic nuclei remained unmodified and were destined to emerge in adulthood. As I shall explain more fully later (Chapter Two), although the analogy between the primitive and the pathological has opened the way to stimulating research, it postulates equivalences which are difficult to uphold and might at times prove misleading.

Bion (1967), on the other hand, presented a model in which psychosis did not represent a return to primitive stages of development, but was rather the expression of an altered capacity to think: the disorder concerned the functions which transformed sensory perceptions into thoughts. For this reason, the patient was unable to work through the events of his mental life on the symbolic level.

Continuity-based and discontinuity-based models

In the analytic theory of the psychotic state, explanatory models based on continuity and on discontinuity exist side by side. *Continuity-based* models present the development of psychosis as the outcome of the operation of mechanisms that are also active in normal development and in the neuroses, whereas *discontinuity-based* models regard psychosis as a radical breakdown of the normal functions of thought and emotionality, these being replaced by mental processes that are totally different and of which little is known (London, 1973).

Continuity-based models, which can also be termed *unitary*, seek to maintain the connection between the analytic theories of psychosis and neurosis, respectively. They tend to interpret psychotic behaviour as unconsciously stemming from intrapsychic conflicts similar in nature to those of neurotic patients. Discontinuity-based theories, on the other hand, are *specific*, postulating as they do that psychosis is a distinct disorder. I shall now give a somewhat partial summary of the development of psychoanalytic thought on psychosis, mentioning the theories that I consider most important. I shall not describe here the development of analytic technique in the treatment of psychotic states, an exhaustive account of which can be found in Rosenfeld (1969).

Sigmund Freud

In Freud's writings, it is possible to find both a unitary theory and a specific theory of psychosis. At times, he explicitly states that the interpretation of psychosis does not differ substantially from that of neurosis:

> The psycho-analyst, in the light of his knowledge of the psychoneuroses, approaches the subject with a suspicion that even thought-structures so extraordinary as these and so remote from our common modes of thinking are nevertheless derived from the most general and comprehensible impulses of the human mind; and he would be glad to discover the motives of such a transformation as well as the manner in which it has been accomplished. [Freud, 1911c, p. 17]

Again:

> The same research workers who have done most to deepen analytic knowledge of the neuroses, such as Karl Abraham in Berlin and Sándor Ferenczi in Budapest (to name only the most prominent), have also played a leading part in throwing analytic light on the psychoses. The conviction of the unity and intimate connection of all the disorders that present themselves as neurotic and psychotic phenomena is becoming more and more firmly established despite all the efforts of the psychiatrists. [Freud, 1924f, p. 204]

Freud describes the mechanism of projection as the externaliza-tion of an intrapsychic conflict into external reality. Thus, for exam-ple, Senatspräsident Schreber's mental illness resulted from a homosexual conflict which manifested itself in the following sequence: intrapsychic conflict, anxiety, projection on to the outside world, and regression to an earlier stage of fixation. On the scale of phases of psychosexual development, in which the more severe disorders lie on the more primitive levels and the mildest higher up, schizophrenic psychosis occupies the lowest level, that of auto-erotism. While these Freudian concepts may appear somewhat simplistic today, nevertheless they contain extraordinary insights, considering when they were formulated.

Psychotic withdrawal and the expansion of the delusional world do indeed correspond to the libidinal decathexis described by Freud. In neurosis, it is repression that produces the symptom; in psychosis, on the other hand, it is libidinal decathexis that leads to a withdrawal from reality and induces regression to the auto-erotic stage.

Elsewhere, however, Freud distinguishes between neurosis and psychosis and outlines a specific theory of the latter. He writes as follows to Abraham on 21 December 1914:

> I recently discovered a characteristic of both systems, the conscious (cs) and the unconscious (ucs), which makes both almost intelligi-ble and, I think, provides a simple solution of the problem of the relationship of dementia praecox to reality. All the cathexes of things form the system ucs, while the system cs corresponds to the linking of these unconscious representations with the word repre-sentations by way of which they may achieve entry into conscious-ness. Repression in the transference neuroses consists in the withdrawal of libido from the system cs, that is, in the dissociation of the thing and word representations, while repression in the narcissistic neuroses consists in the withdrawal of libido from the unconscious thing representations, which is of course a far deeper disturbance. [Freud & Abraham, 1965, p. 206]

From this point of view, Freud characterizes psychosis as an *internal catastrophe* resulting from the withdrawal of libido, a loss which leads the patient to decathect the mental representation of the object, and, consequently, of his link with the world. The catastrophe is followed by a recathexis of libido, which corresponds to an attempt at reconstruction.

In two other important works, Freud (1915e, 1917d) again hypothesizes that psychosis is specific in nature. Taking as his starting point the difference between *thing presentations* and *word presentations*, Freud suggests that in schizophrenia it is *words* that enter into the so-called primary process. Having decathected both the thing presentation and the word presentation, schizophrenics attempt to recover by setting "off on a path that leads to the object via the verbal part of it, but then find themselves obliged to be content with words instead of things" (1915e, pp. 203–204). In this way the psychotic treats words, which are condensed and involve substitutions, as if they were things. These insights of Freud are, in my view, still useful for understanding how words and word associations have the power concretely to potentiate the delusional imagination.

Freud (1924f) writes that under normal conditions the ego is governed by the *reality principle*. In neurosis, relations with reality are maintained as a result of drive repression, whereas in psychosis they are lost because a more radical mechanism, which may be called *disavowal*, is at work (Freud, 1924e). In psychosis, it is not the drive that is repressed, as in neurosis, but the perception of external reality: the psychotic patient obliterates the mental representation of the object. When reality is annihilated because the id triumphs over the reality principle, the ego must find something to replace the lost reality. Delusion then represents an attempt at healing and at the reorganization of reality.

Freud emphasizes on a number of occasions that the alteration produced by psychosis concerns the ego and not the relationship between the three psychic agencies (ego, id, and superego), as occurs in neurosis. In "Fetishism" (1927e), Freud describes the mechanism of *splitting*, which gives rise to an irreducible alteration of the ego and enables two contradictory thoughts to coexist. On the colonizing power of psychosis, he writes:

> They [the pathological phenomena] are insufficiently or not at all influenced by external reality, pay no attention to it or to its psychical representatives, so that they may easily come into active opposition to both of them. They are, one might say, a State within a

State, an inaccessible party, with which co-operation is impossible, but which may succeed in overcoming what is known as the normal party and forcing it into its service. If this happens, it implies a domination by an internal psychical reality over the reality of the external world and the path to a psychosis lies open. [Freud, 1940a (1938), p. 76]

Freud's thoughts on the treatment of psychosis and its outcomes varied greatly over time. He sometimes had recourse to a psychoanalytic model to explain the patient's symptoms, for example in the case of Schreber, yet he also declared that analytic treatment was unsuitable for psychotic patients.

To sum up, Freud neither delved systematically into the clinical aspect of the analytic therapy of psychosis nor described any treatments of psychotic patients. However, he expressed his confidence on various occasions, praising colleagues, such as Abraham and Ferenczi, who undertook such work. For the rest of his life, Freud remained undecided between, on the one hand, a pessimistic view stemming from psychotic patients' observed inability to develop a transference, and, on the other, the more optimistic notion that effective therapy would become available one day. Freud held that the difficulties of treating psychotic patients derived from their narcissistic entrenchment and the consequent denial of dependence on the object.

Rosenfeld (1969) rightly remarks that there was always a dichotomy between the theoretical and clinical levels in Freud. Despite having formulated the concept of the splitting of the ego into a normal part and a psychotic part, Freud did not use this insight in treatment. Neither did he postulate the existence of a conflict between the sick and healthy parts, nor between libidinal and destructive aspects, even though he had identified this in the theory of the life and death drives.

Karl Abraham

Karl Abraham was the first psychoanalyst after Freud to shed light on the genesis of psychotic disorders. Abraham's attempts to understand psychosis (dementia praecox) date from his time at the hospital in Zurich. When he moved to Berlin, his interest shifted to manic–depressive psychosis. I have shown elsewhere (De Masi, 2002) why Abraham was unable to pursue his interest in psychotic patients further after moving to Berlin.

At the Salzburg Congress in 1908, he presented an important paper, entitled 'The psychosexual differences between hysteria and dementia praecox', in which he linked the disease in adults to the vicissitudes of infantile development. This was the first attempt to apply the psychosexual theory to psychotic disorders. Abraham saw in psychotic patients a total break with reality and a complete inability to transfer libido on to external objects.

Whereas hysterical patients were excessively attached to one of their parents, their psychotic counterparts (or rather those suffering from dementia praecox as defined by Kraepelin) showed indifference or hostility towards them. Abraham postulated that the main feature of psychosis was the absence of libidinal cathexis of objects and that object libido, recathected in the ego, was a source of megalomania.

Another interesting observation by Abraham was that the mechanism of repression was lacking in psychotic patients. Consequently, their behaviour was concrete and characterized by exhibitionistic, eroticized, or regressive–faecal acting-out. Moreover, dementia praecox coincided with a regression to the infantile autoerotic stage. A few years later, in his famous contribution on schizophrenia, Bleuler (1911) introduced the concept of autism, which is similar to Freud's and Abraham's description of autoerotism. The correspondence between Abraham and Freud includes some joking references to the fact that Bleuler had borrowed the concept of autism from that of autoerotism. Yet, it should be remembered that the concept of autoerotism was formulated by Freud; it first appears in his letter to Fliess of 9 December 1899 (Freud, 1985, p. 390). Freud stated then that autoerotism constituted the primitive state of sexuality, which could reappear in paranoia.

Whereas delusions of grandeur could be traced back to the afflux of libido to the ego, those of persecution resulted from the patient's terror of the outside world, which became threatening and inhuman. Dementia, Abraham noted, concerned the patient's emotions, which were distorted or blocked, and not his intellectual performance, which could remain intact.

Otto Fenichel

Fenichel (1945) classified psychosis in accordance with the psycho-sexual model. Although neurosis and psychosis both had infantile sexual impulses as their precipitating factor, their defence mechanisms were different. Unlike neurotics, psychotic patients used a very archaic defence, withdrawal from reality, which caused them to regress to primary narcissism, where no distinction existed between ego and id. The regressive collapse of the ego also led to the abolition of the differentiations acquired in the course of psychic development. Psychosis began with regressive symptoms followed by symptoms of restitution, such as hallucinations and delusions, which constituted an attempt to reconstruct reality after the break with the outside world. Fenichel was convinced that the analytic treatment of psychosis was effective because narcissistic regression was never complete.

Melanie Klein

In Klein's view, psychotic disorders had their origins in the initial period at the breast, when primitive anxieties were at their height. Taking Abraham's conception of the oral–sadistic phase as her starting point, Klein (1929) maintained that psychotic patients were imprisoned in their disease owing to an excess of primary sadism. Another contributory factor was excessive primitive anxiety (basically, the fear of being annihilated, poisoned, or devoured), and the consequent defences against persecution (Klein, 1930a). Under the pressure of the twofold threat of the persecutory external object and the patient's own sadistic impulses, the primitive ego, lacking cohesion and stability, tended to fragment. Whereas, in normal development, states of disintegration were temporary because good experiences were able to revive the internalized breast and to neutralize terrifying experiences, this disintegration became irreversible in the development of psychosis (Klein, 1946).

The primitive ego's main defences against psychotic anxiety were the disavowal of internal and external reality, idealization, and splitting of the object. The splitting concerned not only the object, but also the primitive ego, and led to the impoverishment and dispersion of parts of the personality.

Melanie Klein (1929) shared Freud's view (1911c) concerning the fixation of psychosis at the point of transition from autoerotism to object love. In the paranoid–schizoid position, the ego did its best to confront the threat of annihilation using the primitive defences available to a child at this early stage of development. (The analytic literature includes many references to "psychotic parts", "psychotic defences", "autistic nuclei", or structures that function "psychotically" in neurotic patients. These "psychotic" areas of functioning are plainly different from the clinical manifestations of the psychotic state.)

These defences, such as expulsion, disavowal, flight towards the good object, and splitting of the object, were useful in the first phase of growth for structuring the internal world, but were pathological when they persisted excessively in adult life. The same applied to the defences observed in other types of disorder, such as mania, omnipotence, and triumph over, and contemptuous control of, the object, which served to combat depressive–persecutory anxiety.

The primitive defences described by Melanie Klein are psychotic and differ from those in Freud's accounts of neurosis. However, it is important to note that Klein was referring to psychotic-type defence mechanisms and not to psychotic states or disorders. This difference does not always emerge clearly: Klein believed that early defences were psychotic defences. The primitive anxiety an infant had to face was also similar in character and intensity to psychotic anxiety. Again, Klein held that the infantile neurosis identified by Freud corresponded to the working through of primitive psychotic anxieties. When a child was dominated by psychotic anxiety, his attack on the persecutors increased the intensity of his anxiety: his aggressive and homicidal fantasies towards his parents, perceived as persecutory superego entities, increased the level of persecution felt to be emanating from them. This crescendo of aggression and fear formed the basis of psychotic-type anxiety.

The specifically psychotic defence mechanism was projective identification (Klein, 1946): i.e., the projection of destructive and aggressive parts of the self on to an external object. The term "projective identification" came to denote a particular form of identification that established the prototype of an aggressive object relationship. This mechanism, which was closely linked to the paranoid–schizoid position, comprised a projection in fantasy of split-off parts into the mother's body, so as to control the mother from inside. Such fantasies were the source of anxieties such as that of being imprisoned and persecuted within the mother's body.

In psychosis, this mechanism led to the confusion of self and object, and of the internal and external worlds. Since emotions and parts of the self were expelled into other people, areas of emotional void formed in the internal world. When projective identification was massive and prolonged, it became difficult to re-own the projected parts.

The sense of deadness experienced by these patients stemmed precisely from the loss of important parts of the self, the emptying of their emotional world coinciding with psychic death. In its original formulation, projective identification was the omnipotent fantasy of expelling parts of one's personality into an object. The subject thereby perceived himself as bound in a persecutory manner to the object of the projection. (Bion [1967] was later to distinguish between the non-psychotic and the psychotic use of primitive mechanisms, and described the child's use of projective identification for the purposes of communication.)

Klein's model, which traced the disorder's origins back to primitive anxiety and the relevant defences, can be described as *continuity-based*, since psychotic pathology was held to correspond to primitive forms of organization (in particular, schizophrenia was attributed to failure to overcome the paranoid–schizoid position). Her theoretical insights encouraged the application, in the psychoanalytic treatment of psychotic states, of a setting identical to that used for neurotic conditions. Rosenfeld, one of the pioneers of the analytic therapy of psychosis, wrote:

> In our approach to schizophrenia we retain the essential features of psychoanalysis: namely, detailed interpretations of the positive and negative transference without the use of reassurance or educative measures; the recognition and interpretation of the patient's unconscious material; and, above all, the focusing of interpretations on the patient's manifest and latent anxieties. [Rosenfeld, 1965, p. 117]

In particular, Rosenfeld (*ibid.*) described projective identification in schizophrenic patients, who concretely had the experience of entering analysis only to be expelled from it. The mechanisms of splitting and projective identification, which operated in the psychotic state, accounted for patients' lack of a sense of identity, loss of emotions, and difficulty in using symbols.

Paul Federn

Among Freudian analysts, Federn stands out for the originality of his contribution, especially in developing the concepts of the ego feeling and the boundary of the ego.

Federn did not consider the ego to be a separate entity as opposed to the id and the superego. In his view, the ego also contained the psychic self-experience of its functions, which was perceived as a unity stable in time. The unity of the ego—*the ego feeling*—concerned the perceptual continuity of the self, which remained subjectively the same despite all changes over the course of time. The ego feeling could be defined, in ordinary language, as the overall feeling of the living person, which enabled the individual to experience himself as a subject distinct from the external world, and as an object among all other object representations.

The *ego boundary*, on the other hand, distinguished what belonged to the ego from what was outside it. It coincided with the periphery of the ego feeling, the point beyond which the ego did not extend. Federn distinguished two ego boundaries: the external boundary, which separated the ego from the outside world, and the internal boundary, separating the conscious from the unconscious. The boundary that separated the ego from the outside world manifestly did not correspond to the real boundary of the person, but was a psychological characteristic that varied with the phases of existence. In the final analysis, the ego boundary could be seen as a kind of sense organ that automatically distinguished what was *real* from what was *unreal*. If, for any reason, the external ego boundary was lost, external objects were perceived as strange or unreal. Federn's view was that psychosis affected the unity and boundary of the ego, which lost its homogeneity and its spatial limits. In this case the patient could no longer distinguish between conscious and unconscious, and experienced dreams as hallucinations and delusions.

Federn distanced himself from Abraham's and Freud's view that the libido withdrew from reality and became concentrated in the ego, which then hypertrophied. He maintained instead that the loss of reality was a result of the *weakness of the ego* and not its hypertrophy. Unlike Freud and Abraham, Federn thought that patients did not abandon reality, but rather that they developed falsified ideas which altered their perception of their personal identity.

Another important difference concerns the conceptualization of delusional experience. Whereas Freud believed that delusion corresponded to an attempt at reconstruction after the mental catastrophe, that is, to the libidinal recathexis of the object by the ego, Federn maintained that it was due to the falsification of reality and the loss of the ego's boundaries.

Important consequences for analytic technique stem from this model of psychosis. Federn suggested that therapeutic work with psychotic patients should not consist in interpretations of meanings, including transference interpretations, because these added to the confusion of an ego that was already too dispersed. It was, instead, necessary to direct the work towards strengthening the patient's sense of identity, protecting him from excessive anxiety and enhancing his *intentional thought*. The shattering of its boundaries exposed the ego to invasion by hallucinatory reality. In psychosis, the main damage was the loss of cathexis of the ego's boundaries.

As for free associations, psychotic patients were beset by an excess of sense and meaning, so that such associations should not be encouraged but, in fact, limited. One of Federn's most important propositions was that, whereas "in neurosis we want to eliminate repression, in psychosis we want to restore it" (1952, p. 136). It was not a matter of "making the unconscious conscious, but [of] making the unconscious unconscious again" (*ibid.*, p. 178).

Being in the position of the ego ideal, the analyst needed to use the positive transference so as to repair the patient's constitutive deficiency and to offer him a form of identification capable of strengthening his ego feeling. Whereas in neurosis the transference was used to make repressed material manifest, in psychosis it served to establish a therapeutic relationship in support of the patient's identity deficiency. Federn was convinced that the traditional analytic method tended to aggravate the psychotic state, and in this connection cited several cases referred to him by colleagues after the patients concerned had become psychotic in the course of analysis.

His therapeutic method, which aimed essentially to help the patient contain the psychotic state, also involved variations in technique and in the formal setting whereby the analyst even assumed an overtly educational function. For instance, Federn considered that, in the course of treatment, the analyst should take on the role of the representative of reality and should, when necessary, give the patient directions or play a part in his life outside the sessions.

Heinz Hartmann

Hartmann (1953) held that the vulnerability to psychosis was due mainly to the difficulty experienced by the ego in mediating between the drives and reality.

Unlike Freud, who believed that the conflict with reality and the resulting breakdown depended on the intensity of the drives, Hartmann postulated that, in the psychotic, the ego functions that maintained contact with reality were inadequately developed. Schizophrenic symptoms could be seen as due to a selective regression of certain ego functions, such as altered reality testing, intentionality, attention, and affects. In his view, the diversity of psychotic symptoms was attributable to the fact that not all functions regressed in the same way and to the same extent. One of the functions altered in psychosis was language, which was no longer regulated by the secondary process, so that signs and meanings were no longer distinguishable from each other.

To explain the deficiency in ego functionality, Hartmann put forward an energy-based hypothesis for psychosis: the schizophrenic ego was unable to deinstinctualize object cathexis and to liberate the function linked to the object owing to an insufficiency of neutralized energy. In the 1970s, his view of psychosis gave rise to a heated debate in the USA between the advocates of the deficiency theory (primitive impoverishment of the ego) and those who preferred the conflict theory (an excess of unelaborated instinctual energy). The first group included Wexler (1971), and the second Arlow and Brenner (1969). The latter authors held that the neurotic model of conflict and defence was also useful for understanding schizophrenia, and that the two psychopathological situations differed only quantitatively and not qualitatively. Like neurosis, psychosis was a compromise formation, albeit more severe: the regression was deeper, the conflicts of aggression were more intense, and the ego and superego were more seriously impaired. The affective decathexis described by Freud as specific to psychotic patients corresponded to a defensive withdrawal from conflict. According to Arlow and Brenner, delusions and hallucinations, too, could be seen as symptomatic compromise formations, like neurotic symptoms.

Ping-Nie Pao

Pao considered that the terror experienced by schizophrenic patients stemmed from the dissolution of the self, manifested as *organismic panic*, and corresponded to the loss of integration and the sense of personal unity. Once the catastrophe had taken place, the patient created a delusional world, which served both as a defence and as an attempt at reconstruction.

According to Pao, the contents of delusions (the action of perse-cutors, influencing machines, microphones, etc.) referred not to repressed wishes but to the de-animated and mechanical environment in which the patient grew up. Since, in psychosis, the perceptual system was distorted at the primal level by traumatizing experiences, therapy should be directed not towards the resolution of underlying conflicts, but instead at the acquisition of a mental structure. In the acute phase of the disease, treatment should seek to contain the organismic panic due to the dissolution of the sense of continuity of the self. When the panic declined, even though the patient might be able to regain a substantial proportion of the lost ego functions (for example, attention and memory) and to erect some defensive structures, he nevertheless remained marked by the psychotic catastrophe. Only in the sub-acute phase, when psychotic symptoms such as delusions and hallucinations represented an attempt to re-establish the sense of continuity of the self, could the therapist confront the psychotic structure and attempt to "undo" the pathological organization of the self. This was a highly delicate phase owing to the risk of a negative therapeutic reaction, which often followed a premature attempt by the analyst to force the patient to abandon the pathological self (Pao, 1979, p. 188).

W. R. D. Fairbairn

According to Fairbairn (1952), one factor that predisposed to psychosis was an excess of frustration undergone by the child in the course of development. Aggression was not primary, but should be seen as a reaction to frustration and to the perception of oneself as totally bad. The conflict between love and hate unleashed by the traumatic experience radicalized the schizoid position. The patient avoided libidinal cathexis of the object, as he was convinced that his love was destructive. Therefore, he erected barriers between himself and objects because he was afraid of loving. The eventual result was a sense of insubstantiality and futility of the self.

To avoid any link with objects, the ego abolished the perception of the object world. By disintegrating and losing every form of vitality, the ego paved the way for its own dissolution. The libido, withdrawn from the outside world, was redirected on to internal objects. Idealizing himself, the psychotic patient experienced himself as superior until he was forced to face external reality and discovered his own inadequacy.

In manic–depressive psychosis, the conflict was one of aggression, whereas in schizophrenia the central conflict was between loving and not loving, and it is this that lay at the root of the withdrawal from reality.

Fairbairn's position, which is original and stands apart from other analytic theories of psychosis, envisaged a traumatic basis for the disease. The primary object's lack of affective response inhibited the emotional and relational development of the child, who was thus destined to fall ill.

Donald Winnicott

Winnicott, too, stressed the central role of the environment in the development of psychotic psychopathology. In his model, psychosis was *a disorder of environmental deprivation*, which had its onset at a very early stage, when the newborn as yet lacked the experience of a separate and whole self. When not yet capable of perceiving the mother, the baby was in a primary state of non-integration, in which he experienced a complex of sensations and impressions that were only gradually integrated. By actively adapting to the infant's needs, the mother enabled him to exist in a state of protective isolation. Only after he had received sufficient maternal care could the infant succeed in locating his self in his own body; he would then be able to discover his surroundings without dissolution of his identity. If the environment was disturbing or inappropriate, the delicate balance between the individual and that environment was distorted. Extreme situations of insufficiency gave rise to the primitive disintegration anxiety that formed the basis of psychotic development.

Winnicott pointed out that the paranoid–schizoid position identified by Melanie Klein coincided with the condition of an infant excessively frustrated by an unreceptive mother. Only the mother's ability to adapt to the infant, and also to survive his cruelty, could facilitate his development and the integration of his personality.

Winnicott's (1952) original concept of the transitional area threw light on the existence of an area of illusion created by the child and accepted by the mother; a creative area in which subjective experience and the experience of external reality coexisted. Without this transitional area, no contact between the infant's psyche and the environment would be possible. This was a necessary stage of development, but could become maladaptive if the child withdrew into this area completely. In that case, a split could arise between the child's secret inner life and external reality, with the resulting danger of living a false life or of embarking on the course of psychosis (Winnicott, 1971).

An analyst treating a psychotic patient found himself in the same position as the mother of a newborn baby and had to tolerate continual tension. Since maternal care was lacking in a psychotic patient, the analyst ultimately became the only person who could provide the essential elements for development of the true self.

In some of his writings, Winnicott (1954) even conceived psychosis as a defensive organization that protected the true self; the regression occurring in the course of a psychotic episode could thus be seen as a necessary measure for setting the development of personal identity in motion again. Where a transference psychosis arose in the course of treatment, the analyst should not interpret, but should instead wait for the patient himself to draw close to understanding.

Wilfred Bion

Bion's psychoanalytic revolution also opened the way to a new understanding of the psychotic state; indeed, it was precisely the observation of psychotic functioning that enabled him to formulate a new theory of the unconscious and of thought.

According to Bion (Grinberg, Sor, & De Bianchedi, 1974), every psychic experience included what Freud calls the *sense organ* for the perception of psychic qualities: i.e., the particular function of consciousness that permitted contact with internal and external reality. While there might be consciousness of reality, it could also be abolished or evaded. These two opposing modes represented the concrete forms of two types of mental functioning: non-psychotic and psychotic.

Bion (1957) clearly distinguished between neurotic and psychotic functioning. Freud, too (1940a [1938], p. 202), describes two parts of the personality:

> Two psychical attitudes have been formed instead of a single one— one, the normal one, which takes account of reality, and another which under the influence of the instincts detaches the ego from reality. The two exist alongside of each other. The issue depends upon their relative strength. If the second is or becomes the stronger, the necessary precondition for a psychosis is present. If the relation is reversed, then there is an apparent cure of the delu- sional disorder.

The notion of the psychotic personality did not correspond to a psychiatric diagnosis, but indicated a mode of mental functioning that could coexist with others. The patients concerned deployed an omnipotent projective identification that paralysed the functioning of the psychical apparatus as described by Freud. This was the mechanism that enabled them to distance themselves from reality. The omnipotent fantasy that tended to destroy psychic reality itself, or its perception, ultimately brought about an intermediate state between psychic life and death.

According to Bion, the neurotic part functioned by assimilation, introjection, and discrimination, whereas the psychotic part undertook violent projections with the aim of ridding itself of the accumulation of psychic elements it could not "digest". In the psychotic mode, the mind operated as an apparatus that expelled frustrating objects that were felt to be bad (Bion, 1967). The psychotic part was the part of the personality that was incapable of tolerating frustration and the absence of the object: thoughts, which were connected with the perception of absence, were treated as objects to be eliminated.

The intolerance of frustration, which Bion connected with excessive envy in the child, created hatred of any couple-type link: mother–child, analyst–patient, parts of the self, etc. It was the attack on linking that destroyed the symbolic language capable of making the connections that generated meaning.

Psychotic functioning involved the violent projection of emotions, which were experienced as unbearable, and the destruction of the very organs of emotional perception: i.e., of the functions that permitted the recognition of psychic reality. The destruction of the functions of thought and perception and their projection to the outside gave rise to the formation of *bizarre objects*, which were conglomerates of the remains of destroyed organs of perception and external objects. The psychotic patient felt surrounded and persecuted by these objects.

Taking up Melanie Klein's (1930a) insights into the inability to symbolize and those of Hanna Segal (1956) on the impossibility for the psychotic of facing the depressive position, Bion wrote that intolerance of pain drove the patient to destroy the thought function and therefore to deprive himself of the only means whereby he could confront or modify the situation of frustration.

Another fundamental insight of Bion's was that, whereas the neurotic patient used repression to banish negative experience to the unconscious, psychotics destroyed the instruments that would have enabled the unconscious to understand the psychic experience. In Bion's view, after all, the main function of the unconscious was to transform sense data into symbolic elements. If the sense data were not transformed, psychic life would be impossible. This process of transformation took place constantly, in both sleep and waking life, and was mediated by the *alpha function*. In its absence, the dynamic equilibrium between conscious and unconscious functions was altered and the patient was unable to *dream*. Lacking the ability to transform perceptual experience symbolically, the patient felt that he contained within himself concrete things, rather than their images. Therefore, he expected ideas to behave like sensory objects.

A psychotic patient could not repress and unconsciously work through experiential data (he was unable to *dream*) and could not therefore profit from experience. Other authors, for example Abraham and Federn, albeit with different starting points, arrive at similar conclusions about the failure of the function of repression.

What might appear to an observer as a clear manifestation of the psychotic unconscious (an unconscious without repression) was in fact the consequence of the non-transformation of sense data. Owing to the destruction of the alpha function, the psychotic patient was in a state of severe psychic deficiency. The psychotic part of the personality denied temporality and frustration, both of which were tolerable when the principle of causality was accepted. Furthermore, by cutting himself off from reality, the patient ultimately created a frustration even more radical than the frustration he sought to avoid. If he tried to put the fragments of experience together, the repair attempt readily gave rise to a highly destructive superego. The psychotic patient could not accede to the depressive position because that would involve awareness of the vast destruction wreaked.

In Bion's writings, two lines of thought on psychosis, which I shall call *innatist* and *environmental*, respectively, can be distinguished. Although conceived at different times, they continually intersect in his work.

According to the innatist conception, the psychotic part of the personality was a destructive mental state—a violent, murderous force—in which the death instinct and exaggerated *amour propre* fuelled *overweening pride*, often associated with obstinate curiosity and stupidity. Envy, arrogance, and the attack on linking were, for Bion, the primitive elements that destroyed the possibility of a friendly encounter with the object and precluded access to the world of symbols and emotions. Bion attributed these feelings to the power of an internal object, the superego, which originated from psychotic omnipotence and prevented the normal use of projective identification.

The environmental view, on the other hand, emphasized the non-introjection of certain fundamental functions of affective symbolization due to a *defective container*, i.e., the primal object that ought to have received the newborn's projections: Bion (1992) considered that infant–mother communication was mediated by projective identification (originally called *tropism*) used for the purpose of communication; in normal circumstances the mother intuitively understood the baby's non-verbal communication and her response conferred meaning on it. According to this view, psychosis stemmed from the lack of the intuitive function in the object (the mother) whereby the child's communicative projective identification ought to have been received. This lack of receptivity in the mother stripped the infant's communication of its value and reflected unbearable anxieties back on him, plunging him into nameless terror. The infant's capacity to tolerate frustration and develop the symbolic function ultimately depended on the mother's reverie, i.e., her ability imaginatively to intuit the child's mental state. Even if the destruction of the apparatus for thinking thoughts was due to the presence of an omnipotent and guilty world, it was the mother's primal non-receptivity that sowed the seeds of psychosis.

Jacques Lacan

Lacan (1966) addressed the topic of psychosis in many of his works, but it is not easy to summarize his position, as his view of it was in a state of constant flux, ranging from existentialism to structuralism, until he eventually arrived at the original conception that characterized his late period.

A key concept for Lacan in relation to psychosis was *foreclosure*, the impossibility of acceding to the area of the signifier, and hence of symbolization. Unlike neurotic patients, in his view psychotics did not suffer from a symptom but produced a "delusion", because they had never had access to oedipal identification: the *Name-of-the-Father*. Lacan maintained that the Name-of-the-Father was the only position that enabled the subject not only to assume a meaning, but also to assimilate the specific character of subjectivity. For Lacan, the Father did not have real psychological characteristics, but was a metaphorical figure whose foreclosure generated a "hole" in the signifier (the *Law*) and opened the way to the drifts of the imaginary. The Name-of-the-Father was necessary not for learning *langage*, but to gain access to the register of the authentic *parole*. A psychotic patient had no access to the oedipal dialectic because the Father did not act as an organizer of meaning to establish the oedipal law. This foreclosed the possibility of reaching the symbolic function and of creating a symbol endowed with the sense of one's own subjectivity and *parole*.

In the absence of this symbol, which could anchor the subject to *parole* or make the subject the meaning of his own *parole*, the latter ultimately became devoid of sense. Delusion was an attempt at healing which sought to give meaning to *langage*. However, it was destined to failure without a Name-of-the-Father, the only symbol able to identify the subject as the sense around which the play of symbols rotated (Tarizzo, 2003). The subject thus remained deprived of paternal signification on the symbolic level and of the corresponding phallic signification in terms of the imaginary (which Lacan saw as the area of specular and narcissistic identification). Lacking paternal and phallic signification, the psychotic patient could not decode the communications that reached him (Di Caccia & Recalcati, 2000).

Lacan, thus, considered psychosis to be the result of a basic defect that prevented the structuring of the symbolic area. However, his theory did not explore the reasons for this failure or suggest possible remedies, since the basic defect affected the very functions that ought to promote recovery.

Piera Aulagnier

In the view of this author, the vulnerability to psychosis stemmed from early distortion of mother–child interaction. The impact of the mother's mind on the child's was characterized by "primary violence", which was to some extent normal and necessary for construction of the sense of reality. When excessive, this violence could prevent autonomous development, imposing an extraneous viewpoint on the infant and forcing him to use his own means to explain to himself what he could not understand.

It was the mother's intrusion into the infant's mind that facilitated the psychotic development. This was why psychotic patients were themselves aggressive and tended intrusively to colonize the minds of others.

Aulagnier believed that the mother of a child who would later develop a psychosis did not want a child, or rather, did not want *that* child. The child, therefore, was not free to express his own spontaneity, but had to adapt to the mother's wishes. He experienced constant pressure on his psyche from the mother's violent projections. Thought became confused and fragmented. In his attempt to establish order, the child constructed altered representations of himself, his parents, and others; these gave rise to *primary delusional thought*, a necessary but not a sufficient condition for the subsequent development of psychosis.

Aulagnier, thus, postulated a primitive stage of mental representation, which she called a *pictogram*, in which psychic experience took the form of a pleasant or unpleasant sensation that could not be expressed in language. At this first stage, the infant's psyche was in direct contact with the mother's mind and responded to her every thought or emotion. Only at a later stage, when the wish for the other arose, did representations come into being. Psychotic patients did not accede to this second stage, which called for language and thought.

On several occasions, Aulagnier wrote that the pictogram—the primordial element of representation—sometimes could not form. This was the case, for instance, if mother failed to return to the child her own pictographic representation of the mouth–nipple relationship, thus depriving him of an experience of "legitimate and accepted fusion of his [the infant's] pleasure and wish with those of the mother" (Aulagnier, 1984, p. 73, translated).

The common ground

From my necessarily brief and partial summary of the ideas of the authors who have put forward psychoanalytic theories of psychosis, certain common elements emerge; a sort of *common ground* for understanding the psychotic process. Some of these notions can already be found, either clearly expressed or only hinted at, in Freud.

The authors cited share the conviction that psychosis is a very early and primitive disorder, whose origins can be traced back to the primary organization of emotional relations. The damage, though conceived in varying terms (as regression to the primitive libidinal organization for Freud, or failure to develop beyond the paranoid–schizoid position, according to Melanie Klein), concerns the way the ego organizes its perception of the world and its internal relations. A psychotic patient is seen as carrying within himself a primal malfunction, which is destined sooner or later to overwhelm the psyche.

Another point of convergence for many authors is the presence of a disturbance that prevents the exercise of certain mental functions, in particular the ability to use symbolic thought. Whether this is the process of foreclosure (Lacan) or loss of the alpha function (Bion), this dysfunction gives rise to failure of the capacity to understand psychic reality.

Other authors hold that the basis of vulnerability to psychosis is a disturbance of the primal relations that structure personal identity: that is, early alteration of the mother–child emotional relationship. The lack of maternal empathy (Winnicott) or the intrusive violence of the mother acting on the infant's mind (Aulagnier) constitute the early microtraumas that prevent and distort the full development of the infant's internal world.

The hypothesis that psychosis is conflictual in nature and attributable to the dynamic unconscious has now been abandoned. Today, attention tends to focus on the factors that act on the precursors of symbolic thought and on the psychic elements necessary for metabolizing emotional experiences. This is the viewpoint I shall try to develop in the following chapters.

CHAPTER TWO

The primitive and the pathological in psychosis

> But the more we advance in our understanding of psycho-
> analytic problems, the more, I believe, we become impressed
> with the importance of the deeper problems of deficiency and
> deformation of the psychic structures themselves . . . If the
> authors had taken these issues more fully into consideration
> . . . they would probably would have written a vastly different
> chapter on the psychopathology of the psychoses in that case
>
> (Loewald, 1966, p. 435)

Regression and primitive mental states

Analysing the psychotic state of Senatspräsident Schreber,
Freud (1911c) states that the crucial factor in the construction of his delusion was the libidinal regression triggered
by the infantile homosexual conflict with the father. Freud invokes
the psychosexual model, according to which illness represents a
return to a preconstituted fixation point. His view that the primitive
(the fixation point) and the pathological (delusion) were equivalent
prevailed for many years in psychoanalytic theory.

For Melanie Klein, too, psychological growth was characterized by the transition from the primitive forms of thought of the paranoid–schizoid position to the more developed modes of the depressive position. She further suggested that some individuals never succeeded in overcoming paranoid–schizoid functioning: any child with particularly intense basic anxiety and aggression was more predisposed to psychosis in later life. Indeed, Klein believed that all children passed through a psychotic phase, but that only a few overcame it completely.

To sum up, both Freud and Melanie Klein held that psychic illness was characterized by regression to a specific point in infantile development, this fixation point being not random, but determined by the infantile history.

Other theories, too, attribute illness in adults to arrested development or regression to a primitive developmental stage. Kohut, for example, postulates that it is perfectly normal for infants to pass through a state of omnipotence, which, if not endured, causes the cohesion of the self to collapse. This breakdown then constitutes the nucleus for the possible development of illness in adulthood.

Robert Caper's (1998) interesting paper on the relationship between the primitive and the pathological as envisaged in psychoanalytic theories lends itself particularly well to discussion of this issue. (Caper's views were subsequently amplified by contributions from other analysts in the ensuing Internet debate [Williams, 1998].) Caper wondered whether pathological manifestations represented a return to primitive mental states or had a different, specific meaning. He considered that, if psychopathology was seen as a regression to a primitive state, there was a risk of equating the destructive states of the mind specific to mental illness with the normal, primitive states susceptible to development. As an example of such a misunderstanding, Caper recalls that Freud (1905d) had thought perversion was merely a return in the adult to the polymorphous sexuality of the infant; however, contrary to Freud's initial view, the pathological destructiveness characteristic of perversion was, in his opinion, completely different in nature from infantile sexual polymorphism.

The equating of the pathological with the primitive—two areas which should remain distinct—stemmed from the fact that elements of splitting, idealization, and grandiosity were present in both. Furthermore, the characteristic hallucinatory gratification of the infant was quite different from that of a psychotic adult: the child's hallucinatory state was of limited duration; sooner or later a physical need (hunger, for example) would signal the loss of contact with reality. The child's entry into a state of omnipotence did not prevent him from emerging from it and recognizing his dependence on his mother. The perception of separateness existed from birth and enabled the infant to learn from experience and to depend on reality.

Caper contended that psychic development coincided with the progressive diminution of primal omnipotence in favour of a context of more realistic object relations. Continuous communication between the internal and external worlds enabled the child to integrate experiences and gradually to reduce the power of magic thought. In this author's view, a sick person was by no means the adult embodiment of a primitive mental state; instead, illness was the outcome of a state abnormal from the beginning. Although states of paranoia or mania existed in the normal child, they were reversible; they became rigid only in psychotic adults (and psychotic children).

Mentalization in children and psychotics

The Internet debate (Williams, 1998) addressed the issue in greater depth and shed even more light on its complexity. Among the many contributors, Michael Robbins drew attention to the qualitative difference between mentalization in children and in psychotic adults, stressing the importance of using non-psychotic terminology to describe normal infancy. He pointed out that in the psychoanalytic literature the same terminology had often been used for psychosis and for the state of infantile immaturity. The idea that children were *normally psychotic*, or that there was a continuum between normal infancy and psychosis, was endorsed by Freud, Klein, Mahler, and others. In Robbins' view, notwithstanding Melanie Klein's essential contribution to our understanding of the mental functioning of the adult psychotic, the use of definitions such as paranoid or manic, the notion that the infantile mind was split or fragmented, and the theory that hate and aggression were central to the child's world, ultimately equated infancy with psychosis. A child's view of the world was, of course, limited owing to his lack of experience, but it was wrong to portray immature infantile thought as magic, hallucinatory, or delusional. While a child could not discern reality appropriately, infantile thought could not be described in terms of omnipotence or grandiosity, which were concepts normally applied to pathological adult functioning.

Another source of confusion, according to Robbins, was the assertion that the child's hallucinatory wish fulfilment was similar to the psychotic's flight into a drugged mental state. Unlike the adult psychotic, a normal child, within the limits of his capacity, was endowed with curiosity and interest in the world. To sum up, delusion could not be described simply as a belief refractory to learning. Such a view avoided the fundamental question of how it might be possible to analyse a delusional adult or to work analytically with mental states utterly impermeable to contact with others. Robbins hoped that the future might see the development of a psychoanalytic technique suitable for treating psychotic patients, whereby they could be made conscious of the nature of their delusional fantasies and helped to distinguish them from reality.

Unconscious pathological fantasies

In his response, Caper invoked Money-Kyrle's view that mental illness was simply the expression of an unconscious delusion waiting to be transformed. Treating a psychotic adult ultimately meant analysing the anxieties that maintained a split between the delusional part and the part in contact with reality. Since there was no such thing as a patient who was completely detached from reality, only individuals totally incapable of learning from experience should be deemed unanalysable.

Expressing himself now in terms of Kleinian theory, Caper distinguished the unconscious fantasy of omnipotence from ordinary unconscious fantasy: whereas the former made it impossible to learn from experience, the latter constructed hypotheses about the world and was therefore essential to mental growth. An example of such a hypothesis was the infant's unconscious preconception of the existence of the nipple. Hence, the difference between the two types of fantasy was only quantitative. Like the infant's magic thought, which diminished as he developed the capacity to learn from experience, unconscious omnipotent fantasies, too, should gradually integrate with the sense of reality. In Caper's view, even delusional ideas could be transformed into normal unconscious fantasies in the course of analytic treatment. The first step in therapy should be the patient's recognition that the delusion (which was equivalent to the unconscious omnipotent fantasy) was a false construction.

The delusional structure

In clinical terms, the problem of the delusional construction proves to be far more complex than Caper envisages. Whereas Money-Kyrle's view that the pathology stems from an unconscious delusion is correct, the various levels of distortion of reality—the conscious, the unconscious, and the delusional—must be distinguished from each other. In the course of treatment, as the analysand gradually succeeds in perceiving his psychic reality and developing his ability to grasp emotional truth, certain beliefs are found to be false. This is the experience of growth that permits integration and enrichment of the personality.

To my mind, this is feasible only with neurotic patients; it does not work with psychotics, because psychotic constructions cannot be traced back to split-off, omnipotent fantasies that must be reintegrated. The inability to learn from experience, which, according to Caper, distinguishes the psychotic from the neurotic state, is not the central element, since splitting and the refusal to learn from experience form part of many clinical conditions that are not necessarily psychotic. His conviction that the delusional structure is equivalent to an unconscious omnipotent fantasy that can be transformed into a normal unconscious fantasy is not demonstrable, and, indeed, seemingly contradicts his initial assertion of the existence of a clear-cut distinction between normality and pathology in infancy. (I shall attempt in Chapters Eight and Eleven to explain in more detail why delusional fantasies cannot, in my opinion, be transformed into normal unconscious fantasies, and why analytic technique with psychotics should differ from that suggested by Caper. Delusional fantasies are inherently not susceptible to transformation, so that they must be *deconstructed*.)

In my view, the concept of unconscious fantasy does not help us to distinguish clearly between a delusional construction (which, moreover, is in many respects a conscious operation) and other unconscious representations. A delusional patient is unable to tell the difference between truth and falsehood, between his own newly created ideas and ideas derived from the perception of reality.

Furthermore, I believe that the analogy between the primitive state and psychosis is unsustainable, since the psychotic state is very different from a child's fantasy life. Whereas psychosis is a subversion of thought that leads to the disintegration of the mind, the magic world of the infant is open to the unknown and makes for the construction of a personal meaning to be assigned to that world. In a word, the psyche of a normal child is vastly different from that of a psychotic adult; again, the differences are qualitative rather than quantitative.

Defences

Eric Brenman (2002a, p. 39) considers that defences always involve a distortion of perception: "All defences create a delusion or illusion and cannot operate without corruption and mutilation of the perceptual apparatus". (Freud [1940a (1938)], too, considered that defence mechanisms served to keep dangers at bay, but that these same mechanisms could themselves be transformed into dangers.) More specifically, this author believes that in order to live it is always necessary for consciousness to be partially altered, but that excessive defences give rise to an actual emotional deficiency. Defences have a protective function similar to that of the skin, whose protective layer of dead cells must not be too thick, lest the organism suffocate. Considering that the psyche progresses from relatively primitive (paranoid–schizoid) to more developed (depressive) defences, those useful for protecting the primitive ego (for example, omnipotence, projection of the death drive, isolation, or delusion) become pathological once the need to recognize psychic reality is established. Pathology consists in the use of prim- itive modes of defence at a time when the individual ought to be resorting to more appropriate defence mechanisms. Brenman points out that when psychopathology rears its head, a patient may readily turn back to the worship of "primitive gods". Traumatic experience, too, tends to potentiate the primitive parts of the mind, which, in general, fuel the defences. This was Brenman's reply to a question of mine at the launch of the original Italian edition of *Recovery of the Lost Good Object* (Brenman, 2002b), a collection of his theoretical papers and clinical supervisions, in Milan in September 2002. (The English version appeared in 2006.) In sum, Brenman shares the view of the post-Kleinian authors that there can be no pathological defences other than the omnipotent ones deployed by the primitive ego.

Psychopathological constructions

In this book, I postulate that severe pathologies are not only a matter of primitive defences (although these do, of course, exist), but that it is also essential to consider the action of *psychopathological constructions*. In defences such as repression or projection, the unconscious perception of the defensive transformation undertaken is preserved, whereas in a psychopathological construction consciousness is radically altered. Psychopathological structures form silently in infancy and their pathogenic potential finds expression only later in life; often aided by emotional traumas, they soon take on a developmental momentum of their own.

This point can be clarified by reference to a contribution of mine (De Masi, 1988) on the various possible configurations of the love transference in analysis. (Freud himself theorized that the erotic transference was a *defence* against analytic dependence.) My view is that, whereas the idealizing type of love transference re-evokes an infantile experience that could be seen as a defence with potential developmental implications, sexualization of the transference constitutes a psychopathological construction that opposes any relational development. While the first form of love transference can be seen as a defence against a state of depression, the sexualized transference corresponds to a state of mental excitation that tends to destroy the analytic relationship. In other words, in the pathological construction the defensive character tends to be secondary to the function of excitation that colonizes and perverts the mind. A theory in which psychopathological constructions are seen as structures different from primitive defences has important implications in terms both of one's clinical approach and of analytic technique.

Colonization

Whereas *neurotic defences* might be said to limit emotional perception and thereby to bring about an equilibrium that tends to be constant, *psychopathological constructions* (which could also be termed perverse or psychotic defences) might distort the perception of psychic reality and even completely destroy it. Their aim is to construct a neo-reality that appears superior and desirable; for this reason their colonizing action is not obvious to the patient, who is passively attracted to them. Constructions of this type are encountered in severe mental states such as perversions, anorexia, drug addiction, and psychoses.

One psychotic patient fought against states of desperate loneliness by plunging into a fantasy withdrawal: a lit cigarette in hand, she created for herself the illusion of being a sheikh surrounded by courtesans in an ecstatic experience of pleasure. On emergence from this mental state, she felt depersonalized; overcome by panic, she could remember nothing about herself and the world. She referred to these states as "mental heart attacks".

Idealization of destructive parts of the personality

The author who opened the way to the understanding of psychopathological constructions was Herbert Rosenfeld (1971), with his theory of *destructive narcissism*. Rosenfeld postulated that certain severe pathologies stemmed from the idealization of a bad part of the self, whose operation was split off from that of the rest of the personality. This structure dominated the patient and seduced the more healthy parts. (The concept of destructive narcissism cannot, in my view, be generalized, but must be used in specific contexts. It is not a structure of the internal world in normal or neurotic personalities, but a psychopathological construction observed in some borderline, perverse, or psychotic patients.) In order to enslave the healthy part, the pathological structure presented itself as a kind of saviour, hiding its destructive purpose. Submission to the sick part thus became blind, as any failure of compliance was punishable with the loss of the promised happiness and a return to the condition of suffering.

Destructive narcissism cannot be seen as the expression of primitive mechanisms of idealization (it is not a defence connected with the primitive paranoid–schizoid position), but represents a new pathological construction that distorts psychic development. Donald Meltzer describes a similar process, which he sees as very different from a defence against anxiety:

> Where dependence on internal good objects is rendered infeasible by damaging masturbatory attacks and where dependence on a good external object is unavailable or not acknowledged, the addictive relationship to a bad part of the self, the submission to tyranny, takes place . . . I have come to the conclusion that *the intolerance of depressive anxieties alone will not produce the addictive constellation of submission to the tyrant.* [1973, p. 105, my italics]

O'Shaughnessy (1981, p. 363), too, attempts to distinguish these defences from *defensive organizations*, which she locates on the boundary between the paranoid–schizoid and depressive positions:
Unlike defences (piecemeal, transient to a greater or lesser extent, recurrent), which are a normal part of development, a defensive organization is a fixation, a pathological formation when development arouses irresoluble and almost overwhelming anxiety. Expressed in Kleinian terms, defences are a normal part of negotiating the paranoid–schizoid and depressive positions; a defensive organization, on the other hand, is a pathological fixed formation in one or other position, or on the borderline between them.

Perverse transformation

I should like to refer briefly to a perverse, masochistic patient who, among other pathological manifestations, habitually inflicted severe corporal punishments on himself whenever he made a mistake.

This patient dreams that he has on his payroll the Nazi criminal Adolf Eichmann, who appears dressed in white while preaching to a group of people. (This dream is taken from the clinical material presented at a seminar on borderline pathologies held in Venice in September 2003 and chaired by Janine Chasseguet-Smirgel.)

It is obvious from this dream that the perverse sadistic structure personified by Eichmann is seen as good and is fuelled by the patient himself (Eichmann is on his payroll).

The element of confusion concerns the denial of the criminal character of Eichmann, who appears innocent, dressed as he is in white and trying to attract disciples.

In this case, the power of the sick and sadistic part stems from the perverse transformation of the superego, a transformation that makes destructiveness appear innocent and demands to be espoused by the patient's healthy part. Since the seductive action of the psychopathological structure stems from the pressure of a perverse superego (De Masi, 2002), the analyst's task is to clarify for the patient the confusion between the healthy and sick parts and to analyse the submission of the former to the latter by describing the nature of the psychopathological structure which dominates him and the means used to seduce him.

Manipulation of the organs of perception

Psychosis and withdrawal into a state of pleasure are, in my opinion, synonymous. If the attraction to psychosis were not initially pleasurable, the pressure in the direction of psychosis would be incomprehensible.

As Freud pointed out (and Bion reminded us), we possess an *organ of consciousness* capable of understanding psychic reality. Within limits, we can manipulate and alter this organ, as happens in all defensive processes. Brenman reminds us that for this reason every defence operates by restricting and altering perceptions. The manipulation of the organs of psychic perception might reach extreme levels, to the extent of creating special worlds in which the patient is captured: for example, states of sexualized well-being, perverse pleasure, or delusional realities.

In the long term, the withdrawal is never idyllic; it usually affords an exalted break, which, however, is followed by a disastrous lapse into anxiety, for the psychotic defence's alteration of the organ of consciousness proves to be a catastrophic operation: in order to preserve omnipotence and persevere with the flight from reality, the patient is forced to wreak increasing violence on the organs of perception, destroying them and ultimately being left with no defence at all. That is what happens in the psychotic state.

The blue world

Sohn (1995) describes a patient who had assaulted an elderly man, a complete stranger to him. His mental state was characterized by two types of functioning. On the one hand, he could evoke a fantastic world—the "blue world"—with a wonderful woman who gratified his every wish; simply conjuring her up would provide him with extraordinary sexual experiences. Unfortunately, this world would not last long; it would end suddenly, and then came the terrible "black world", where there was no good, but only infinite desolation.

Why had he assaulted that poor fellow? His blue world had suddenly collapsed when he failed to receive a benefit he urgently needed; he had been told to come back the following week. At this point, the patient had tried and failed to evoke the woman of his fantasies. He had then noticed this elderly man, who seemed totally oblivious of the drama inside him. Overcome by terrible rage, he had attempted to eliminate his victim.

This case is mentioned to exemplify the fact that particular mental states are likely to be encountered in psychosis. The patient's blue world was self-created, and amounted to a psychotic withdrawal, a drugged mental state. The means of creating and continually reproducing it have catastrophic effects, with which the patient is ultimately unable to cope.

CHAPTER THREE

An example of psychotic transformation

"As he lay wide awake, vast processions passed in mournful pomp before his eyes, and a never-ending succession of ancient, ceremonial buildings soared skyward. Yet soon his day-dreams merged into those of night, and everything his gaze conjured up in the gloom lived again as he slept, in uncanny and unbearable splendour. . . . Each night, he would plunge headlong into sunless chasms of unimaginable depth, from which there could be no hope of return. Even when awake once more, he remained a prey to all-consuming sadness and despair"

(Baudelaire, 1860, p. 208f., translated)

The psychotic journey

Psychosis can be thought of as a "journey" characterized by specific developmental phases involving the triggering of processes leading, once set in motion, to mental explosion. At first, the patient retains a degree of awareness that he is ill, but this is gradually lost. Entry into the psychotic state is merely the end result of a slow process of transformation: the alterations in the perceptual apparatus and in the consciousness of the self that take place silently over the course of time eventually become visible even to an outside observer. Psychosis may appear clinically as early as in infancy, when bizarre behaviour or learning difficulties might signal a process already under way.

During the crisis, the organs of perception and of thought conform to unpredictable laws and modes of functioning. The patient still has some healthy nuclei that retain a degree of perception of psychic reality, though their functions are paralysed. The process of restoring normal functioning can begin from these small islands of health. Once the psychotic episode is over, it leaves scars or seedbeds of pathology that are likely to give rise to further instances of decompensation. The possibility of overcoming the disorder depends not only on the time that has elapsed since the start of the process, but also on its gravity: if it is too severe, the patient will be unable to retrace his steps.

The psychotic transformation has a number of salient features. First, psychosis arises long before the appearance of unequivocal clinical manifestations such as hallucinations and delusions. Second, the process tends to be unstoppable, involving changes in the perception of the self and of individual identity; phenomena affecting visual or auditory perception (hallucinations) or thought are secondary to the alteration of the self. Third, the psychotic transformation can be divided into three stages: initial, central, and final. At first, the experience is usually pleasurable; it is only later that the process of perceptual alteration assumes a devastating and terrifying character. In the final period, sensory production becomes totally autarkic.

The foregoing may appear to conflict with the views of other authors (for example, Pao, 1979) to the effect that the delusional state is characterized primarily by anxiety. In my clinical work, however, I have found that catastrophic anxiety arises only when the self-induced sensual pleasure or the grandiose experience is no longer present; patients then lose the capacity to control the transformation of perceptions that they had, in fact, actively brought about. Even Senatspräsident Schreber, before he was overcome by the catastrophic experience of the transformation of the world and by the delusion of persecution centred on Flechsig, had been captivated by the sensual pleasure of becoming a woman in the act of coitus. Unless the initially fascinating nature of psychosis is borne in mind, it will not be possible to understand the attraction of psychosis and the patient's "passive" submission to it. The pleasurable aspect of the delusional experience often lies hidden from the observer, since the patient does not spontaneously convey it.

A fourth consideration is that a psychotic episode sometimes begins with a state of ecstatic revelation, which, unlike similar states of consciousness, goes on to induce psychic changes that are not readily reversible. By acceding to *higher* mental states, such as ecstasy or telepathy, the patient comes into contact with the *divine* and the *omnipotent*. The onset of psychosis often consists in a withdrawal involving a benevolent, seductive voice that promises the patient total bliss. At a second stage, however, the same voice acts as a terrifying dictator that dominates his mind.

Fifth, psychotic functioning is in dynamic equilibrium with its non-psychotic counterpart, but the system tends to become unbalanced with a bias towards the former. Last, the psychotic condition is completely different from that of neurosis. Whereas the latter leaves the levels of organization and the structure of the personality intact, psychosis tends to alter the functions of the perception of identity and the emotions by means of ongoing parasitic mental productions.

John Perceval

To illustrate the entire course of a psychotic episode, I shall now give a brief account of a crisis as reported by the protagonist himself, who described his experience as a patient who became psychotic, lived with his psychosis, and eventually emerged from it. John Perceval, a nineteenth-century English nobleman, was committed to a lunatic asylum at the age of twenty-nine. Released three years later, he wrote an autobiographical account documenting not only the phases of psychotic delusion, but also the transformations that preceded them. The book was published anonymously in 1838 with the title *A Narrative of the Treatment Experienced by a Gentleman, During a State of Mental Derangement: Designed To Explain the Causes and the Nature of Insanity (and to Expose the Injudicious Conduct*

Pursued Towards Many Unfortunate Sufferers Under that Calamity).
The book was republished by Gregory Bateson in 1961.

The American psychoanalyst, Edward M. Podvoll, presented a
commentary on the case of John Perceval in his book *The Seduction
of Madness* (Podvoll, 1990), on which I shall draw in this chapter. In
my view, the account illustrates the character of psychosis as a
process, with points of transition and specific transformations. The
biographical reconstruction clearly demonstrates both the perceptual distortion that marked the onset of the psychotic episode and
the patient's journey of emergence from it.

John Perceval was a solitary young man who, despite his
humanistic inclinations, embarked on a military career, which he
abandoned after a few years. Having left the army, he began to
question himself obsessionally about his moral integrity and to
torment himself over the permissibility of his actions. His quest for
spirituality led him to attend meditation groups, to help the poor
and the sick, and to give himself over to prayer and vigils. Eventually attaining a state of ecstasy, he experienced a new mental
condition of harmony and pleasure. He felt inspired by the Holy
Spirit, which urged him to surrender his own will and submit to
divine power. With soothing words, it encouraged him to make
contact with the world "beyond the visible". Thus, he acquired the
power to make contact with spiritual presences that revealed themselves to him through the voices of people he met. He tried to
perform miracles, but became depressed when he failed. He then
went with a prostitute and contracted a venereal disease.

He now became tormented by guilt. A voice ordered him to put
his hand into fire, while others told him to sing through the night
or to assume contorted, back-breaking postures.

Perceval was forcibly committed to a mental hospital. He was
not aware that he had lost his reason, but thought he had been
locked up in an infernal prison for his crimes. Inner voices told him
that all his suffering stemmed from higher beings who wanted to
purge him of his sins: his task was to save not only himself but
others, too, from the fires of hell. Menacing voices informed him
that others were laying down their lives, whereas he himself was
too cowardly to put an end to his.

Although thoroughly under the sway of delusion, Perceval
retained a modicum of doubt. In brief lucid moments, he wondered

if what he was experiencing was real or only a dream, and whether, instead of moving towards spiritual perfection, he was, in fact, going mad. This uncertainty, which had the potential to bring him back to reality, was promptly called into question by divine voices, which declared that doubt was sinful and accounted for his lack of progress along the path of spirituality. If he hesitated and failed to obey, the "voices" would terrify him with threats of eternal torture. So, he cast aside all doubts before they even arose and plunged headlong into the delusion, which now proved to be increasingly deceptive (Perceval was later to see the perverse manipulation of doubt as "original sin" *par excellence*). From then on, he began to lose control of his imagination: words and thoughts were transformed into visions. He could be transported to other spaces or times, to celestial or infernal realms; forgotten, previous lives would reveal themselves to him; every sensation, every sound, every taste, or even the act of breathing gave rise to concrete events, such as shots, shouts, laughs, or weeping. Terrifying perceptions tormented him relentlessly for months on end.

Islands of lucidity

Perceval's return to psychic integrity began with some unexpected intervals or "reawakenings", brief moments of insight when he became aware that what he was experiencing was a dream. At these times, he realized he had been committed to an asylum and saw with dismay the self-deception to which he had fallen victim. These islands of awareness were of very short duration. It required a constant effort to stay alive, as the moments of lucidity were immediately swallowed up by a new version of the delusion. An ongoing, inexorable lie (which is, after all, what delusion is) was in effect always on hand to swamp and re-absorb what little truth emerged.

Realizing that the insights he had in the delusion-free moments conflicted utterly with what the voices told him, Perceval sought to break away from his automatic obedience to the hallucinatory commands. For example, when the figure of a naked woman appeared before him, claiming to be his sister and beckoning to him to come close, he decided to stay absolutely still, inwardly insisting that *she* approach him. When he stood firmly by this idea, the vision disappeared. Trying to remember precisely when his dog had died, he asked his brother, and noticed that his memory, which contradicted the delusion, was correct. On another occasion, the sight of his certificate of baptism helped him to reject the voices' assertion that he was not his mother's son.

Emergence from psychosis

Although progress was short-lived, since the delusion constantly created new perceptual distortions, Perceval nevertheless succeeded in making one important observation. He found that if he concentrated on an external object while listening to a "voice", the voice would be transformed into an indistinct buzz. If, on the other hand, he lapsed back into his state of mental absence, he would hear the voice again. He then understood that the hallucination appeared whenever he was distracted and created a mental void, which allowed the "voice" to expand within it. It was the state of mental absence that permitted a sense impression—for instance that of a draught—to be transformed into a dialogue with a voice.

He now realized that it was he who was responsible for the appearance of hallucinations, even though they seemingly presented themselves of their own accord. Even when they manifested themselves suddenly, the voices to some extent anticipated a thought of his own. He found that the more anxious he felt, the more likely he was to turn a sense perception into a hallucination. From then on, the hallucinations became more indulgent, sometimes assuming a friendly guise and wishing him a speedy recovery. Perceval sensed that he had to distrust all the voices, even those that claimed to be his friends. As if gradually awakening from a dream, Perceval little by little developed the perception of the existence of the outside world, which enabled him to emerge from the refuge in which he had confined himself. On leaving the asylum, he hesitated greatly before setting down his memoirs, fearing as he did that the mere memory of the psychotic crisis might plunge him back into madness. After completing the book, he devoted the rest of his life to protecting and defending the rights of patients in British mental institutions.

The fascination of psychosis

Whereas Freud used the memoirs of Senatspräsident Schreber to attempt a dynamic explanation of psychosis, John Perceval's account allows us to observe in detail the transformations occurring in the course of the psychotic process.

The idea of losing his identity in order to reach a state of psychic beatitude gradually came to dominate Perceval's mind. The annihilation of his self was mediated by the mystical experience—the "surrender" of his will to ecstatic enlightenment. (Not all mystics become psychotic, but sometimes the ascetic quest leads on to psychosis [Gilberg, 1974; Hamilton-Merritt, 1976]. Ghent [1990] sees the asceticism of the mystic as a means of discovering the unity of being in the absence of time. Perceval, tormented by anxiety on account of his identity problems, underwent the mystical experience, but forced it to an extreme pitch and ultimately found himself in thrall to psychosis.) Only then did Perceval's anxiety cease. Intoxicated with pleasure, he went on until he became one with the divine and the omnipotent. Surrendering himself to new, "higher" psychic experiences, he ultimately entered into a mental world beyond his control. He seemingly had no regrets about the wrecking of his mind, but there was also no turning back.

Perceval's psychosis manifestly took the form of a two-stage process, proceeding from heaven to hell, from celestial ascent to the plunge into terror. The structure of the psychotic organization, after all, resembles an obsessional system that swings between the promise of pleasure and the threat of eternal punishment. The ascent towards grandiosity and the freedom of omnipotent fantasy ultimately prove to be a system that demands complete submission.

The intoxicating state of well being that constitutes the first stage of psychosis expresses the triumph of omnipotence over the perception of an unbearable subjective reality. This initial exaltation is followed by catastrophic anxiety over the destruction wreaked on one's mind (the world) and by a persecutory sense of guilt. In the second phase, there are very few moments of felicity, while at the same time the superego's intimidation becomes absolute.

Perceval distanced himself increasingly from the world of emotional relations; his mind closed in on itself and his sense organs were saturated with self-produced perceptions. Through the hallucinatory animation of his physiological functions (respiration and heartbeat), the organs of perception (those of sight and hearing in particular) filled his sensory world. Perceval unconsciously withdrew into his body, which became the source of all sensations and the screen on to which his hallucinatory constructions were projected.

Perceval's account shows how difficult it is, even in the phase of reawakening, to emerge from confusion, to distinguish truth from falsehood, and to keep hallucinatory seduction or intimidation at bay. When the terrifying, dictatorial voices grew weaker or fell totally silent, they were replaced by ones that soothed and charmed. Delusion changes its form in order to keep its victim in thrall. It is a system of lies which must, if it is to continue to hold sway, produce a never ending succession of false perceptions that seduce the patient and isolate him from the rest of the world. Yet, its power also depends on the patient's passive participation. Perceval intuitively realized that, to avoid losing his islands of lucidity, he had to remain particularly vigilant, and forced himself to do so by the exercise of his will. By remaining mentally active, he regained his intentionality and slowly recovered his capacity for thought. In this way, he again became able to form hypotheses about the meaning of what was happening to him and gradually emerged from the prison of delusion.

As stated earlier, this account is an excellent illustration of the preparation, evolution, and possible resolution of the psychotic process, whose salient features may be summarized as follows: (a) it is a process in a constant state of flux, which gradually develops from partially reversible to relatively fixed stages; (b) the fascination of delusion stems from the lure of pleasure and seduction in a specific mental state that promises superiority and omnipotence; (c) the patient surrenders to the psychotic nucleus and can escape from it only in particular circumstances; (d) in the course of the process, the psychotic superego gradually shifts its ground from seduction to threat; in this second guise, it intimidates and persecutes the patient; (e) an important phase in the mind's recovery is the triggering of the patient's attention to, and observation of, the workings of his mind (the "islands of lucidity"), but this process is initially tortuous and fragmentary.

The unconscious and psychosis*

> "I began having what I don't think are dreams, since they were not like any dream I have ever had, or read of . . ."
>
> (Philip Dick, from an interview with Ursula Le Guin, July 1986; in Sutin, 1989)

> "At that time almost the whole of my life was not experienced as such but as a film or as a reflection of the film projected by my mind on to the screen of my unconscious. Unfortunately, the unconscious can only feel and does not see, just as the eyes can only see and do not feel, and because the unconscious does not have eyes of its own to see inside, into its fantasies, but can only feel itself, it sees the internal images as delusions outside through eyes it lacks inside."

These words were written to me a year after the end of a patient's analysis and refer to the memory of the psychotic state that had dominated the analytic picture for a long period. What was the patient telling me? Why was he talking about

---

* This chapter is a reworking of a paper originally published in the *International Journal of Psychoanalysis* (De Masi, 2000a). For a summary of the Internet discussion, see Roberts (2000). A shortened version in Italian is included in Rinaldi (2003).

the unconscious that had no eyes to see inside itself? Which unconscious was he referring to? His words seemed to me to provide a suitable opening for this chapter on the unconscious, whose aim is to examine some of the relations between analytic theory and psychosis. I contend that, by starting from the study of the unconscious, we can clarify the difference between neurosis and psychosis and construct an analytic approach more suitable for the latter condition.

Before turning to the central issue of my subject, I think it is worth pointing out that there are considerable differences between the various theories of the unconscious, the first object of analytic study.

The unconscious: singular or plural?

Should we speak of the unconscious in the singular or the plural?

The French philosopher Michel Henry (1985) holds that Freud did not delve in sufficient depth into the nature of the unconscious, even though he developed a theory of its existence and laws of functioning. In his view, the Freudian concept of the unconscious, which is at once ontic and ontological, is ill-defined. In the ontic sense, it represents the seat of the drives, of their representations, of the primary process, of the mechanisms of displacement and condensation, and of the symbolic contents of the infantile and phylogenetic past, whereas in ontological terms it is described as the negative of the conscious. Henry wonders if it is possible to describe one of these concepts only without a simultaneous detailed consideration of the other: in his view, the characteristic aura of indeterminacy surrounding the psychoanalytic unconscious is due in part to Freud's failure to undertake a parallel investigation of the concept of consciousness. The unconscious is, thus, an ontologically indeterminate term, so that its psychoanalytic conceptualization can readily lapse into ontic naturalism.

Besides the difference of opinion between philosophers and psychoanalysts on the nature and importance of the unconscious in mental life, psychoanalysts themselves disagree on the matter: Klein's unconscious is not the same as Lacan's or Jung's, and differs again from that first outlined by Freud. In recalling that Freud defined the work of analysis as *making the unconscious conscious*, Baranger (1993) notes that the term "unconscious" is not devoid of ambiguity even in Freud himself, for the unconscious of his 1915 theory, whose correlate is repression, is expanded in its scope in his contribution on splitting of the ego in the process of defence (Freud, 1940e [1938]). As Baranger says, behind one and the same word, *unconscious*, lie the different concepts of the principal analytic schools. By the *deep layers of the unconscious*, Melanie Klein means an organized mass of archaic fantasies that are present and active at every moment of life. Conversely, when Lacan tells us that *the unconscious resists any ontology*, he means that the unconscious is not a thing.

Following this brief introduction, I should like to develop three propositions. *First*, psychoanalytic theories and the techniques derived from them differ from each other because they are based on different conceptions of the unconscious; *second*, the unconscious is not a unitary structure: the various theoretical models refer to different unconscious realities, describable as different functions of the mind; and *third*, the various models are not interchangeable: each calls for confirmation in the specific clinical situation and in analysis of a specific unconscious function.

Let me stress that the various theoretical approaches, based on different functions that are all present in the unconscious, may correspond to different areas of psychopathology. To arrive at a correct analytic technique, it is therefore necessary to identify *the most suitable model of the unconscious for understanding the nature of psychosis*.

I now summarize the views of the unconscious presented to us by Freud, Klein, and Bion. My elementary account admittedly fails to do justice to the complexity and profundity of the authors' ideas, but my aim is to compare and contrast the various approaches rather than to discuss the individual models in depth.

Freud's dynamic unconscious

Freud uses the term "unconscious" to refer to two different kinds of psychic experiences of which the subject is unaware: thought processes that have easy access to consciousness, which are pre-

conscious, and those that can be recovered only with great difficulty, which belong to the unconscious proper. Whereas, from the
descriptive viewpoint, there are two types of unconscious, in dynamic terms there is only one (Freud, 1923b). Topographically, the
term *unconscious* denotes a system of the psychic apparatus made
up of contents that are barred from access to the preconscious-
conscious system by repression. Objects are stored as unconscious
representations linked by memory traces.

The Freudian unconscious is, therefore, a psychic locus having
specific mechanisms and contents. The contents are the "undis-
guised" drives, instincts, and affects, which are regulated by the
primary process, condensation, and displacement, and are recog-
nizable only through derivatives that have access to the preconscious–conscious system in the form of compromise formations
distorted by the censorship. Fantasies are the unconscious mental
representations of the drives. The unconscious is the reservoir of
primitive wishes and instincts from the personal and phylogenetic
past, but is also the locus of the primal fantasies which structure the
subject's infantile experiences.

The first split between the unconscious and preconscious is
effected by infantile repression. The characteristics of the unconscious system are those of the primary system, involving the
absence of negation and doubt, indifference to reality, and regula-
tion by the pleasure–unpleasure principle. In Freud's second topog-
raphy, the unconscious comprises not only the id, but also part of
the ego and superego. Repression is not the only mechanism in
which the unconscious is embodied; there are many others, too.
Splitting, negation, and disavowal are all defence mechanisms that
sustain and mediate conflicts between different psychic structures
or between the ego and reality; they contribute to the formation of
the unconscious and are themselves unconscious mechanisms. In
perversion, for example, splitting of the ego results in the coexis-
tence of two opposing conceptions of reality, each unaware of the
other.

Alongside the dynamic unconscious, whose basis is repression
and the conflict between instinct and culture, Freud described
other forms of unconscious functioning. In *The Ego and the Id*
(Freud, 1923b), he writes that, whereas it is true that everything
repressed is unconscious, not all the unconscious coincides with the

repressed. A portion of the ego, too, is unconscious; not in the sense that it is preconscious, but that it belongs to the non-repressed unconscious. In my view, Freud is thereby anticipating some present-day conceptions of the non-conscious components of emotional perception and of the unconscious roots of the self. While stressing the highly developed unconscious functions of emotional communication, Freud (1912b, 1915e) does not consistently develop these insights, and nor did others after him for a very long time. Analytic theory has come to place more emphasis on the repressed unconscious originating in man's animal heritage: the unconscious described in *Civilization and Its Discontents* (Freud, 1930a), which attributes human unhappiness to the irresoluble conflict between nature and culture.

The Kleinian unconscious

While continuing to espouse Freud's theory of the unconscious, Melanie Klein contributed two significant innovations: the notion of unconscious fantasy and the introduction, alongside repression, of the concept of splitting of the object and, later, of splitting and projection (projective identification). In her theory, unconscious fantasy differs from unconscious representation. It is not only the psychic representative of the drive, but also a mental representation that includes physical perceptions interpreted as relations between objects, and the corresponding anxieties and defences. The Kleinian unconscious is made up of relations between internal objects perceived concretely (Isaacs, 1952), and fantasies about them. The fantasies may be elaborated or modified by manipulation of the body (masturbatory fantasies), or produced actively through the imagination. They are unconscious in that they are knowable not directly, but, in accordance with Freud's ideas, through clinical material (interpretation of tics, fantasies, and play). However, unlike Freud, for whom fantasies are gratifications of instinctual impulses that cannot find pathways for discharge, Klein holds that a child is always able to achieve hallucinatory wish fulfilment, and accompanies the relationship to reality with continuous fantasy activity.

Innate fantasies, derived from the instincts, are seen as primarily unconscious. They include a knowledge of the nipple and the mouth, and represent all mental activities; for instance, perceptual activity is represented as the incorporation of external reality through the sense organs. In unconscious fantasy, the relations between, and the significance of, the mental objects (good and bad) are structured by splitting in accordance with the quality of the relevant bodily sensations.

The spatial metaphor is emphasized in Klein's description of the unconscious: in projective identification, unwanted contents, including parts of the self banished from consciousness, are projected outside, deposited in, and confused with, an object, and subsequently reintrojected. Furthermore, the concept of the unconscious is extended through projective identification to the bipersonal field: the projection into another person modifies the perception of the subject who projects and distorts the perception of the object that receives the projection. In one of her last contributions, Klein (1958, Chapter Eleven) describes an unconscious that is inaccessible and incapable of elaboration; she postulates the existence of separate, split-off areas that are not amenable to normal transformations: cruel and primitive aspects of the mind, thrust down into very deep layers of the unconscious (again the spatial metaphor!), where they persist as potential and inaccessible generators of madness.

Bion's unconscious

Whereas Descartes had seen the mind and consciousness as a unity and excluded the experience of animals, Freud's formalization of the unconscious as the seat of the instincts and primitive emotions helped to re-establish the link between human beings and animals. Where is the animal heritage to be found in Bion's unconscious?

In Bion, the unconscious forfeits the ontic connotation of place: it is a function of the mind and not a space for depositing the repressed. Thus, when walking, we are conscious of doing so, but unaware of how we perform the walking function. If we were so aware, our minds would be clogged up with perceptions and we should not be free to walk.

The contact barrier and the *alpha function* serve to free the mind from excessive sensory stimuli. Dreams are the psyche's modus operandi in waking life: their function is to establish the contact barrier through which *beta* elements are transformed into *alpha* and sensations become emotions. At the beginning of life, this function is performed by the mother through her capacity for reverie. The concept of repression is replaced by that of a semi-permeable membrane, a kind of unconscious organ of consciousness, which allows the processing and knowledge of the world and emotions. For Bion, the antithesis is not between the repressed (Freud) or split-off (Klein) unconscious and consciousness, but between waking and sleep, between what is and what is not conscious on the level of awareness. The unconscious is a metabolizer of psychic experiences, and, if it does not function satisfactorily the mind will be unable to produce thoughts (the semi-permeable membrane and the alpha function). (Bion's Grid, by analogy with the Mendeleyev table of the chemical elements, investigates the relations between the elements of psychoanalysis, whose structure is not directly accessible.)

In this conception, the spatial metaphor has been dropped and with it the notions of repression and splitting, together with the guilt and anxiety at what has been done to the relational objects. The patient may be conscious but unaware, in accordance with the theory of thoughts without a thinker.

In psychotic states, thoughts lack a thinker owing to the damage sustained by the alpha function. Again, "thinking", for Bion, coincides with the possibility of "dreaming". A dream is not only the process whereby the unconscious is made conscious, but also the means of moving on from the paranoid–schizoid position (expulsion) to the depressive position (assimilation). Preverbal unconscious material must be constantly subjected to dream work, which operates outside of consciousness. Bion distinguishes Freud's concept of "dream work" from his own. He writes:

> [Freud] took up only the negative attitude, dreams as "concealing" something, not the way in which the *necessary* dream is *constructed*. . . . *Freud* . . . states that a dream is the way the mind works in sleep: *I* say it is the way it works when awake. [Bion, 1992, p. 33]

Dreams, like the unconscious, are intrapsychic and interrelational communications, and not constructions to be interpreted. The unconscious, through dreaming, provides the new supplies of symbols and images that transform sensory experience into thought. Far from being the product of repression, dreaming, like the unconscious, is a function that moulds and records emotions, a daytime activity that is always present.

Some present-day conceptions of the unconscious

(A more extensive treatment of this subject [in Italian] can be found in De Masi, 2000b.)

Contemporary psychoanalysis is seen to emphasize the non-conscious component of our existence in the world—the cognitive and emotional aspect—at the expense of the animal, drive-related, and sexual heritage with which Freud was, albeit not unequivocally, concerned. This central individual nucleus of human experience features prominently in the theories of many authors, including Winnicott, with his concepts of the potential space of the self and the true self, Kohut, Bollas, and the relational and inter-subjectivist analysts.

The concept of the self, which is not to be found in Freud's theory, was anticipated by Ferenczi, who sensed the existence of unconscious functions necessary for psychic development, which were mortified by adult intrusion into the child's private space. Whereas Freud notes that patients are compelled to repeat what they are unable to remember, Ferenczi (1929, 1933) demonstrates in his contributions on abused children that post-traumatic stress gives rise to confusion and shame and that a hated child may incorporate a wish to die as a result of his early affective experiences.

Studies of memory and the effects of trauma (Fonagy, 1999) show that, when it precedes the development of the systems of emotional memory, trauma cannot be represented as a story either consciously or unconsciously.

Bollas (1987, 1992) uses the concepts of *existential memory* and the *unthought known*. The former refers to the link that evades representation, a memory recorded in everyone's being. Bollas holds that children internalize the "maternal idiom" of care, seen as a complex mode of being and relating. Relational experience, in his view, becomes experience of the self. He mentions the need to recognize the part of the self that lives in a world without words.

Emde (1989) likewise mentions a pre-representational affective centre of the self stemming from early experiences with the mother, which is similar across cultures and individual lives and guarantees the perception of continuity in the course of development, notwithstanding the progressive changes to which we are all subject.

Stolorow and Atwood (1992) expand the concept of the unconscious to include even the part of the personal history that, never having been confirmed, cannot become experience of which we are aware. According to these authors, not only omnipotent and destructive parts, but also good and constructive impulses, are rendered unconscious where these conflict with the vision of the child's care-givers; in this way, much infantile awareness and "wisdom" becomes unconscious and unavailable.

A similar view is expressed in Winnicott's reference to some patients' need to defend the *true self* from the destructive action of the environment by the construction of a *false self* that is activated in social relations. The conflict is between intimate truth and social falsehood: modern man must keep his intimate knowledge unconscious in order to defend it. Social pressure claims its victims. In this way, Winnicott offers an alternative version of the "discontents of civilization".

These hypotheses facilitate understanding of how infantile intersubjective experience is introjected and of the importance of the environment's response. Projection and distortion by the adult care-giver are introjected by a child as prohibitions or threats that make for "not knowing" (Bion's −K): that is, mental blind spots.

This brief overview of models of the unconscious in contemporary psychoanalysis shows how analysts' attention has shifted from an unconscious that operates on the basis of repression to what instead remains outside the realm of awareness and to what a person "knows" unconsciously. Even the selection of psychic experiences is not conscious. Shevrin (1986) describes it as something that "leaps" into consciousness, something prepared for by a complex and unconscious process. Research on attention has shown that the brain relates to emotional activities before relating to consciousness. The mind grasps an event emotionally even before that event enters the area of awareness, and is able to record and store information on a level outside a person's awareness.

The unconscious of the neurosciences

I am convinced that psychoanalysis, which has from the beginning demonstrated the importance of the emotions and of primal affective relationships, could benefit from a comparison with the findings of the neurosciences. Recent neuroscientific research on the emotions, an area long excluded from behaviourism, can make a valuable contribution to our own consideration of the unconscious. Behaviourism, after all, concentrated on the individual's problems of cognitive learning.

The psychologist John Kihlstrom (1987) coined the term *cognitive unconscious* to describe the subterranean processes that are the main stock-in-trade of the neurosciences. These are unconscious processes that range over many different levels of complexity; for example, routine analysis of the physical characteristics of stimuli, remembering past events, using grammar or syntax, imagining things that are not present, taking decisions, and many other processes (Pally, 1997).

To what extent does neurobiological research bear out analytic intuitions and in what respects does it differ from, or contradict, them? And can the objects of the neurobiological discoveries be deemed the same as those of psychoanalysis? LeDoux (1996), one of the best known neuroscientists, acknowledges that Freud was absolutely right to define the conscious ego as the tip of an iceberg. The experimental neurobiologists confirm that emotional experience includes much more than the mind knows about.

The link between emotions and the unconscious is one of the most important points of convergence between psychoanalysis and the neurosciences, which have shown how emotions are formed through unconscious mechanisms. Having established that the pathways from the emotional to the cognitive system are more robust than those in the opposite direction, the neuroscientists believe that the unconscious has a preponderant influence over our behaviour as we tackle the vicissitudes of life. States of consciousness arise only when the system responsible for awareness is put in touch with the systems of unconscious processing, an activity which may remain forever unconscious.

The system responsible for the generation of emotions has been identified experimentally and found to comprise important sub-systems (located respectively in the amygdala, the mammillary bodies, the striate nucleus, the hippocampus, and the thalamus), each of which performs a different function in the triggering of different integrators of emotions.

For obvious reasons, the most comprehensively studied emotion is fear. Fear leads back to trauma and its important role in memory, amnesia, and repression or, conversely, anxiety. An excessively high level of anxiety can demonstrably block memory and even damage the hippocampus.

The experimental data prove beyond doubt the kinship between the emotional unconscious of the neurobiologists and the analytic unconscious. Whereas neurobiologists and psychoanalysts alike now reject the Cartesian idea of the equivalence of mind and consciousness, the emotional unconscious of the neurosciences nevertheless appears remote from the psychoanalytic unconscious.

The dynamic unconscious and the emotional unconscious

While neuroscientific research confirms some aspects of Freudian metapsychology, it refutes others. For instance, the unconscious of the neurosciences has no place for drives, repression, and splitting. According to the neurobiologists, traumatic experiences are stored in memory systems that are not accessible to consciousness (implicit memory) and are not the outcome of repression in the Freudian sense. However, neurobiological research bears out some other data of psychoanalysis, confirming as it does that the emotions have an unconscious life, separate from the higher processing systems (i.e., those present in thought, reasoning, and consciousness).

The *unconscious* of the neurosciences coincides with *that of which the subject is unaware* and not with the repressed; being simply the emotional unconscious, it is far removed from the Freudian dynamic unconscious. This shows that, in both our language and our practice, the terms *unconscious* and *unaware*, although referring to different realities and functions, are used interchangeably. How many emotions, after all, are conveyed in the transference and, in particular, in the countertransference, by communications of which the protagonists are unaware?

It has long been known that significant and constantly active communication takes place between the analyst's unconscious and that of the patient, and that the patient might, although unaware of it, perceive certain non-verbal communications or unconscious mental aspects of the analyst of which the analyst is not aware, which are registered and appear in dreams in subsequent sessions. This "unaware" perception bears witness to the ability to grasp correctly one's own and the other's mental state through the emotional unconscious, *an unconscious that has eyes and can see*. It is surely this kind of unconscious perception, when not detected and brought into awareness by an appropriate interpretation from the analyst, that underlies the psychoanalytic impasse.

One of the earliest reported examples of the analytic impasse is Freud's Dora case (Freud, 1905e). Dominated as he was by the idea of understanding the material in terms of seeking out the repressed, Freud interprets the second dream, which accompanied Dora's decision to break off the analysis, in terms of the dynamic unconscious—uncovering the latent content—rather than as an unconscious communication. In reporting the dream, Dora tells how she saw a deserted square with a monument in it, how she returned home to find that her father had died, and how she did not attend the funeral but took refuge in her room. Freud interprets Dora's complexes and her love for Herr K, but takes no account of the communicative significance of the affective desert in which Dora found herself, of the monument to the important man that Freud was constructing for himself, and of the indifference with which the patient characterized the breaking off of her analysis. Dora was using the dream to communicate her impressions and her intention to break off the analysis, hoping that Freud would be able to understand. Freud himself stresses the importance of the emotional unconscious as something capable of directing the analyst's listening: the analyst, he writes, "must turn his own unconscious like a receptive organ towards the transmitting unconscious of the patient" (Freud, 1912e, p. 115–116).

Some references to the theory of technique

Even if each analyst has a model of his own, which may or may not be reflected in the various parameters of the unconscious outlined above, the various techniques ought not to conflict with each other. A good analysis should explore all simultaneously operating aspects of the unconscious. I contend that the analyst must identify the type of unconscious involved in the patient's psychopathology and the type of analytic communication to be used: we need to know which unconscious we are addressing.

In parallel with the theoretical realization of the importance of the analytic relationship as a transformational function, analytic technique has changed progressively. I shall now outline the main characteristics of the analytic techniques arising out of the different conceptions of the unconscious, which in turn support different models of mental disturbance and different therapeutic strategies. The three groups very broadly correspond to the evolution of the concept of the unconscious during the course of the development of analytic thought.

1. An analyst working with the Freudian dynamic unconscious interprets repressed contents. This technique stems mainly from the discoveries about dream dynamics and the unconscious conflict that underlies symptoms. The manifest content becomes understandable through the unveiling of the latent content. Interpretation means uncovering the underlying content; analysis of the transference, which refers back to the repressed of the past, is therefore of central importance. Freudian technique comprises mainly interpretative interventions intended to make the unconscious conscious and to reduce the severity of the superego by the transformation of archaic unconscious fantasies.

2. The importance attributed by Melanie Klein to the mechanisms of splitting gives rise to a modification of technique, which concentrates on recovery of the split-off and projected parts of the personality and on transference interpretation of the here and now. The analyst serves as the recipient of the projections and split-off parts. Through systematic analysis of the transference, Kleinian analysis sets out to help the patient to recover an image of the internal world in which libidinal aspects hold sway over their destructive counterparts. The libidinal aspects can emerge only when the split-off parts of the self—which are unwanted owing to the unconscious destruction and envy they

contain—have been experienced and recovered and reparative processes have been initiated.

3. The emotional unconscious implies that a high proportion of emotional communication is unconscious and that perceptions of the emotional reality of the analytic couple are mediated by non-verbal communication. The notion of projective identification for the purposes of communication is paramount in this context. The capacity for construction and restitution by the container, the analyst who receives the analysand's unconscious and "unaware" communication, is of fundamental importance. Particular significance attaches to the analyst's countertransference and emotions, the level of symbolic and emotional communication, and the type and quality of dreams. Much of the theoretical discourse on the analytic relationship (Mitchell, Greenberg, and Ogden) and on the analytic dialogue (in Italy, Nissim Momigliano and, for certain aspects, Ferro) results from the implicit assumption of the existence of an emotional unconscious that communicates, or of two unconsciouses speaking to each other on a level beyond the participants' awareness.

Which unconscious is relevant to psychosis?

Bion's view of the nature and function of the unconscious as the metabolizer of thoughts and emotions (the emotional unconscious) oddly and unexpectedly anticipates the neuroscientific theory of the unconscious processing of emotions. The neurosciences describe the conscious and unconscious aspects as serial and parallel functions. Consciousness seems to operate serially, one step at a time, whereas the unconscious mind is made up of a large number of different systems working in parallel. The serial processors create representations by manipulation of symbols, the only entities of which we are conscious. At a lower level, processing takes place subsymbolically with codes that cannot be deciphered by consciousness. The neurosciences tell us that the emotions are not only unconscious but must be transformed in order to become conscious. That is to say, in Bion's terms, the preverbal and presymbolic unconscious material must be continually subjected to dream work (the contact barrier, beta elements, and the alpha function), which operates outside consciousness. How indebted we still are to Bion for his visionary and revolutionary intuitions!

For Bion, the unconscious is a function of mind, an unaware memory that processes experience, characterized not so much by repression as by communicative semi-permeability. The conscious content is the fruit of a process of which we are never conscious; we are conscious only of its result.

For the sake of simplicity, I have attempted to distinguish two unconscious systems, the *dynamic* and the *emotional*. (This distinction throws light on the vexed question of wishful dreams and traumatic dreams. The former are the product of repressed wishes in the dynamic unconscious, while the latter communicate a suffering not yet worked through in the emotional unconscious.) The first corresponds to the repressed unconscious discovered and described by Freud, while the second is the unconscious intuited by Bion and confirmed by the neurosciences, which relates to *that of which we are unaware*. What place is to be assigned to these two models of the unconscious and what is the relationship between them? Must the Freudian model be deemed obsolete?

If different models explore different aspects of the psyche and different fields of human pathology, it may perhaps be postulated that Bion and the neurosciences are concerned with what "lies below", whose functioning does not enter consciousness because it is "unaware consciousness". We must accept that there are structures and functions of our minds of which we are unaware, whose constitutive components are unknowable, but which make emotional life possible. A further distinction must therefore be made, between the *unconscious*, that of which we are *unaware*, and the *unknowable*. We can never know what a *beta* or *alpha* element or a presymbolic emotional element consists in. An important contribution to this subject was made by Sandler & Sandler (1987), who postulate the existence of unconscious functions, objects, or representations that can be *conceived* but not *perceived*. One of these is the *past unconscious*, which contains the vicissitudes of the infantile self, which has a history and an organization that is crystallized in the very first years of life, but which is not accessible to consciousness and can be known only through hypotheses.

So, if the emotional unconscious exists alongside its dynamic counterpart, Freud tells us what happens when the system "below", which makes psychic life possible, is operational: only then can a personal unconscious permeated with conflicts or relational wishes come into being. Unlike the emotional unconscious, which serves the purpose of knowledge but is not knowable, the dynamic unconscious can be brought to the light of day. The emotional unconscious, in this view, is the precondition for the existence and operation of the dynamic unconscious, which is engaged in an ongoing relationship with the former.

"Unaware" consciousness

The emotional unconscious is fuelled by affective life and early infantile relational experiences; it constantly constructs the sense of personal identity, determines the subject's mode of relating to the world, generates the capacity to perceive and deal with emotions, and defines *the unaware consciousness of existence (of the self)*. "Higher-order consciousness depends on building a self through affective intersubjective exchanges" (Edelman, 1992, p. 150).

> Tragedy becomes possible—the loss of the self by death or mental disorder, the remembrance of unassuageable pain. . . . Ironically, the self is the last thing to be understood by its possessor, even after the possession of a theory of consciousness. [*ibid.*, p. 136]

The concept of the self, which is not found in Freud's theory, was put forward by Winnicott and Kohut with a wide range of semantic connotations. It is used here with no theoretical reference to these two authors, to throw light on the unaware (unconscious) roots of everyone's personal identity and individual meaning. Whereas the function of consciousness is proper to the ego, self-awareness is a function of the self.

The components of this unaware consciousness of self are damaged in the course of psychosis. Whereas neurosis is the result of inharmonious functioning of the dynamic unconscious, psychosis stems from an alteration of the emotional unconscious: that is, of the mental apparatus that can symbolize emotions and use the function of thought. A possible example of the failure to distinguish between the unconscious levels is Freud's analysis and interpretation of the illness of Senatspräsident Schreber. Schreber's psychosis begins with a state of sexualization, based on a delusional wish to be a woman in the act of intercourse and the subsequent conviction of being penetrated by rays of God in an ecstatic state. Persecutory elements enter into the relationship with God and with Flechsig, the psychiatrist in charge of his case. Using the model of the dynamic unconscious (unwanted content, repression, and return of the repressed), Freud "considers" Schreber's delusional state in terms of an expression of the relationship with the father (God) and with the unconscious homosexual component. Psychosis, like neurosis, is interpreted in accordance with the theory of dreams and the revealing of unconscious contents. Note, too, that Freud equates Schreber's transsexual delusion (he was sometimes caught wearing women's clothes) with unconscious homosexuality.

During the course of the psychotic process the emotional unconscious undergoes a series of transformations, initially gradual and later radical, that completely destroy its function of intrapsychic and relational communication.

As the basis of the potential space of the self and an entity necessary to our unaware perception of psychic identity, how does the emotional unconscious come into being? What happens when the conditions for its formation are altered or inappropriate at the beginning of life? Why does psychological and emotional life collapse into psychosis at a certain juncture? Even a partial answer to these questions would take us further in understanding the nature of the psychotic state, the conditions that pave the way for it, and its consequences.

As we know, in the normal developmental process, a child becomes increasingly aware of the lack of something that is unknown, but necessary for his peace of mind; he senses that there must be a mind outside himself, which he does not possess and which is capable of receiving him. In the chapter of *Cogitations* headed "The tropisms", Bion (1992) writes that the development of personality depends on the existence of an object similar to the breast, into which the tropisms (projective identifications) can be projected. If this object does not exist, disaster ensues for the personality, which ultimately becomes structured in terms of loss of contact with reality, apathy, or mania. The sense of self stems from the successful restitution, by an object endowed with sensitivity and emotional receptivity, of the projections in search of meaning.

This aspect of the experience of the child's relationship with the primary object accounts for the environmental element in the formation of the psychotic part of the personality: in this case, the child does not learn to internalize a "breast-mother" who provides psychic containment and uses emotions in order to understand.

Arguing along these lines, Fonagy and Target (1996) consider that patients with severe personality disorders inhibit a phase in the normal development of mental processes—namely, the reflective function—thus making it impossible for them to understand the symbolic qualities of other people's behaviour. At any rate, the psychotic process proper makes use of further destructive processes, which are as yet little known, and among which the omnipotence of perception features prominently. Failure to introject an object that understands emotions distorts growth and impedes the development of a function fundamental to the constitution of our "innate" sense of existence.

The crucial point is the constant deterioration of the apparatus (the emotional unconscious) that was damaged from the beginning, through the agency of a system (the psychotic construction) that prevents the subject once and for all from coming into contact with the perceptual part of the self. *In psychosis, the unconscious is blinded.*

The destructive onslaught is not direct. The perceptual alteration system includes omnipotent and illusional mental transformations: manic states, drug addiction, or masturbatory withdrawal underlie a mental catastrophe (the psychotic breakdown) subsequently experienced as extremely guilt-inducing.

Personal identity is altered, disorganized, and destroyed by an anti-emotional pathological organization that devalues and kills emotions, distorts psychic reality, and continuously transforms the subject's mental state. Psychosis may be seen as a destructive way of dealing with mental pain, *a psychic strategy directed towards self-annihilation* (De Masi, 1996), which leads imperceptibly to the crossing of the threshold of tolerance and to the final destruction of personal identity. This self-destruction, whose origins lie in the subject's earliest object relations, becomes the tragedy enacted in the psychotic state, when the patient no longer possesses the unity and potential space of existence whereby he can feel alive, whole, and separate from others. The psychotic patient must face his own psychic death, the unbearable pain of the destruction that has taken place, confusion with the rest of the world, which rushes in on him through hallucinations and delusions, and the anguished search for his own self in others.

A corollary of the loss of the functions of the emotional unconscious is that the patient is deprived of the capacity for self-observation and awareness of his mental and emotional processes. One of the major obstacles to progress in analytic therapy is the extremely high level, in the psychotic process, of the state of unawareness, due to the impossibility of making practical use of the unconscious emotional function. *The patient is conscious but unaware of what is happening to him.* (If thinking is to be possible, an apparatus to "contain" thoughts must be developed. In the absence of this apparatus, there may be consciousness but there will be no awareness. In psychosis, it is impossible for the subject to *be aware of what appears in consciousness* [cf. the "film projected by the mind on to the screen of the unconscious" described by the patient mentioned at the beginning of this chapter].)

Meltzer (1984), who creatively expands some of Bion's formulations on the relationship between psychosis and thought, investigates how dreams succeed in producing symbolic forms appropriate for representing emotional experience and hence truth. In his view, psychopathology of the process of dreaming coincides with the distortion of thought—that is, with the formation of hallucinations and delusions. Lies, too, like hallucinations and delusions, are a distorted representation of emotional experience, and correspond to a self-induced poisoning of the mind.

I shall now present and comment on two case histories in order to illustrate my views.

Giovanni

A "normal" patient, too, may mistake the time of a session, try to understand the reason for his error, and possibly feel sorry. Giovanni, however, was not "normal"; at least, he did not appear so when, after spending a fruitless twenty minutes or so in the waiting room (having arrived that early for his session), he insisted, immediately upon lying down on the couch, that he had got the time right and that it was I who was late. Once I had succeeded in clearing up the error, I asked him what his thoughts had been during his wait. A "normal" patient might perhaps have said that, while waiting, he had imagined that the analyst had come under the spell of his predecessor and lost track of the time, or perhaps that he had been unable to end the session on time. But Giovanni told me that, on seeing a well-dressed man leaving, he had realized that I had carried on over time so as to talk to an executive of the firm in which he had worked abroad: he had guessed his identity from his smart attire. Since Giovanni had left the firm and not been in touch since, it obviously wanted to know where he had hidden and had therefore sent someone along to my consulting room to find out.

The explanations about his wait had had no time or place to form in Giovanni's mind. The certainties stemmed from his recent past, which was characterized by a delusion that had transformed his perception of the reality around him. Although Giovanni was unaware of it, his false perceptions embodied his anxieties in concrete form.

When I then tried, in the session, to examine with him the sequence of thoughts that had passed through his mind during his wait, the patient said he had realized subsequently that a "little worm" had slipped into his brain while he was waiting and suggested to him something that he had not hesitated to see as true and real. This "little worm" seemed to lie at the root of his tendency to relapse into a psychotic state.

Giovanni was a twenty-six-year-old graduate engineer. He had spent the previous two years abroad completing his training, having won scholarships as a brilliant and highly promising worker in his field. After graduation, he had decided to go abroad to study and work, not only for professional reasons, but also for the sake of his "maturation", as he put it. He had wanted to separate from his family, in particular, from what he called the "maternal river bed", a complex of affective relations that he had experienced as immature and over-dependent.

According to my reconstruction during the course of the treatment, Giovanni, the eldest child of a mother who was good but lacked emotional resonance and a father who had always urged him to assert himself, had been unable to see himself as a child. Following the birth of his sister and a number of cousins, he had felt compelled to uphold his prestige as the eldest by force. In order to stand out, he had had to impose his will on the younger children and assert himself *vis-à-vis* his parents with his intellectual performance. He had kept himself going in adolescence with idealized friendships.

Working successfully in the multi-national corporation that had engaged him in the foreign country, Giovanni gradually became convinced that he could quickly become its leader. Once he had risen to the level of worldwide president, he could implement a plan to get rid of all the world's ills, such as poverty, racism, and war (by association, this was reminiscent of the part he had played at home since early childhood in pacifying his constantly quarrelling parents). To confirm the reality of his own power, he had needed to be able to conquer women. One day, however, he had clashed with a foreign colleague, who had then stolen his girl. He had tried to overcome the difficulty by persuading his rival to stand aside, but manifestly to no avail. Giovanni's impotent rage had then assumed colossal proportions. Having had no response, he had lived in ever-increasing fear of possible secret reprisals from his rival and colleague (who had meanwhile disappeared) or compatriots in league with him. This episode had ushered in a progressive delusional state in which he had seen all people of his rival's nationality as possible persecutors who were out to kill him by any means, including poison gas.

Meanwhile his parents fetched him back from abroad and arranged for him to go into hospital, where he was treated with drugs. After his discharge, Giovanni was no longer suffering from delusions and felt reassured by his return home. The psychiatrist in charge of his case advised him to have analysis. The psychotic episode seemed to have been a "journey" in which his mind had been progressively colonized by an anti-emotional, arrogant system that had first made him omnipotent and then caused him to feel threatened and helpless.

In some of my initial interventions, I stressed the effort that he had consciously made very much earlier to transform his personal identity, and also pointed out the analogy between the fear that his life was in danger and the anxiety about his own psychic self, which seemed to have been worn down by an anti-human system of extreme arrogance. The problem as presented in the analysis was complex and could not readily be tackled by reconstructive inter-pretations.

Although Giovanni had now resumed work (he would get up in the mornings and meet people with whom he carried on a dialogue), he nevertheless lived in a potentially "other" reality, or rather, there were two adjacent realities, one of which could unex-pectedly spill over into the other: two worlds coexisted, as if belonging to different minds, and the two perceptions, normal and psychotic, could alternate. When the delusional state was upper-most, Giovanni was afraid of being poisoned in the bar where he went for his lunch break. If an acquaintance told him that he "knew" the location of his house in the country (because he lived nearby), Giovanni sometimes felt that he had been discovered by the "organization" that was persecuting him: the acquaintance might, after all, be a spy. If I spoke about him in the analysis, link-ing up with things he had told me about his past or merely using my intuition, I realized that I became an object of suspicion for him: I knew much more than he imagined, was endowed with telepathic powers, and therefore belonged to the organization that was spying on him and wanted to eliminate him.

As the analytic work progressed, "psychosis-free intervals" enabled him to gain a better understanding of the power exerted over him by the psychotic state. In the past he had been convinced that he had to conquer, to "possess" (he now said this almost with a sense of shame). The clash with his foreign colleague had been catastrophic because it had called into question the dominant and omnipotent part of himself that always had to come out on top. He now understood that the alteration of his state of mind had served to construct a megalomanic world when he was faced with an impoverished self which he was afraid did not even exist: in the place of a self that had not formed, Giovanni had constructed mega-lomanic defences that had altered his psychic truth and preached the freedom of arrogance.

Afterwards he had felt threatened by the very system he had created. Whenever he succeeded, in the analysis, in gaining some insight and felt able to understand the psychotic world, he noticed that this world became more threatening. When he was apart from the analyst, the psychotic organization would become more capable of dominating him.

However, areas of freedom and thought enabled him to realize that, in his manic race for success, he had taken no account of himself, and he was now aware that he had no perception of personal identity, did not know what real qualities he had, what objects he loved, and what he could develop. He had always been concerned about what others thought of him, but not about what he thought of others, or about what his own emotions were in his personal relations. Giovanni's gradual emergence from psychosis now enabled him to confront the identity problems that had preceded and determined his illness. This new awareness came about in a relatively benign situation, since the breakdown in this instance had not involved substantial psychic mutilation.

Giovanni's case helps us to understand the qualitative difference between psychotic and neurotic mental functioning. The latter is still governed by the properties of the dynamic unconscious, which admittedly undergoes quantitative alterations (e.g., excessive use of repression, or an unbalanced relationship between the various psychic agencies), but the alterations are never structured and progressive in such a way as to destroy perception.

Psychosis alters the unaware elements that underlie the construction of psychic reality. Hence the aim of *making the unconscious conscious* remains appropriate for a neurotic patient who, while repressing truth, preserves it unconsciously, and does not destroy it. The destruction of meaning in the psychotic state stems from an attack—not experienced as such—on the functions of learning from emotional experience, and generates an ever closer dependence on an omnipotent system that proves to be a parasitic production of the mind (my patient's "little worm").

Paolo

This case, which is not unlike my first example, shows how the patient is unaware of his psychotic functioning and hence how important it is to direct the analytic work towards bringing about an awareness of the meaning of the psychotic organization, which tends to engulf the self and destroy the sense of reality.

Paolo, aged twenty-four, was the only son of separated parents and had always lived with his mother. Although he was a lively, seemingly communicative boy, he had had relational difficulties in the past, and had been unable to adapt to the regular rhythms, schedules, and tasks of school life. A tendency to withdraw and to minimize the difficulties and demands of life, as if he were living in an infantile dream world, had often caused him to fail.

Having had a passion for rock music since his teens, he had joined with some others of his own age to form a band, which had begun to enjoy a degree of success among young people before his psychotic explosion. Paolo participated spasmodically in his group's activities, and dreamed of becoming a rock star (this, for him, represented an extraordinary change of status, success, fame, and power. However, he seemed unable to understand that success in the world of entertainment was difficult, conditional not only on improvement of one's technical skills, but also on the ability to maintain empathic relations with other people. He often interpreted conflicts as deliberate attempts by others to exclude or attack him, cut him off, and humiliate him.

Paolo exhibited clear-cut psychotic symptoms in the course of a problematic relationship with a girl—his first real love relationship—while working with his rock group. The relationship was stormy partly because of his partner's difficult character, and it consumed his energy to such an extent that he felt on the point of losing his mind. He therefore sought other relationships, and went with two prostitutes. After confessing this to his girlfriend, he felt that he had committed a catastrophic act that had entered the public domain, for which he felt constantly accused. In this delusional atmosphere, Paolo decided to seek psychological help, and at first felt relieved by it. During this period, his difficulties with the rock group came to a head, and the band went on tour without him. The ensuing sessions came to be dominated by the figure of Peter, a rock musician he absolutely worshipped and spoke of as a brother, an imaginary twin, someone with whom he desperately wanted to meet up but did not know when that might happen. Paolo "knew" that Peter was in Milan; he had met him in the street and they had greeted each other. Paolo seemed anxious and disorientated, and sometimes positively afraid. It was not easy to enquire about his state, as his replies were evasive. He often skipped sessions, telephoning me from home and giving me the impression that he was disorientated and in a state of persecutory anxiety. The analytic communication was very fragmented and it seemed to me that the patient was unable to talk about what was happening and did not trust me. Members of his family reported that Paolo would leave the house in the middle of the night or go wandering on the edge of town. Systematic psychiatric intervention became necessary and antipsychotic therapy had to be resumed. The holidays were approaching, but I knew that his father was not far away and that Paolo was receiving psychiatric attention, and so I was able to leave him in a relatively protected situation. When the analysis resumed after the holidays, it became possible to "work" on the delusion, now without the emergency of the acute psychotic state. The figure of Peter remained dominant in these sessions. Paolo told me about his music, about his certainty that he would be working with him, and would pursue his music to depths down to which even Peter had not delved. He described idyllic moments of union with him during the holidays. A few weeks later, he told me he had decided to go to Florence for an important international music festival. I then asked him whether he would be meeting Peter. He said no. I added that it seemed easier to meet Peter when he was fused in with him (he had "seen" him a week earlier in the window of the block over the road) than when he was separate from him. Paolo said he really did see Peter, who saw him from a distance and would then run away. I told him it was when he felt he did not exist that he saw Peter, an imaginary twin, who protected him and promised to save him, like a mirage generated by the need to survive, which then dissolved if one approached it . . .

He replied that Peter was there but ran away because he did not wish to trivialize the meeting. Their meeting would be extraordinary and would transform his life. I remarked that Peter was like a messiah who held out the promise of a complete transformation of his existence—something different from and far above the analytic work he was doing with me. The patient confirmed this and went on: "Just imagine when he comes to pick me up: all the papers in England will be full of me . . . Yes, it really is true!" I continued to press him, asking why, if this were so, he gave himself things to do, tried to get involved, came to analysis, and was even thinking of getting a job. "Because, when Peter comes," he replied, "I shall follow him, and I think I would then feel guilty at the life I have left behind here." I pointed out to Paolo that he "knew" that the meeting with Peter was tantamount to becoming someone else: in the exchange, he would lose the real Paolo and was afraid of losing him for ever. He answered, "My idea is that I can become Peter and he me." It was clear that, concealed behind the wish to turn into something grandiose and false that drove him to enter into a delusional world, lay the impulse not to exist or to die psychically, obliterating his failing self.

I noted that the patient on this occasion was listening to me very attentively. In fact, by this stage of the therapy, Paolo was in the process of distancing himself from Peter; he could be snatched out of his world, but at other times not, as in this session.

The function assumed by Peter in Paolo's mind was very complex. Peter was not only his "protector" but also his "dominator". He would often tell him all the things he had to do and give him orders; he would suggest, for example, that if he really wanted to meet him in the musical Eden (lots of money, power, and girls), he would have to submit totally to him; or he would command him to have sex with a girl he could see before him in the presence of her boyfriend. Whenever Paolo attempted to extricate himself from his power and expel him from his mind, Peter threatened to kill him. The period of persecutory anxiety was bound up with this aspect of the relationship with Peter: because Peter threatened him with death, he was afraid for his life. At a certain point in his development, the psychotic representation moved into the world of intimidation and the protective figure was transformed into a dictator of the mind. Paolo recognized that Peter's world was a trap, a prison, from the recesses of which he could communicate only by silent and secret means if he was stay alive. For the time being these channels of communication were present mainly in the analytic relationship.

It is very important in analytic therapy to reach a stage at which the patient can "see" the psychotic construction, as seemed possible for Paolo at this time.

Consequences of the destruction of the emotional unconscious

I have presented these two cases to draw attention to the fact that there is no possibility of analysing a patient without making him aware of the objectives of the delusional structure. One must confront the parts that have remained outside the system, prevent them from being attracted by it, and help them to "see". This is possible only at certain moments in the analysis. The psychotic solution exerts a powerful attraction, and it is therefore understandable that the patient—since it is the only solution remaining to him—defends it tenaciously and distrusts the analyst. It is the power of the psychotic mode of functioning that explains how easily the patient may lose insight even if, during the course of therapy, he has become capable of introjection and integration. As we shall see later, years of precious analytic work can sometimes melt away like snow in the sunshine.

As it progressively becomes more powerful, psychotic functioning extends its dominion to memory. Freud had already shown that the emotional experience of the present modifies the past, which is constantly remodelled. In the psychotic state, the alteration of the perceptual apparatus is capable of continuously modifying the past, too, recreating and recataloguing it as a new, ever-changing reality. What is lost at the same time is the plasticity of memory that enables the intuition of the present to enrich and integrate with the experience of the past. This applies particularly to the working through of a psychotic episode, which is resistant to any reworking.

Owing to the lack of a place in the mind for depositing, working through, and utilizing memories, and hence of one of the basic conditions for the synthesis and integration of thoughts and emotions, particular modalities apply to the attempt at recovery from the psychotic state. After the breakdown, the patient, lacking a genuine capacity for transformation, tends to re-establish the previous equilibrium, putting together shattered parts of the personality. The psychotic repair (reconstruction) takes the form of gluing together parts of the personality by omnipotent and violent means (Steiner, 1991) without regard to the patient's personal history and the reasons for the crisis, and is, therefore, doomed to failure. For this reason, one of the main functions of analysis is to support the patient in the quest for more appropriate means of healing.

The alteration of the emotional unconscious in the psychotic state gives rise to qualitative alterations in the dynamic unconscious; for example, it produces a psychotic superego that seemingly lacks any kinship with its neurotic counterpart. As I shall explain in the next chapter, the terrifying quality of psychotic superego objects cannot be compared to the neurotic superego, which stems from the introjection of the parent figures, albeit with various degrees of distortion. Like a kind of catastrophic magma that alters the lie of the land and undermines the buildings constructed upon it, the psychotic state impacts on the emotional unconscious and at the same time devastates the Freudian dynamic unconscious. The destruction of the emotional unconscious, which is accompanied by nameless anxiety, has lasting repercussions on the capacity not only to think, but also to dream. I shall attempt to show in the next chapter that the dreams of psychotic patients are not, as theorized by Freud, linked by association to hidden thoughts or emotions, but remain concrete objects; they cannot therefore be interpreted so as to uncover their latent, symbolic meaning.

In this chapter I have distinguished the dynamic from the emotional unconscious and have sought to show that the psycho-analytic theory of psychotic states is based not on the dynamic unconscious, but on the much larger area of that of which the subject is unaware. The *psychoanalytic unconscious* may be said to comprise a number of distinct unconsciouses: the dynamic uncon-scious and the emotional unconscious, the defensive unconscious functions that alter perceptions of the self and the "unaware" and vital emotional functions of the self. Since the "system above" (the dynamic unconscious) does not coincide with the "system below" (the emotional unconscious), psychoanalytic treatment of the psychotic state cannot use the dynamic theory, which, I repeat, is derived from the therapy of neurotic patients. The usual interpre-tative posture is not only not useful, but also liable to confuse the patient, in view of the profound alteration of the constitutive elements of the emotional unconscious in the psychotic state.

Once the psychotic breakdown has occurred, analytic therapy consists essentially in an attempt at non-omnipotent reconstruction, with the aim of restoring the functioning of the emotional uncon-scious, so as to give the patient back his awareness, thereby helping him to reconstitute his self-perception, his personal identity, and the functions that support it. This process of reconstruction, involving confrontation with the reasons for, and methods of, destruction of the self, entails enormous pain and is potentially catastrophic; it is a challenge to the darkness from which we ourselves still have much to learn.

Analytic treatment of such patients presupposes painstaking investigation of the primal processes (the child's earliest relations with his objects) which alter "unaware" consciousness and the potential space of the self, and which, in combination with other, subsequent defences that abolish awareness, give rise to self-destructive mental tendencies whose outcomes are often not easily reversible. We must concentrate on these as yet badly understood special mental states, which pave the way for the psychotic break-down and the quite typical processes governing the balance between destruction of the emotional and cognitive functions and the attempt at reconstruction that follows the catastrophe.

The following chapters are devoted to an in-depth examination of these matters, which are, in my view, crucial to clinical and theoretical research in the field of psychosis.

CHAPTER FIVE

The meaning of dreams in the psychotic state*

"The god created dreams to show the way to the dreamer, whose eyes are in darkness"

(Egyptian Papyrus Insinger)

Imprisonment in psychosis

The *Schizophrenia Bulletin* of the US National Institute of Mental Health includes a section, "First Person Account", open to patients and their families. In some of these articles, patients diagnosed as psychotic discuss the way they live and their problems. (A collection of accounts by these patients and members

---

* This chapter substantially coincides with the paper by Paola Capozzi and myself published in the *International Journal of Psychoanalysis* (Capozzi & De Masi, 2001). The Internet discussion appeared in the same journal (Werbart, 2002).

of their families has been published in Italian by Bertrando [1999].)
One of these descriptions seems to illustrate particularly well the
state of mental imprisonment in which some patients live even
when they have succeeded in recovering a part of their social
capacity.

The patient concerned writes:[1]

> "Over the years I have had many 'mad' thoughts, but my main
> delusions, of grandeur—mediumistic phenomena—and persecu-
> tion, have remained constant. These delusions are supported by
> such vivid hallucinations that I cannot usually distinguish them
> from reality, except by saying to myself that none of this is real, that
> what the people I love and trust tell me is true, that I am unusual
> only because I am schizophrenic, and that everything I think about
> the supernatural is due to an illness."

This statement helps us to understand how the relationship
between the healthy and psychotic parts of the personality resembles a precarious compromise that can break down from one
moment to the next. The delusion is always present as a *second
system* that can be activated at any time.

The psychotic condition cannot be seen as something static, in
balance with something else (from this point of view, the notions of
the *psychotic part* and the *neurotic part* of the personality, used first
by Katan [1954] and later by Bion [1957] may be misleading), but is
in fact an entity endowed with a dangerous power, for the
psychotic world can colonize and engulf the healthy one at any
time.

To preserve their psychic equilibrium, some patients eventually
decide not to experience their own emotions. As another patient
puts it, "Flat emotions are an obvious compromise to reduce
psychotic symptoms. As a result, one feels emotions at a lower level
than a normal person would."

The kind of improvement to which this patient aspires (which
can also be secured by spontaneous remissions or by treatment with
drugs only) is anti-analytic in that it runs counter to the purpose of
therapy, which is to recover the unity and completeness of the
self. However, we know that any attempt to recover emotions and
vitality entails the risk of relapse, and that, when the analytic
process facilitates integration and a closer approach to the patient's

emotions, a fresh crisis is possible. Attempts at improvement and integration will therefore always be risky.

"Keeping the emotions flat" is a defence deployed by the patient because even pleasurable experiences might be felt too intensely to be tolerable. The state of inhibition that often characterizes the therapy of these patients for long periods might also result from underlying confusional states which make it impossible for the patient to distinguish the meaning of his emotions, so that vital aggressive aspects are confused with destructive explosions. This emotional paralysis often conceals the activity of a confusing and terrifying superego. This problem arises in a particular form in patients whose living and passionate infantile world was met with crushing responses from adults.

It is, therefore, essential for analytic therapy to create the conditions whereby the psychotic nucleus can be confronted, with a view to reducing its power. Until the underlying delusion has been understood and transformed, the psychotic experience continues to bring about a state of intimidation that holds sway over the patient, who sees himself as a person whose liberty is restricted, a prisoner who can feel relatively safe provided that he does not overstep certain limits and move on to dangerous ground.

Dreams without associations

One of the complex and paradoxical aspects of the analytic therapy of psychotic patients is that, for long periods, the psychotic functioning is invisible in the clinical material, and that, when it emerges, it does so suddenly and unexpectedly, after the transformation into "psychosis" has taken place. My intention is to show that exploration of the dreams of certain psychotic patients might prove useful for understanding their psychosis and contribute to the analytic work of modifying the delusional state. Dreams prove to be a useful instrument for the comprehension of psychotic constructions when other possible channels of analytic investigation are lacking.

As we know, one of the difficulties encountered in analysing the dreams of psychotic patients is the absence of associations. Since these patients are unable to make significant connections to their dreams, they bring them into their sessions in such a way that their meaning cannot be analysed or explored in depth.

Clinical aspects of psychotic dreams

Freud (1911c) notes that, at the time of onset of Senatspräsident Schreber's second psychotic episode, Schreber dreamed more than once that his old nervous disorder had come back. Once, in the early hours of the morning, while he was in a state between sleeping and waking, the idea occurred to him that it must be very nice to be a woman submitting to the act of copulation. In Freud's view, such patients are struggling with the same material as will feature in their psychosis. Schreber later had the delusion that he had been transformed into a woman and was being fertilized by divine rays. Subsequent authors (e.g., Katan, 1960) have observed that the psychosis might begin with a dream and that psychotic patients do not distinguish between dreams and psychotic symptoms.

On the relationship between dreams and psychosis, it is worth rereading the report by Mack (1969) on an American Psychoanalytic Association panel held in Boston in 1968. Among the participants, Frosch (in Mack, 1969) wonders whether there is anything specific about the mental content or affective quality of a psychotic dream. He concludes that a definitive answer cannot be given, because some dreams exhibit nothing specific, whereas others include a persecutory content in which the psychosis is expressed. Frosch considers an important and characteristic aspect of psychotic patients to be their inability to distinguish dreams from reality: their dreams are so vivid that they are confused with the events of the day. Postulating that dreams might be an attempt to forestall the illness or to control the conflict, Frosch enquires as to the further significance of dreams that herald psychosis. Dreams of disintegration of the world might reflect the disintegration of the ego, or, alternatively, they could represent the way in which the ego reacts to drives directed against the external world and the self.

Finally, in the view not only of Frosch but also of Katan, dreams sometimes not only impel the dreamer into psychosis, but actually become part of the delusion, so that they are incorporated into psychotic behaviour (the dream then being the construction of a

delusional reality). Frosch thinks that, in these cases, ego deficiencies allow the emergence of pathological phenomena in the waking
state, or else excessive instinctual pressure is present. As a result of
the ego deficiencies, the dream may be accepted as reality.

Atkins (in Mack, 1969), too, considers that psychosis may be
anticipated by certain dreams, which in this case will be of two
kinds: those expressing the regressive and ego-disorganizing potential and those containing elements of defence and delusional restitution. In the latter type, the manifest content exhibits a consistent
defensive construction similar to delusion, erected in an attempt to
counter the threat of disintegration.

The relationship between dreams and psychosis is complex
even on the simple phenomenological level.

Certain authors (for example, Racamier, 1976) have described
some clinical characteristics of the dreams of psychotic patients.
The first relates not so much to dreams themselves as to the activity
of dreaming, which, in acute psychotic phases, becomes confused
with external reality. In psychotic dreams, especially in the acute
phase of psychosis, there is often no distinction between the waking
state and that of sleep, and between hallucinations and dreams; nor
is there any distinction between delusions, hallucinations, and
nocturnal events that might be called dreams, to which they are
often psychically equivalent. In these acute phases, dreams may be
experienced as real events.

The second characteristic concerns the *psychotic dreams* occurring not infrequently in the therapy of borderline patients or in the
intervals between psychotic episodes. These dreams feature violence, sexual sadism, sudden aggressive explosions, and monstrous
nightmare figures, which sometimes worry the patient but more
often alarm the analyst.

Finally, there are aspecific dreams, i.e., ones indistinguishable
from those of neurotics.

Theoretical problems

Analytic theory has investigated the meaning of dreams by linking
them closely to the dreamer's mental functioning.

For Freud (1900a), the dream work consists in fulfilling, albeit in disguised form, an unconscious wish that would otherwise disturb the dreamer and interrupt his sleep. Dreams also serve to reduce and modulate the tension of the drives and to express drive-related wishes in manifest form through the distortion of the censorship (Freud, 1923c). Dreams enact a conflict of which the patient is not conscious, but their interpretation allows the conflict to be resolved by making it conscious. The interpretation of dreams thus constitutes the royal road to a knowledge of the unconscious and to the understanding and subsequent transformation of psychoneurotic disturbances. Translation of the manifest content into the underlying latent thoughts is made possible by a knowledge of the mechanisms of the dream work, such as condensation and displacement. This work transforms the latent dream thoughts, which are unacceptable to the ego, into the manifest content.

The only exceptions to this dream-work process are traumatic dreams, which are a repetition of the traumatic experience in which the function of fulfilment has failed (Freud, 1920g). They are an attempt to master the traumatic event, but, like the repetition compulsion, are one of the phenomena that led Freud to theorize the existence of the death instinct.

Freud (1940a [1938]) considers psychosis to be analogous to a dream because it exhibits the prevalence of the drive-related wish and of the primary process, the lack of the notion of time, the absence of contradiction, and hallucinatory wish fulfilment. On this basis, Freud interprets the latent content of Schreber's psychotic delusion as a persecutory state that conceals repressed homosexuality.

Modern hypotheses on the relationship between dream mechanisms and the mental functioning of psychotic states have not confirmed this equivalence, but, in their enrichment and supplementation of the Freudian model, throw light on the modalities of psychotic thought. There are indeed mental states that abolish the function of imagination, in the sense of the capacity to represent wishes and emotions, and which therefore interfere with the function of dreaming. It follows that the *meaning of dreams differs according to the patient's mental state*. This clinical problem arises particularly with patients, such as borderlines and psychotics, whose state of integration constantly varies.

The meaning of dreams

It can be postulated that the function, meaning, and use of dreams differ according to the mental state and structure of the analysand, and that *different mental states give rise to different dreams* with diametrically opposite meanings. It should also be borne in mind that today we see dreams very differently from our predecessors. Dreams, for us, are a particular manifestation of the symbolic function, a first step in the process of thought. Whereas Freud considered dreams to be the hallucinatory fulfilment of a repressed infantile wish, and repression to be the engine of the psychical apparatus, Melanie Klein held that it was not the repressed that gave life to dreams, but instead the dynamic between internal objects formed by splitting and by projective and introjective identification.

Further insights on dreams and the process of dreaming were contributed by Bion, who saw dreaming as an activity that creates thoughts rather than as a limited functional regression that reveals a repressed content. Riolo (1983) points out that, whereas a dream for Freud was the distorted representation of an already existing unconscious meaning, Bion saw dreams as attempts to generate a new meaning on the basis of the perception of an emotional experience. According to Bion, in order for the perceptions of an emotional experience to be used for the production of a dream, they must take on the characteristics of thought; that is, they must be transformed by the *alpha function*. If the alpha function is damaged, the *beta elements* will remain unmodified and emotions will be experienced as sensory objects, so that the patient cannot dream. Both dreams and the unconscious are products of the differentiation effected by the alpha function: beta elements are non-thoughts that cannot become a part either of consciousness or of the unconscious; they can be neither known nor repressed. Dreams constitute a barrier, or *alpha screen*, which creates consciousness and continuously differentiates it from the unconscious. Dreams are the royal road to the unconscious and constitute evidence of the functioning of the alpha screen and the contact barrier. However, if the contact barrier is destroyed and replaced by the *beta screen*, it is no longer possible to distinguish conscious from unconscious, to repress, to remember, to think, and, hence, even to dream. In Bion's view, the destruction of the alpha function makes it impossible to store experience.

Dream-work-alpha enables neurotics to experience psychic reality by way of unconscious thought, which always remains active. For Bion (1992, p. 19), "the dream-work we know is only a small aspect of dreaming proper—dreaming proper being a continuous process belonging to waking life". The dream work turns reality into a dream and thereby constitutes the foundation of its experience through the function of the alpha elements integrated in thought. Hence, a neurotic dream of reality does not correspond to a psychotic's omnipotent fantasy, but is the opposite of it. In psychotic states, "dreams" remain attempts at construction (from chaos to the formulation of meanings), but these are doomed to fail and remain unused because the function of thought is lacking.

Many analysts have noted the particularity of the manifestation of dreaming in psychosis, but have interpreted it in different ways. Bion (1967) had already pointed out that dreams in the psychotic state perform a discharge function for unelaborated emotions. Green (1977), too, suggests that the purpose of dreams in psychosis is not so much to express the fulfilment of a wish as to evacuate, to rid the psychical apparatus of an excess of painful stimuli. Segal (1991) asks what happens to dreaming and dreams when the ego is temporarily or permanently unable to carry out the task of producing a normal or neurotic dream. In order for dreams to perform their function of elaboration and insight, the benign interaction of projection and introjection must accompany the constructive container–contained relationship. In this author's view, the classical theory of the function of dreams takes it for granted that the ego is capable of appropriate repression and that the subject possesses the capacity for symbolization, which in turn calls for repression. If, however, excessive projective identification is present, concrete thought—confusion between the object and its symbolic representation—will result. Only the perception of separateness and the working through of mourning allow the development of the capacity for symbolization. Segal draws attention to the technical problem involved in analysing dreams in which the dream work is defective.

Another relevant contribution is that of Pontalis (1977), who holds that dreaming indicates the successful development of the area of illusion: that is, of a potential space in which a dream can be created as a transitional object. In the absence of this area, which Roussillon (2001) calls the *appareil auto*, subjective perception of experiences would be impossible. In other words, dreams express the capacity to symbolize and are an essential stage in the process of attaining subjecthood. Both of these French authors refer to Winnicott's insight concerning the importance of play and of the potential space for the constitution of the self.

Dreaming as acting out

My own view is that it is utterly useless, if not counter-productive, to analyse dream content as if it referred symbolically to something else. A convincing and extreme example is that of a sadomasochistic patient who had succeeded, during the course of his analysis, in giving up perverse fantasying in the waking state, but who for a while used night dreams to enter the perverse dimension that was closed off while he was awake. Dreams, for this patient, constituted not "dreaming" but a form of "acting out". As soon as the vigilance of conscious life gave way to the onset of sleep, he began to perform actions in dreams, whereby he again achieved a similar perverse satisfaction to that of the former sadomasochistic representation of waking life. Instead of actively summoning up fantasies with his eyes open during the daytime, he "dreamed" them at night.

In such cases, it is superfluous to analyse dreams, but the operation of dreaming is seen to throw important light on the dreamer's mental functioning.

Segal, too, refers to Bion's model and his concepts of alpha and beta elements, as well as that of a mother capable of containing the child's projective identifications. Discussing two of her borderline patients, she mentions predictive dreams, that is, ones that foreshadow action, in which what has been dreamed is to be acted out. The acting out of the dream is totally literal and is performed down to the slightest detail. Rather than substituting for acting out, these dreams contain every detail of what is to be acted out. Predictive dreams would seem to operate in the same way as the definitory hypotheses described by Bion (1962b). They differ from evacuative dreams, in which certain internal perceptions of the patient are successfully got rid of, in that they appear to remain in the psyche as a bad object that must be eliminated by acting out the dream.

Dreams in the psychotic state

In Bion's terms, psychosis is not a dream, but its opposite. Not only do psychosis and dreams not coincide, but the dreams that occur in the psychotic state are *not*, in fact, dreams, even if they appear to be so, but instead concrete facts or acts of evacuation of parts of the self. These patients' dreams cannot be genuine dreams because they are not the result of a process of symbolization and because there is no internal mental space to contain them. These dreams, thus, no longer conform to the rules applicable to the unconscious laid down by classical metapsychology: they are not subject to censorship and their manifest content does not refer to a latent content. What may be regarded as the psychotic unconscious is not, in fact, such, because there has been no dream work (which is the precondition for the representation, symbolization, and thinkability of the unconscious). In this context, dreams may be fragmentary and meaningless constructions, but may at the same time represent the beginnings of the construction of an internal space and constitute a potential communication.

The general validity of the traditional Freudian view of dreams is not denied, but the conditions for its complete application are lacking in psychotic patients.

A useful approach in our terms is that of Meltzer (1984), who investigates how dreams succeed in creating symbolic forms suitable for representing emotional experience and hence truth. Exploring the path followed by dreams in the attempt to construct the meaning of an emotional experience, he shows how these experiments sometimes succeed in solving the problem and sometimes fail. In the latter case, the dream process becomes psychopathological, resulting in the formation of hallucinations or delusions. Like hallucinations and delusions, lies are a distorted representation of emotional experience. The psychotic experience is underlain by a distortion of truth of which the patient is unaware, due to attacks on the organs of perception that prevent the use of conscious awareness.

Blechner (1983) suggests that, in the dreams of borderlines, the unconscious cannot be regarded as an entity with specific contents and processes (e.g., repression), as in classical theory. Borderline dreams express a quality of psychic experience in which conscious awareness is lacking (and here the term "unconscious" is used mainly adjectivally). In this author's view, as a borderline patient improves, the dreams, whose content tends to be very concrete in the early phases of analysis, become less sharply delineated and more complex, exhibiting a greater capacity for symbolization.

In more recent contributions, Blechner (2000, 2001) notes that a quick perusal of the psychoanalytic literature reveals examples of dreams incorporating psychotic material. Referring to a patient of Arieti (1963), who had emerged from a persecutory delusional state, he notes that a dream had heralded progress in her psycho-analytic therapy. Resnik (in Bateman, 1996) too draws attention to the role of dreams in borderline pathologies, where they often constitute attempts at reconstruction.

Hypotheses on the clinical material
of psychotic patients' dreams

Aldo

A young psychotic patient, Aldo, in analysis during a period of remission, pointed out to me in every possible way how difficult he found it to communicate his "dreams", as if they were among his most intimate and private possessions, which, he said, he was afraid I might destroy or annihilate.

Aldo once told me that he had *dreamed of a church with a tennis court*. This was at a time when, feeling better, he had taken up this sport again, having greatly enjoyed it during his teens. The patient added nothing to this statement, and I, too, felt unable to say anything about this dream.

In subsequent sessions, he went on talking about his pleasure in playing tennis, and said that he had entered for a tournament orga-nized by his club. Eventually, however, it became clear to me that he was totally and delusionally identified with the then world champion, John McEnroe. An instance of delusional behaviour acted out in his parish church later revealed that he also saw himself as a reincarnation of Jesus Christ. Only then did it become possible to understand the communicative value of Aldo's "dream", in which he had concretely described two aspects of the content of a grandiose delusion, sport (the tennis court/McEnroe) and mysticism (the church/Christ).

As I was later able to understand, the "dream" represented the psychotic solution that the patient wished to keep to himself lest I destroy it and prevent his flight into delusion. It then occurred to me that, although he had improved (or perhaps precisely because of the improvement), Aldo had become desperately aware of the severity of the disturbance and of the impossibility of a genuine reconstruction of the self, so that he was again impelled towards a delusional solution.

As with other patients, for Aldo, too, the moment of improve-ment and clarity corresponded to a precarious equilibrium that could easily break down and plunge him back into psychosis. My point is that in such cases the patient dreams of something that is going to happen, which is only indirectly connected with the analytic relationship but concerns his future mental functioning; for example, the development of a new psychotic state, the themes of which are foreshadowed. In other words, I postulate the existence of *predictive* dreams that anticipate the onset of the psychotic state and specify the basic elements that will be contained in the delu-sional construction. According to my hypothesis, such dreams arise when the psychotic crisis is not yet manifest.

My patient, Aldo, who brought the dream with great difficulty and without associations to the tennis court and the church, produced his "hallucination" in a session, but it was not possible to work on it because I was still stubbornly convinced that the dream referred symbolically to something else. While emerging from the megalomanic state heralded by the "dream", the same patient subsequently brought another dream, which could be seen as repre-senting the psychotic transformation and persecutory guilt.

> Aldo had been invited to the home of an analyst couple who allowed him to get into their double bed with them. There he became turned on as he performed a series of twisting and turning movements, ending up in a blissful state of pleasure. Then the figures of his parents

appeared, faded and far away in the distance. Eventually, he found himself surrounded by deformed basset hounds with their heads wrenched back, which complained that he was responsible for their deformity.

This time, Aldo said he felt that the little deformed animals in the dream had to do with himself and were like little selves of his own. In the dream, the patient had visualized the state of masturbatory pleasure that had underlain the onset of the delusion of omnipotence, but he was now aware of the destructive quality of this process, which was responsible for causing mental damage and for weakening the analyst and the parents.

The entire process of psychotic transformation, which had come about "in silence", could be visualized only retrospectively, once the patient had become capable of transcribing it in the dream images.

Since a distortion of the truth outside the area of conscious awareness lies at the root of the psychotic disturbance, understanding dreams in this situation is always an awkward and complex matter; owing to the distortion of reality contained in them, it is difficult to make use of the dream content even when such dreams seem to be attempts at communication.

Because the distortion affects the organs of perception, Meltzer (1984) seeks to equate lies and delusions. However, whereas in the case of lies the alteration of truth is conscious and the attempt to distort the truth is intended to confuse the other person, in psychosis the first person to be confused is the patient himself, who shows his agreement with the liar.

Yet, if the psychopathology of the process of dreaming coincides with the distortion of thought and the formation of hallucinations or delusions by mental self-poisoning, valuable traces or signs of the origins of this poisoning might perhaps be found in the dreams of psychotic patients. I postulate that "dreams" in the psychotic process have a specific meaning: they are the patient's way of describing the mental states characteristic of his psychosis, of allowing the dreamer and the analyst to understand and anticipate the nature of the psychotic poisoning, or, conversely—albeit with more difficulty—of describing a possible exit from it. Sometimes, in the optimum case, they may constitute an attempt to make delusional contents assimilable; that is to say, to dream the psychosis in order to act it out again in the potential space of the analytic relationship.

Claudio

I shall now present a dream in which Claudio, a patient in a persecutory psychotic state, repeats the persecutory psychosis by representing it.

> He is in a dark tunnel like that of an underground railway and is trying to get back into the open by climbing up a ladder. The ladder is very long and weird, as if in a painting by Miró. While climbing in the dream, Claudio meets a man with a notice saying: "These last five minutes will be the most terrible of your life"; and the persecutory prediction immediately comes true. As he climbs, the patient feels a spray of liquid on his shoulders; he is then surrounded by a group of threatening men, who grab him by the shoulders and violently plunge him down a steep slope.

Claudio had begun the session by talking about Marie Cardinal's book *The Words to Say It* (1975); this had comforted him, because he had read that at a certain point in her analysis the woman patient described had emerged from the nightmare of hallucinations and begun to dream.

What distinguishes the experience of the dream brought in the session from the ordinary experiences of persecution afflicting the patient virtually every day? For the sake of brevity, I shall disregard all the implications of the delusion in terms of Claudio's history and personality structure, as well as the possible transference meanings, and concentrate on the new element introduced by the dream. In it, the persecutory experience, which seemingly repeats the persecution of waking life, takes on a new meaning precisely because it is dreamed, and the patient who constructs the dream becomes the bearer of intentionality. The intention of the dream is to convince the patient (and the analyst) of the ineluctability of persecution: the delusional part delivers him up, in a state of terror and total isolation, into the hands of his enemies. No one comes to his aid, nor, in the dream, does the patient ask for such aid.

However, if, as Claudio had indicated in advance by his reference to Marie Cardinal, a dream is a communication, a space shared with the analyst, then the delusion no longer arises in a place of total isolation. By interpreting the dream as propaganda of the delusional part and describing its power, the analyst was able to show the patient that it was actually a part of himself that created the delusion and believed in it.

Enumerating other episodes when the delusional intuition appeared out of the blue, Claudio said that a "click" would sound in his mind and that when this happened there was no escape. If the click did not occur, there would be no terror and he would not be a prey to delusion. I replied that the click was facilitated by a mental configuration that thrust itself forward and conquered his mind when he withdrew into fantasy and believed himself to be alone against the world. When he isolated himself, he lost all protection and perception of friendship. He would then enter into the world of the "enemies", who would subject him to incredible force and confront him with ever more refined and sophisticated persecution systems, which only his own fantasy (represented in the dream by the weird ladder) could create, for example, dust, smells, television cameras, and the like. The weird, surreal ladder corresponded to the fascination exerted by the psychosis, which had him in thrall so that he risked discovering too late (the "last five minutes") that he had wasted his life in the dark tunnel of delusion.

A few months later, during a period of manifest improvement, the same patient brought a very long dream in which, at the Olympic Games, a male Italian athlete was taking part in a difficult event and he felt impelled to help him. A group of female athletes were performing movements in which they flew up into the air and defied the laws of gravity. He watched them in admiration but knew that he would not be able to imitate them. Later, a group of athletes were engaged in an event in which he, too, would have liked to take part.

Notwithstanding the many grandiose elements in the dream (the Olympic Games, strange movements, and events with heroic winners), Claudio himself—associating to how worried he had felt at a difficult match which his national football team did eventually win—expressed the good atmosphere which not only appeared in the dream, but which he himself experienced when he recovered the area of relationship, co-operative playing, and possible identification with coevals. On the evening before, he had indeed experienced a similar atmosphere of well being, which he had been able to contrast with that created by the persecutory solution.

It should be noted that, for Claudio, the two dreams were not only dreams as such, but also two possible mental dispositions of the waking state that conditioned the perception of reality.

Ada

(The analyst in this case was Dr Paola Capozzi.)

I shall now present some excerpts from the analysis of a case which bears out the hypothesis that certain dreams "predict" psychosis before the psychotic crisis actually becomes manifest.

Ada was twenty-three years old and had, while still at high school, already suffered from fits of anxiety and periods of isolation, anorexia, and obsessional dieting; she had been referred for analysis by a psychiatrist who had treated her when she was hospitalized for several weeks after a bizarre attempt to ingest objects, which had been thwarted by her mother in time to stop her suffocating herself.

During her few weeks in hospital, the patient had had threatening auditory hallucinations and delusional ideas of guilt. The diagnosis on discharge had been uncertain, somewhere between borderline pathology and incipient schizophrenia.

Having felt empty and abulic at the beginning of her analysis, Ada said that, before her admission to hospital, she had felt herself to be very intelligent, lucid, and creative, and had immersed herself in reading the great authors, in particular, Virginia Woolf. In a crescendo of excitement, she had conceived the idea of being Lucifer, the bearer of light, God's chosen angel. Later, she had felt demoniacal, the bearer of all the world's evil, and had understood that the only way to ward off the imminent end of the world was to do away with herself. She had then suddenly lost her mental lucidity. The exalted state of the psychotic episode, although it had aroused anxiety, had also seemed to constitute a special, extraordinary condition, and was remembered not without nostalgia.

This patient's therapy can be divided into two parts. The first was characterized mainly by anxieties without psychotic symptoms, while in the second she again lapsed into psychosis. In the first year of her treatment, Ada had not presented any psychotic symptoms, the material having instead revealed depressive and collapse-of-identity anxieties. Given the seriousness of the case, the analysis seemed to be going well, and transference interpretations, especially of her fear that the analyst might be unable to understand or support her, enabled her temporarily to overcome the various moments of emptiness and anxiety.

Although the analysis was going well, the impression might even then have been gained that things were going "too" well, and that, as regards improvement, Ada was being in part very obliging towards her analyst, almost as if she were conforming to the latter's therapeutic expectations.

At any rate, notwithstanding her belief that she had devoted a great deal of attention to the material, the analyst was surprised by a fresh psychotic episode that began after the patient had consented to her father's insistent demand for her to go away with him. This had involved her missing a week's sessions. During the trip, Ada had fallen ill again, suffering from the delusion of being sexually excited by her father, who was seen as the Devil. The trip was broken off, and the patient was readmitted to the psychiatric clinic. The virulence with which the psychotic symptoms resurfaced showed that all the analytic work thought to have been accomplished had been swept away in an instant. The analyst wondered how she could have overlooked the persistence of the psychotic situation on such a massive, unmodified scale. The analysis had manifestly proceeded up to that point in an excessively reassuring climate inconsistent with deeper penetration into the patient's psychotic functioning, which had continued to exist and to exert power over her.

Upon the resumption of her analysis, Ada said that she had experienced the trip as an incestuous event. It had seemed to her indecent for her father and herself to be there among a group of couples. People had taken them for a husband and wife on honeymoon. The double bed in which they had slept had also appeared to her to be an enormous red vagina, suggesting "sinful" thoughts towards her father. During the psychotic episode she had been terrified of the analysis and of her analyst; she had thought that the analyst would be furious because she had broken certain laws or destroyed her (i.e., the analyst's) brain. Already in the previous months, the patient had every so often fleetingly mentioned that she felt she was entering into the analyst's thoughts.

The separation from the analysis had constituted a dramatic discontinuity, in which the previous psychotic episode had been repeated. In the new delusional episode, the patient seemed, by the incestuous flight with her father, to have acted out an attack on the mother–analyst, who had been transformed into a damaged and vengeful figure. For this reason, the patient had felt guilty towards the analyst and threatened by her, representing as she did the psychotic superego bent on revenge.

At the height of this destructive state, Ada had felt diabolical (as in the first episode, in which she had been Lucifer), in league with the figure of the father, who also represented a part of herself—the part that urged her to plunge into a manic, sexualized reality.

Confronted with the fresh psychotic episode, the analyst realized that she had arrived on the scene "after the event", when the psychic catastrophe had already taken place. Because she had been unable to oppose the father's wish (which, moreover, had sounded to the patient like a diktat), the analyst must have been put in the position of a feeble mother swept aside by the paternal sexualization. The psychotic episode induced the analyst to review the prior analytic material; in the light of the events described above, her attention focused on a series of dreams that seemed particularly meaningful, in which the patient had mentally anticipated and virtually predicted the psychotic episode that was to ensue shortly afterwards. These dreams had remained unanalysed partly because they were so terrifying that the patient had been unable to produce any associations to them, and partly owing to their intrinsically "alien" quality. With hindsight, it was easier to understand these dreams as a communication of the psychotic mental state to which both analyst and patient had closed their eyes.

Two pre-crisis dreams whose meaning could have been recognized were indicative of the erotization of the feared father figure, as subsequently manifested in the delusional explosion.

> We are ski-ing in the mountains, and are to go to our rooms in the evening. I hope to end up in the room of a boy I like, but instead find myself going into the room of Father X, an Italian teacher. He makes to seize hold of me, I run away, he follows me, and the house turns into a castle. Wherever I go, fires break out . . .

> My family are at home having an orgy; they seem to be drunk, and there are people jumping on the beds. My family are amused to see me

turn up in this awkward situation. I act furious, and try to get my creams and make-up. But I can't do it, because I am somehow hanging up, my hands tied, as if in a pornographic film.

In these dreams, Ada had described how, by transforming her parents into perverse objects, she was able to create an orgiastic state of mind and consequently trap herself in a sexualized world. Her acquiescence ("I am somehow hanging up, my hands tied") lay at the root of her imprisonment in psychosis and her total loss of the perception of human relations.

Further clarification of the complexity of the psychotic anxieties and persecutory guilt that followed the annihilation of Ada's healthy self was afforded by another dream, which she brought in terror a few months after the second psychotic episode:

My sister and I are prostitutes in a brothel. Each of us has a speciality; one of us goes to bed with murderers. We are expecting Robert De Niro from *Cape Fear*. Everyone is terrified because he is a savage murderer. We wait; an Indian prostitute ties herself to the foot of the bed, saying that she must suffer the death penalty because she neglected her child so as to become a prostitute. A general silence descends and I burst out crying to the depths of my being in enormous sadness.

This dream is particularly touching because it portrays the punishment that threatens the patient when she has no choice but to submit to the power of the psychotic part, which is represented by the invasive, terrifying figure of a murderer (Robert De Niro and *Cape Fear*). The patient feels not only guilty but also bewildered and horribly depressed at the devastation in progress ("crying to the depths of her being in enormous sadness").

Given all the possible limitations due to the complexity assumed by this treatment, Ada's dreams became a particularly valuable medium for the understanding of altered mental states that could not otherwise have been revealed and worked through. The comprehension of these dreams helped in the construction of an analytic relationship that laid the foundations for preventing further psychotic implosions, the analyst now being more capable of discerning the expression of the psychosis in dreams. It was, after all, always possible for Ada to lapse into psychosis, and the analysis of her dreams confirmed that the patient's communication had to do with this problem, which it was important to confront.

Some dreams had already described the mechanisms of transformation of psychic reality, of the control exercised by the psychotic part, and of the drugged mental condition, all of which were central to the creation of the psychotic state. Here are some examples.

> I am at a Salvador Dalí exhibition. There is an empty anteroom with columns similar to the giraffe-like necks of Dalí's women. I ask Dalí to go with me into a room because I am afraid. He accompanies me into another room and gives me a piece of a sculpture of the Virgin Mary to eat; there is a notice that says, "Now it is too late". I ask him to take me home because I have not got my car keys. The car turns into an escalator, going up; it is like an elastic band that you have to pull with your hands. It is very steep; I laugh like a madwoman and fall back down.

> I have to go and see Di Pietro, a university lecturer, about the subject of a thesis I am to write; he suggests one on surrealism. In the waiting room I am very worried because I know nothing about surrealism; I would rather have written a different thesis.

> I am in my father's village. My father is at home, copying some of my notes with his left hand. He thinks they are shorthand symbols, but actually they are only scribbles . . .

In this case, Ada mentioned her attraction to Dalí's paintings and to surrealism, to the automatic writing that "liberates the unconscious", and to mental logorrhoea. She herself said that in the past she had had periods of writing mania, in which she would scribble away for days on end. In some of these periods, her mind would create continuous links, where she would constantly think of everything with great lucidity, in a state of uninterrupted intense mental activity accompanied by a huge sense of exaltation. The scribbles in the dream were the exalted and surreal production of the psychosis, which transformed reality and presented itself as superior; the father who copied them suggested that the patient thought her father and the analyst should copy and admire them and take inspiration from her. The madness idealized in this way excited the father, whereas a part of the patient knew that the scribbles were only faeces.

(It is interesting to note that the figure of Di Pietro [the famous Italian anti-corruption judge] in the dream represents an exciting and persecutory superego, of a kind that, as also pointed out by Rosenfeld [1978], confuses the patient by first exciting her and then making her feel guilty and persecuting her.)

This was a particularly important dream because it led to the reconstruction, with the patient's participation, of her entry into the psychotic state, which had been responsible for her first admission to hospital. In that situation, the patient had felt particularly lucid and creative and had had the idea of being Virginia Woolf. The state of exaltation, initially perceived as a positive, uplifting mental openness, had subsequently become destructive. The patient had then felt herself to be Lucifer, the transgressive, negative bearer of light. This biphasic sequence is characteristic of the psychotic mental state. The patient is first excited and then plunged into persecutory, self-destructive guilt.

Later dreams described the dominion of the psychotic part over the rest of the personality, exercised through threats ("an evil devil joined our group and told us that we must cut the veins out of dolls drawn on a piece of paper, using scissors. I absolutely did not want to, but was afraid of rebelling") or erotized allurements ("I can see my sex organs from a distance and they look very small. Then they open and I can see the tubes and an alien, who seems to be wink-ing. I feel sort of surprised, like 'Aha'").

The bizarre transformation of objects—in this case, in particular, of the parent figures—is also evident:

I'm flying . . . Then I'm on the phone to my mother, but I don't tell her that my father is there because I am confused by the racket he is making. Instead, I tell her that an ornament has got broken. It is a glass cock in the form of a human being, dressed like one of those decent characters from a Manzoni novel. I'm very fond of this object, in the way that one is fond of dolls. I put it in a glass crusher that vaporizes it and what come out are substances of different colours that recombine in the form of a doll that looks like me and flies . . .

There is also seduction with the promise of omnipotent mental states:

F. is running with his head only and is much faster than I am. I say to myself: just look at that, it's amazing!

Finally, awareness appears, with the beginnings of repudiation of the delusional nucleus, represented as a destructive criminal gang:

> Two boys know how to fly, and I do too, but not so well. They summon me into a room to show me that they have destroyed the carpet, which is like the skin of the house. I call my aunt, who is so upset that she gets drunk; she tells me I am mad to let these criminals into the house—and meanwhile they have also wrecked the bodywork of the car.

Together with the other factors favouring change, this type of analytic work on dreams contributed to the successful outcome of the analysis, because it enabled the analyst to make the patient receptive to the danger and to confront the silent, omnipotent allurements of the psychosis. The analyst having understood the psychotic transformation described in the dream and communicated it to the patient, she was able to recognize and internalize it at a time when Ada was still able to use her mind, i.e., before the onset of a fresh crisis. This method also made it possible to reconstruct and understand the two previous psychotic episodes.

The analytic work was pursued in two complementary directions, involving, on the one hand, the reconstruction of the psychotic episode so as to make it understandable at a time when it was threatening to reappear, and, on the other, confrontation of the attempt at omnipotent reparation whereby the patient sought to abolish the catastrophic sense of guilt that followed the psychotic episode. The therapeutic work concentrated on these points with a view to breaking the vicious circle between irreparable damage and manic reparation (Salvador Dalí), and to sweeping away the patient's collusion with the psychotic part.

Analytic reception of psychotic dreams

Owing to the nature of the psychotic process, the dreams of psychotic patients present very complex problems of reception to both members of the analytic couple. On the formal level, these dreams possess all the characteristics described by Racamier. They may be very short, like visual flashes, or extremely long and full of transformations, a symbolic interpretation of which is not feasible.

Patients always have great difficulty in associating to them, sometimes displaying a sense of alienation, surprise, or alarm at their
terrifying and incomprehensible content.

The dreams reported here, on which I have concentrated, are
connected with the patients' condition in so far as they *describe the
psychosis*, so that they offer valuable material for the therapeutic
process.

Quinodoz (1999, 2001) describes dreams that "turn over a page",
dreams that are full of anxiety and whose primitive content frightens the dreamer. In this author's view, notwithstanding their
regressive aspect, these dreams may be seen in dynamic terms as
signs of progress: despite their primitive content, they may constitute attempts at integration and reunification of parts of the patient.
Although he was considering mainly the problem of dreams in
neurosis, Quinodoz (2000) believes that similar processes take place
in the dreams of more seriously ill patients when they attempt to
put together the scattered parts of their personality. In these cases,
too, the anxiety appears to be connected with the attempt to represent and reintegrate parts of the self. Dreams featuring psychotic
parts might be attempts by the patient to reunify split-off, scattered,
or not readily integrable experiences, which nevertheless manage to
achieve representation. Although I agree with this author on the
progressive, integrative meaning of these dreams, it is difficult to
say how far the anxiety accompanying "psychotic dreams" results
from the difficulty of integration and to what extent it is due to
perception of the threat from the delusional nucleus that terrifies
the patient.

Grotstein (1981) states that dreams perform a fundamentally
important function in allowing psychic life to be observed. For this
to happen, however, an unseen observer must be preserved to
annotate the plot and verify and validate its truths and messages.
Psychosis, by altering the structure and coherence of the mind,
represents the failure of this function. The dreamer who dreams a
dream and the one who understands it may together be deemed a
unit that maintains the stability of the sense of personal identity, by
constantly integrating emotional experience and conferring meaning on it. The dreamer who understands the dream is a representation of the internalized maternal container, which apprehends the
narrative urgency and modifies the story so as to allow a solution

to be found. However, if this object is felt to be damaged, dreams are experienced as malevolent oracles, resulting in the psychotic experience. The realm of −K, or hallucinatory transformations, is established.

Dreams and delusional transformation

One of the difficulties presented by the understanding of dreams in the psychotic state is precisely the absence, in the patient, of the dreamer who understands the dream, which, as a result, becomes indecipherable. The dream no longer represents a dialogue between the dreamer and someone who understands it, but sometimes instead only the product of a sensory experience that bears witness to the collapse of the mind.

Meltzer (1973) described the processes of mental sexualization that occur in certain psychotic conditions, perversions, and drug addictions, when patients succeed in creating an excited masturbatory mental state likely to distance them from reality. The entry into such a mental state is clearly experienced and anticipated in some of the dreams I have described. My point is that these patients (like Ada) *are not consciously aware* of this process because the transformation is so invasive and overwhelming that they are prevented from warning of the danger or asking for help.

Since working with the delusional nucleus of the personality is the analyst's purpose in the treatment of a psychotic patient, such "dreams" are important because they afford access to the area of the delusion. Psychotic "dreams", which remain totally lacking in meaning for the dreamer, must first be understood by the analyst as a delusional transformation occurring in the here and now.

My patient Aldo, who overcame powerful resistances before eventually revealing that he had dreamed of a tennis court in a church, said nothing either about the content of the dream (he had no associations) or about its quality. It was only with hindsight, when the content had been acted out, that I was able to say that it had described a delusion several days before it invaded his mind. What had been "dreamed" had then been translated completely into reality. The patient described the *delusional transformation as if it were a dream*. I was deceived, because I had received his communication as a dream and not as an explicit delusional declaration.

In all the cases presented, "dreams" coincide with hallucinatory constructions; the "dream" and its content refer not to the meta-phorical discourse of the dream work, but to the concreteness of the hallucinatory construction. They constitute the delusional reality in concrete form, and that is why they cannot be understood by the patient even if they are represented so vividly. For this reason, even if the delusional reality is clearly *represented*, the term "representa-tion" is inappropriate because it presupposes a capacity for symbol-ization. The point I wish to stress is that, whereas some authors treat delusions as if they were dream material, it is, in fact, neces-sary to *treat this dream material as if it were a delusion*. The significance of the clinical material reported here lies in the fact that the dreams not only anticipate the content of the psychosis, but also precisely describe the functioning of the psychotic part and its exciting, confusing power to destroy the patient's mental health.

Meltzer (1973) drew attention to some important aspects of this situation: for example, that the (destructive) psychotic part of the patient's personality presents itself as promising protection from pain by arousing sensuality and vanity, while concealing the sadis-tic and brutal facets.

The clinical value of psychotic dreams

As we know, in the analysis of borderline or psychotic patients, failure to recognize the elements of the analytic communication connected with the action of the psychotic part increases the risk of delusional breakdown. For instance, underestimating the messages appearing in dreams or other material concerning an initial erotic transference may encourage the development of a violent delu-sional erotic transference. An "absent" analyst colludes with the patient's impotent, subjugated self.

The failure to take account of patient Aldo's "dream" of the church and tennis court, leaving it uncomprehended and uninter-preted, may have convinced him that the analyst's mental absence granted him permission to proceed freely along the path of delu-sion. After all, in his next dream the patient described how he had been allowed to get into the marriage bed of an analytic couple and to do whatever he wanted there.

The overlooking of the sexualization in Ada's dreams might have weakened any possible defence against the advance of the erotic delusion. In this case, the analyst had allowed the patient to go away without understanding the situation, abandoning her to the power of the sexualized internal father and the subsequent action of the destructive superego. This being the case, the analysis of Ada, who was fascinated by Salvador Dalí, concentrated for a long time on understanding the dreams in which this situation was clearly represented; the analyst sought to make the patient see how she was acting out the delusional nucleus, how it transformed reality, and how it seduced her mind, aligning herself with the level of functioning present at that particular time. Concentration on the communication of the "dream" made it possible to show Ada how the psychosis (Salvador Dalí) was seducing her vanity, convincing her that she was special and idealizing the world of surreal transformations. In other dreams, the seduction tended to follow the path of sexualization (the Alien in the masturbatory vagina).

The fascination of the "surreal" also appears in the themes and dreams of Claudio, the patient with the persecutory delusion: the painter connected with the weird ladder is Miró.

Clinical experience suggests that there are only a small number of themes that describe the entry into psychosis. The most common are those describing the fascination of the surreal and the weird, sexualization and perverse excitement, or the drugged mental experience. These themes are described clearly and without disguise in the dreams.

It is never easy for an analyst to discern promptly a dream's communicative meaning, and so the use of the dream becomes a highly complex operation. Reception by the analyst may help the patient to escape from the psychotic trap, whereas, if the analyst does not "understand the dream", the patient feels even more impelled in the direction of psychotic colonization. Indeed, one of the clinical difficulties in the cases presented here is precisely the docility with which the patient is trapped in the psychotic world. In this process, the analyst must pay close attention to the patient's propensity to act as a subordinated, consenting object and not to offer any resistance to the pathological process. Steiner (1982) considers in this connection that the psychotic part gains control by persuading the rest of the personality to enter into a "perverse" relationship.

Another reason why the analyst is deprived of dreams and associations is that psychotic patients' "dreams" contain the delusional nucleus, which presents itself as the *only exciting and seductive reality*, a way of escaping or fleeing from the analysis and the analyst that might destroy the "dream". Whether dreams betray the patient's submission to the seductive power of the psychosis or bear witness to his resistance to the delusion, they will always be clinically important; indeed, they may sometimes be the only communication that makes psychosis representable, describing its self-destructive and exciting nature. It is certainly helpful if this work can be done on dreams rather than in the midst of the psychotic crisis, given that all awareness of the catastrophic and destructive character of what is happening is lost during such a crisis.

Let me conclude this chapter by recalling the statement made at the beginning concerning the difficulty of using the associative method where the dreamer's mental state is approaching that of psychosis. Such difficulties make the therapy of psychotic patients particularly arduous.

Whereas the dreams I have described allow direct access to the psychotic transformation, it must be borne in mind that they do not immediately give rise to increased insight because the patient's conscious ego is in thrall to the delusional part. Conferring meaning on these dreams sometimes serves only to uphold the patient's unstable equilibrium, preventing him from plunging into the delusional vortex.

The analyst must concentrate for long periods on the specific mode of functioning of a patient battling with psychosis, and must establish a complex and thoroughly well structured setting tailored primarily to the nature of the ongoing process. In this sense, the meaning of a dream in the case of psychosis, which refers not to the search for a symbolic content but to the constitution of the psychotic state, might be the vehicle of a communication essential for working on the psychotic nucleus and on the tendency to lapse into delusion. It is possible to work at a later stage at length on "dreams" that contain the representation of the psychosis and the way in which the patient allows himself to be fascinated by it.

In conclusion, if delusion is a specific, omnipotent "dream" that transforms psychic reality, a psychotic "dream", which also represents the pressure of the delusion that is colonizing the ego—which is inclined to submit to it—may become one of the means at our disposal of drawing attention to what is happening, with a view to warding off the catastrophe and helping the patient to escape the threatening and seductive grip of the delusion. Such an approach to psychotic "dreams" may make patients receptive to the danger of psychosis and facilitate a more favourable development of the analytic process.

Note

1.   Translator's note: these extracts are here translated from the Italian.

CHAPTER SIX

Intimidation at the helm: superego and hallucinations in the analytic treatment of a psychosis*

> "Perhaps this is the bottom line to mental illness: incomprehensible things occur; your life becomes a bin for hoax-like fluctuations of what used to be reality. . . . The madman experiences something, but what it is or where it comes from he does not know"
>
> (Dick, 1981, p. 26)

I n this chapter I shall attempt to describe the progress of a hallucinatory state that developed during the course of an analysis and to illustrate how the patient's self was recomposed in a process whereby his confusing and destructuring superego evolved into one that was more characteristic of melancholia. In the course of my exposition, I shall describe the psychic experience resulting from the action of the psychotic superego, involving, for example, condemnation, accusation, and mental terror, and I shall show how the process of recovery was thereby impeded.

---

* This chapter is a reworking of a paper originally published in the *International Journal of Psychoanalysis* (De Masi, 1997).

I shall, therefore, tell of the road travelled by the patient in order to emerge from the psychotic state, the obstacles overcome, and my own frequent moments of difficulty and loss of bearings; finally, I shall consider the constant recourse by patient and analyst alike to the analytic method as the only possible therapeutic approach.

My account covers an eight-year span; the analysis was conducted in the usual setting and there were four sessions a week.

Alvise's psychotic breakdown

Alvise had had a severe psychotic episode, for which he had been admitted to hospital for two months and undergone drug treatment. He came to me for analysis at the age of twenty-five after two years of psychotherapy following his discharge from hospital. Both the psychiatrist who had treated him during this period and the patient himself had realized that the psychotherapeutic work could not proceed any further. The same psychiatrist subsequently continued to provide medication until it ceased to be necessary at an advanced stage in the analysis.

The psychotic breakdown had caused the patient to break off his studies just as he was about to graduate in computer science; he had left Milan, where he had been at university, and returned to the town of his birth to live with his parents.

Alvise had been born to an ill-matched couple. The mother, who was much younger than the father, had tried to return to her own parents immediately after the wedding because she had felt unhappy and isolated in the relationship with her husband. The birth of the child may have motivated her to persevere in the marriage.

I have no direct information on the first years of the patient's life, but it seems that the birth of a sister when Alvise was five had broken up a close relationship between him and his mother. From then on, he had had to face periodic separations from his family and the experience of educational institutions that imposed strict discipline. In this connection, he recalled that he had one day kept some food in his mouth until he got back home because he had not dared to refuse it.

Alvise was sociable at primary school. However, although taller and stronger than his coevals, he could not defend himself if attacked. He was afraid of his own violence and managed to fight only when his mother told him to retaliate. He had had periods of anxiety from an early age, fearing, for example, that there might be a devil in his room. When he was once told off by the priest for missing catechism classes through no fault of his own, he took fright and refused to go back to the church.

Alvise remembered that in his early childhood he had often been punished after violent arguments with his mother; when she had told his father about this, he had asked him to behave himself. However, the punishments inflicted by the mother seemed out of proportion to the naughtiness of her son. I gained the impression of an overbearing and authoritarian woman, worn out by the two children and finding it difficult to cope in particular with the older one's impetuous and rebellious temperament.

The father, a kind but isolated and rather odd person, had remained aloof from his infant son's upbringing and had barely related to him. However, owing to a shared passion for sailing, father and son had met at weekends or on holidays during the latter's adolescence.

At secondary school, the boy showed a precocious tendency to be independent and to assume polemical positions against teachers and authority figures. During this period he joined far-left student groups with a view to becoming their leader. The patient had worked out an elementary political ideology, in which capitalists were like parents engaged in perpetual battle with their children, took everything for themselves, and wanted to crush the proletariat. Because his parents sought to control him by prohibitions, Alvise experienced their presence as a useless burden and an obstacle to his adolescent appetites.

At the age of eighteen, when it was time for him to go to university, Alvise had left home and settled in Milan. He had chosen computer science as his subject because of his inclination towards abstract thought and mathematics. Although potentially a brilliant student, he had obtained mediocre results owing to his fear of examinations and to breaks in his studies. He had practised many sports, such as skiing, sailing, swimming, and fencing, in the last of which he had made something of a name for himself at national level. He had an athletic physique and took his training very seriously. He also liked music and, while at university, belonged to a band which had unsuccessfully tried to go professional.

Another important aspect of Alvise's life at this time was his reaction to post-flirtation separations: he would plunge into a kind of melancholic state that would go on for days but would then often melt away as if by magic.

It was precisely one of these episodes that paved the way for the psychotic breakdown. The patient had broken off a relationship—the most important of his life so far—with a girl of his own age. Attracted by women in his music set, who seemed to him more beautiful and fascinating, he had suddenly lost interest in his girlfriend and separated from her. He had thought he would be able to conquer other women and compete with his friends, whom he saw as better than himself at seduction and in sexual performance (he suffered, for example, from premature ejaculation).

After hearing that the girl he had abandoned had found a new boyfriend (she had had an abortion between the two relationships, having become pregnant by Alvise), he had tried to return to her, but this had not been possible.

At this point the young man had rediscovered the agonizing pain of separation and had sought to get rid of depressive feelings by devoting himself obsessively to his studies, sport, and music, abolishing his emotional life and looking only for thrilling sexual relationships. He relied greatly on his friends in the band and felt at one with them; he tried to deny the conflicts within the group and the bullying sometimes inflicted on him, and assumed a very formal and obliging manner in order to succeed.

At one point, he had suddenly conceived a violent rage against the group, and in particular against the leader of the band, a friend whom he had idealized in his teens but who was in fact very overbearing and a drug addict. So, he had broken with his friends and returned home. He had felt very depressed and asked his parents for help. His father, a doctor, had referred him to a psychologist specializing in psychosomatic medicine, who had failed to grasp the seriousness of the situation. Neither Alvise's family nor his friends fully appreciated the patient's state. He tried to keep his head above water by his own resources but became more and more desperate inside.

The breakdown culminated in a suicide attempt: while on holi-day, he jumped off a flyover while under the delusion of harbour-ing a devilish power within that made him totally destructive. Other diabolical presences were also at work, often in the form of animals such as black dogs, while the world proclaimed forthcom-ing mass suicides through the sound of bells or gunshots. Alvise had felt that he could enter telepathically into other people's minds and make them commit suicide; believing that he was in contact with God (terrifying divine forces revealed catastrophic truths to him), he was convinced that no appeal could lie against his convic-tion. During the psychotic crisis Alvise's guilt at his own destruc-tiveness was so catastrophic, and his fear of the doctors who might unmask him so acute, that, having first done everything possible to avoid hospitalization, he accepted the psychiatric diagnosis and his subsequent admission with a degree of relief. Being mad was admittedly shameful, but did not involve such disgraceful guilt as being devilish and dangerous. When in hospital, he was able to "act crazy" so as to hide his diabolical nature from the doctors. The patient subsequently took refuge in mutism because he felt too confused and was afraid of confusing the doctors.

Analytic therapy

It is difficult to describe and convey the dramatic sense of the analytic relationship, the efforts of both parties to understand and achieve toleration of catastrophic emotions, as well as the patient's constant anxiety that he might not "make it", might be mad, or might become even more confused as a result of the treatment. Although the themes illustrated in this paper might seem to have appeared and developed in orderly succession, in fact, they arose in stormy and unpredictable fashion, so that I found it difficult to anticipate them in time and to contain the anxieties appropriately and promptly.

My ambivalence about accepting such a serious case for analy-sis was clear to me from the first interview. I remember that, as I listened to him, I wondered if analytic treatment was really indi-cated. I hesitated because of the psychotic episode with its dramatic outcome and the patient's precarious state. I was encouraged to try by his sincere request for help and his inner conviction that the analysis could truly benefit him.

The anxiety about not "making it", which was present between us from the beginning, was in fact a leitmotif of the first few years of therapy, characterized as they were by alternating phases of excitement and unforeseeable psychic collapse that were also experienced in the transference.

One of the psychotic defences I got to know at an early stage of the analysis was the production of an excited, sexualized mental state. Once, at the end of a session during which he sarcastically noted that I seemed to him to be depressed (in fact, I think I was merely in a state of thoughtful concentration), he immediately offered me a homosexual relationship to buck me up: my role was to be a depressed and impotent object in which to deposit the sick part of himself, whereas his was to treat me by his own methods. Sometimes, however, partly owing to excessive weakness or uncertainty in my interpretations, the equation between the analyst and the sick part of himself aroused too much concrete and realistic anxiety in Alvise.

The following substantial extract from the clinical material conveys something of the anxiety that pervaded certain sessions.

About a year after the beginning of the analysis, with his session barely over, he rushed home convinced that I had telephoned his father to say that the analysis had failed. He was afraid that, following my call, his parents might have disappeared and left him to his fate. Then he had phoned me from home, saying that he was "going too fast" and that he wanted to "swell up" and hurl himself from the window. In the next session he told me that he had gone to a restaurant, where the waiter had taken a long time to give him his bill. Alvise had regarded this as a clear token that he was considered to be a total failure, but the waiter had then come and he had noticed that he was being seen as a normal person. This had made him even more anxious.

I interpreted to the patient that he had felt neglected in my answers in the previous sessions and that this had made him feel that he had been driven out. He replied that my comments in the last session about the terror of not "making it" and of falling to pieces again had sounded too reassuring to him. I told him that, noticing that he was being treated very much as a healthy person, he had

seen me as denying reality and concealing my own state of desperation. Alvise agreed, and said that telephoning his father meant that I
regarded him as a "turd". He also told me that in the previous
session, when he had asked to go to the lavatory, I had said, "Of
course", in an irritated voice. I replied that he experienced me as a
person unable to keep calm in the face of his critical and malevolent
thoughts (the faeces he wanted to deposit in the lavatory). I
reminded him of the aggressive excitement that may have caused
his mother to be intolerant and violent when he argued with her; his
seeing me in this way had raised his anxiety to an intolerable pitch.

The patient told me that after the last session he had thought that
the analysis was driving him mad, and that a friend and neighbour
said that analysts did make people go mad. I answered that perhaps
my tendency to reassure him had confirmed to him that I, too, saw
analysis as a dangerous instrument. He responded that he had felt
he was going "too fast" in his frantic eagerness to make progress
(he revealed that he had a secret plan to get better within the first
year of analysis and that the deadline was fast approaching), and
that the realization that this was impossible, coupled with my over-
reassuring attitude, had made him think that we were both using a
pretence of certainty to deny the anxiety about not "making it".

I later understood that the fear of going mad came over him
when he confused himself with me during the session and when
the confusion persisted during the interval between sessions,
causing him to produce meaningless thoughts all by himself. I
succeeded in helping Alvise by describing to him what I defined as
pseudo-analysis, as distinct from what might really happen
between us in the sessions. Furthermore, I explained, in trying to
obtain from me the capacity to think, because he felt deprived of
this capacity himself, he could no longer distinguish between his
own thoughts and mine. When in this state, he felt claustrophobic
and did not want analytic contact, so as not to become mixed up
with me again. A part of the negative emotions that sometimes
assailed him on returning from the breaks between sessions was
made up of the anxiety and fear of losing the state of precarious
individuality he had achieved.

A particularly painful aspect of Alvise's subjective experience
that arose at this time was his inability to perceive a sense of bodily
and psychic individuality. During the sessions he felt as if he

"lacked a cranium", and sought to fill himself with my words in order to achieve bodily and psychic completeness. In the outside world, having lost the perception of the boundaries that made him a separate individual, he felt that he had no defensive "shield" and was therefore a prey to other people and liable to be run through by the presence of others. His mind worked like a gutted gut, unable to assimilate, and capable only of being an irritated and explosive surface that gave rise to chaotic perceptual turbulence. He had consequently begun to move about in a world replete with hostility. On his way to his sessions, he engaged in endless eye-contact duels with passers-by, whom he stared out with a view to entering their minds and thereby countering the thoughts "people" conceived about him.

Likewise, before lying down on the couch, he would make a careful inspection of my face and expression in order to assess possible negative signals emanating from me. The world about him seemed violent and dangerous, like a jungle dominated by homici-dal violence. He had stopped driving because he was afraid that someone might crash into him, and sometimes he was concerned for his physical safety while walking in the street.

Owing to the confusion between good and bad experiences and the constant transformation of meanings, personal relationships induced such anxiety that he gradually withdrew into a life of isola-tion. The decision to withdraw also seemed to be connected with a need to protect himself and with the insight that a long period of reconstruction of his person would be necessary before he could confront life and human relations.

Another important problem was the impact of emotions on him. If they appeared, even within the "analytic shell", Alvise was compelled to transform his mind so as to abolish them. Strong emotions—in particular, anger and rage—were like crashing break-ers; he literally had no internal space or means of mental contain-ment for them, so that, when they arose, they were accompanied by agonizing pain and the anxiety that he might fall apart again.

Progress, too, was feared. Mental activity and the acknow-ledgement of capabilities on his part were liable to become so excit-ing that he would be thrown off balance; he lacked a mind that was strong and organized enough to sustain improvement, which thus had to be immediately evacuated.

Until recently, his relational life had been confined to the analysis. Apart from his contacts with his family, Alvise left home only to come to his sessions.

After the first two years of therapy, I, for my part, had noticed substantial changes: in particular, a better analytic relationship had become established, in which the patient was able to refer with greater certainty to a stable and constant object. Good feelings emerged and persisted for longer.

The exclusive concentration on the analytic relationship gradually allowed him to have the experience of being held together by, and kept in the thoughts of, someone. In the transference he began to live a protective union with me, followed by a sense of sadness at separation. Because he seemed to me uncertain about this point, I helped him to distinguish between, on the one hand, "being with me" and, on the other, "putting himself inside me and confusing himself with me" as he had done before.

I was also able to interpret how, during separations, he lost contact with me and again saw me as a cold and scientific analyst, and how he swung in the transference between two mutually exclusive systems (good and bad) of emotional truth and emotional reality.

The hallucinations and their course

In the first two years of the analysis Alvise tended to feel hated and despised by people (such perceptions often arose in respect of myself!), so that he avoided contact with neighbours, strangers, and, later, also friends. The patient felt that people were "reading" his thoughts. For instance, he mentioned snatches of conversation between patrons and the barmaid in a bar he visited before his sessions, from which he inferred that they knew all about him, including his thoughts. In a second phase, all these perceptions became organized as auditory hallucinations. Alvise had become a negative entity that lived in the minds of others and was universally despised.

The hallucinations would arise without warning, attacking him with disparaging accusations and plunging him into a state of terror. The "voices" assailed him in many areas of his personality;

for example, they might suddenly call him "gay", or accuse him of being "mad". The space that had been opened up terrified him because the "voices" could emerge from it.

When he came to analysis, he would travel in railway carriages with small compartments in which he could protect himself. Once, when the train had only coaches with big compartments, he was overcome by terror and missed his session. The hallucinations could occur anywhere and at any time.

I must say that this new development in the patient left me feeling bewildered and annoyed. On the basis of my past experience as a psychiatrist, I was afraid that Alvise might prove to be one of the many cases in which the patient emerges from a psychotic episode only to succumb to chronic auditory hallucinations. At first, therefore, I regarded the hallucinations as an unfavourable and undesirable event, and noticed that I hoped to see them disappear as soon as possible. At the same time, however, I was induced to penetrate more deeply into the mystery of hallucinatory thought and to try to understand how it might come into being. In other words, I realized that the hallucinations could not disappear by magic, but only by dint of consistent analytic work. In listening to him, I wondered about the possible meaning of these senseless accusations and this quirk of the moral sense. What was he telling me, for example, when he said that he was unable to step out of his house because the young people in the neighbourhood, whom he saw as vulgar and uncouth, would have thought him mad owing to the differences in cultural background and language between them (the patient was not conversant with the local dialect)? Would I ever be able to discover in the cryptic, hallucinated message a communication or meaning that could be shared? The "voices" sometimes resembled an indiscriminate campaign of denigration, an attempt to destroy his personality. When in the throes of a hallucinatory attack, the patient reminded me of Job standing before God, overwhelmed by terror and without guilt. However, I must repeat that I, too, felt as overwhelmed and paralysed as Job.

I interpreted the hallucination as an attempt by a cruel part of himself to colonize and intimidate him, but realized from his reply that it was difficult to help him. Alvise saw my interpretation as proof that, denying the reality of his perceptions, I distrusted him and thought him "mad". Upon every attempt at interpretation, I found that it was taken for granted that the hallucinatory world was one of concrete reality, an idea that could not easily be overcome. I could not regard the hallucinations as a fantasy to be interpreted and transformed. Here, fantasy was fact. The patient really was seeing people who spoke ill of him and hearing neighbours make comments or insinuations about his madness, and he was not prepared to believe that this, too, was a result of his own bad relations with other people and his inability to see these in terms of conflict.

The problem was not only to understand, but also, and in particular, to supply interpretations that would take due account of the patient's capacity to comprehend them. I knew that a forced or unilateral interpretative intervention could very easily give rise to misunderstandings and psychotic contamination of the analytic relationship.

Whereas I could count on the patient's receptivity in other areas of our relationship, I became increasingly convinced that, with regard to work on his hallucinations, the only possible approach was to maintain an unsaturated space that would allow for the patient's limitations as well as, first and foremost, the complexity of the clinical situation. Even if the hallucinations permeated the transference and influenced my countertransference, they seemed to involve a mental activity that went beyond the analytic relationship and its conflicts. I felt that there was much to be discovered and that only the patient could make the decisive contribution.

I sought to observe reality as the patient saw it, to accept and describe it, and to encourage the patient to think about what was happening. I was, thus, surprised to learn that sometimes the "voices" also spoke in an enigmatic language of their own about the analytic communication and its stumbling blocks or failures. For instance, one hallucinatory attack occurred after a session in which I had been unable to interpret the state of self-induced sensual pleasure, which the patient had described as one of well being. Left alone after the session, and with the state of euphoria at an end, Alvise had been bombarded with hallucinatory accusations from passers-by ("he's mad, he's drugged out of his mind!"). I told him that the "voices" had punished him for misleading me, but in the session they had perhaps allied themselves with him so as to confuse me.

On another occasion, the "people's voices" spoke of his coming to analysis, attacked him for it, and tried to condemn him: they knew he was coming to me, and so it was clear to everyone that he was "mad". Another time he described a hallucinatory attack, just before he arrived for his session, in which the voices advised him to attack me because I was a botcher and a pompous old fart. I told him that the aim of the "voices" was to discourage him and at the same time to do violence to the analytic relationship, after which he would feel destructive and guilty.

Once he described a hallucinatory attack (with the usual comment "he's mad, mad as a hatter!") after an argument with his mother, who had seemed to him overbearing and intrusive. In this case it was clear that the "voices" were confusing him about the nature and quality of the emotions he was experiencing: they told him that he was in the throes of a violent fit of destruction when the emotion he was actually experiencing was rage, which was admittedly violent, but due to incomprehension.

I realized in this case that Alvise was destroying the possibility of feeling alive and aggressive in an attempt to placate a superego that was threatening him with a hallucinatory attack. He said that if he were to rebel against the "voices", he would be persecuted even more; he felt that an aggressive counter-attack on the persecutors would have brought back the confusion and the catastrophic sense of guilt. So he could only submit with resignation to the aggression of the "voices".

I remained attentive and vigilant for a long period and kept my mind open to any possible way of helping him or of bringing about insight, until one of the rare dreams in the analysis made it possible for us to think together about his hallucinations and for the first time to stand apart from their terrifying power. In my view, it was precisely this countertransference attitude that helped to provide the patient with a space to think, something that was made possible by the dream.

Alvise told me he had dreamt that he was in a Navy hospital that greatly resembled a concentration camp or lunatic asylum. There were other inmates, who all seemed to be normal people. Beside him was a serial killer, who frightened him. The camp commandant appeared and told Tony Curtis, a fellow prisoner, to be quiet; Tony Curtis went limp.

Alvise tried to leave the hospital/concentration camp, boarded a bus that failed to move off, and began to wander aimlessly through the countryside.

The patient associated himself with Tony Curtis, a genial, rebellious young man. As we worked on the dream, I pointed out to him that the camp commandant, by ordering him to be quiet, was trying to kill off these characteristics and reduce his personality to nothing; after all, at the end, Tony Curtis appeared drained and totally passive. I added that there were exuberant young men and murderers together in the same camp and that the naval officer not only failed to distinguish between the mad killer and the rebellious young man, but also targeted the latter.

Emphasizing that the camp commandant, who represented the destroying agency, was attacking the vital aspects and not the murderous ones, I showed the patient that in this figure he was describing the hallucinatory pressure that was tormenting him, annihilating his personality, and could not distinguish between his rebellious vitality and murderous destructiveness.

I was convinced that the dream marked a step forward. I saw it as an attempt to recover and reintegrate his former rebellious personality. However, this process was failing. In the dream, it seemed that Alvise thought he had been led into disaster on account of his rebellious personality, as the young man had been attacked because he was regarded as dangerous.

This inability to distinguish between reactive vitality and murderous aggression was a problem that had prevented progress for some time, keeping him passive and destroying strong, vital emotions. It was as if these two positions were too close together, so that each could flip without warning into the other, something that terrified him. I also connected the dream with the previously analysed moments when he had experienced me, the analysis, and my interpretations as manoeuvres demanding an adaptation or abolition of his individuality. I reminded him how difficult it was for him to see our relationship as a dialogue between equals, in which to develop and live, rather than as a kind of submission. I linked the drama experienced in the dream to the climate of violence in which he seemed to be immersed in reality, which frightened him and made him submit to the yoke of subjection.

This dream, to which we returned on many occasions at important junctures in the analysis, in my view tellingly represented the
threatening power of the psychotic superego over the entire personality and opened the way to an understanding of the hallucinatory
terror. The dream portrayed a violent entity that assaulted him at
moments of rebellion: Alvise had introjected an annihilating object
that had become a part of himself. Intimidation and accusation had
hitherto cut the patient off from curiosity, understanding of his
conflicts, and exploration of psychic reality.

It seems to me that the interpretative work on the destructuring
and confusing nature of the superego was central to the analytic
development of this case. This development allowed the catastrophic anxiety and guilt (for a long time projected into external
objects and reintrojected in the form of hallucinations) to be gradually transformed into the capacity to think about the damage
inflicted and into the assumption of responsibility.

In this situation, the perception of personal responsibility was
out of the question for Alvise, dominated as he was by an overwhelming and terrifying superego. When he had to confront conflict and guilt, he was confused by the superego and no other course
was open to him than withdrawal and self-annihilation. It was only
later that he became capable of confronting the anxiety resulting
from the perception of the loss of his own personality.

An attempt at reparation

A dream in the second period, in the fifth year of the analysis,
revealed to us his incapacity to confront loss other than by violent
and self-aggressive methods. He said that in the dream he was with
a sixteen-year-old girl with whom he was in love and, whereas he
was with her at night, during the daytime he frantically did his best
to forget about her. Then the girl suddenly disappeared, leaving
him a prey to destructive rage against himself owing to his lack of
foresight and the pain he had experienced.

The dream seemed to be a new version of the depressive anxiety of the period just before the psychotic breakdown, portraying as
it did the pain that had assailed him after he was abandoned by the
girl he himself had rejected and neglected. I considered that the part

of him that was capable of experiencing emotions was exposing him to pain and narcissistic rage.

I interpreted that the lost girl represented the healthy, relational part lost in the psychotic state of manic excitation. I also said that the dream not only demonstrated his reaction to loss, but also described the self-aggressive, disparaging hallucinatory attacks. I connected the hallucinated voice with the narcissistic rage that prevented him from accepting and grieving for his loss. After all, the "voice" now confined itself almost exclusively to contemptuous comments about the feeling of sadness that afflicted the patient when he compared his present state with that of the past. Alvise explained to me that any feeling of dejection could be perceived by "others": any unsteadiness of voice might give him away and make him appear mad. He was, therefore, compelled to defend himself against sadness, sometimes by destroying his very self and his feelings, and sometimes by aggression against himself.

Working with the patient, especially in the intervals between hallucinatory episodes, I was later able to identify a specific time, tantamount to a period of incubation, when the accusing, destructive voices first came into being. Whenever, outside the sessions, he happened to feel sad and isolated from everyone, this caused hatred and violence towards the rest of the world to grow within him. The culmination of the paroxysmic hate coincided with the collapse of the psychic boundary (the loss of his psychic "cranium" and "shield"), resulting in perceptual holes that were the source of the "people's" aggressive and violent thoughts which ran him through and terrified him.

We gradually came to understand that the mental state into which he withdrew, in which the sadomasochistic isolation of a victim was mixed with hate, was the fertile soil for the production of the hallucinations.

Psychoanalytic hypotheses on hallucinations

I shall now connect these ideas with the work of other authors who have described the technical problems of the treatment of psychotic states and discussed the hallucinatory state in analytic terms.

As we know, working with a patient who has had a psychotic breakdown presents complex problems of technique. Once the psychotic catastrophe has occurred and the capacity for symbolic thought has been destroyed, the patient must try to restore the unity of his fragmented ego and to reconquer the use of his mind. The analyst must assign meaning to the various elements of the psychotic process, distinguishing them from each other and placing them in the correct developmental perspective.

The phase of the analysis described above falls precisely within this specific context. During this period, the analyst's delicate task is to preserve the therapeutic relationship while taking account of the psychotic—not neurotic—functioning at the patient's disposal.

The experience of hallucinations is preceded by loss of the perception of psychic reality and of the sense of spatial and personal identity. The patient lives his life enclosed in his bodily monad, in a hostile dimension that separates him from the rest of the world. Hence, his thoughts and anxieties will present themselves as a dialogue or altercation between persons and not as something relevant to his internal world.

The process of analytic restitution is, therefore, complex: the patient "feels" thoughts but cannot think them. The analyst must concentrate for a long time on the patient's hallucinated world before he can succeed in supplying a progress-facilitating meaning.

Some authors take the view that, in the course of the psychotic process, the hallucinatory accusations that follow the actual breakdown allow the mind, by means of splitting, to assume a more stable structure than it had in the confusion of the acute psychosis. In this phase, perceptions become organized in such a way that a weak, subjected self is separated from a bad world looming over it.

Bion (1957, 1965) considers hallucination, like psychosomatic illness or mental functioning in the form of "basic assumptions", as a means of evacuating excess sensory stimuli and intolerable anxiety. In hallucination, the working of the sense organ used for the hallucination is reversed. Undigested *beta* elements are expelled together with pieces of the ego and superego. The massive hallucinatory evacuation also serves to avoid worse situations, such as confusional states or more dramatic psychotic experiences.

Pao (1979) notes that during the acute phase of the illness, the patient, while unable to confirm this verbally, is in a dream-like hallucinatory state. In the sub-acute phase, hallucination presents itself in completely different form because terror is reduced and the structure of the ego functions is beginning to re-establish itself; the perceptual disturbance affects mainly the auditory sphere and the "voices" are experienced as ego-dystonic. It is only at this point that the hallucinations can express conflicts and needs, and may therefore prove useful for understanding the patient.

Ogden (1982), in his study of the process of reconstruction during the therapy of psychotic patients, maintains that the schizophrenic conflict is resolved in stages. The first is that of non-experience, with the predominance of hatred of reality and the wish not to have any experience. In subsequent stages, the balance gradually shifts towards the desire to live, but the patient's thoughts then become painful and terrifying. In this context, the hallucinations appear as reified and projected representations of fragmented thoughts. The result is the creation of bizarrely distorted external and internal worlds.

For Pao and Ogden, hallucination, dreadful and terrifying as it is, constitutes a virtually obligatory stage of personality reconstitution in the therapy of psychotic states.

My own view is that, as analysts, we may be privileged to help the patient in his attempt at recovery if we hold fast to the conviction that the communication of a problem is inherent in even the most bizarre hallucination. It may sometimes be possible to understand this communication only at a later date, when, by virtue of the gradual recovery of the capacity to think brought about by the work of analysis, the psychotic superego has been stripped of the terrifying, distorting, and obstructive elements expressed through the hallucinated voice.

The hallucinatory dialogue

For example, I understood only later that the "voices" of Alvise's young neighbours, which told Alvise that he was "mad" because he was refined, betrayed his "knowledge" that his "refinement" was partly an affectation aimed at conveying an ideal image of himself to others. This was the "kernel of truth" in the communication that was distorted by the superego's terrifying and accusing propaganda.

The voices might express a truth in distorted fashion as in the present case, or egg him on to destructive violence and then ferociously criminalize him. The voices that tormented him on his way to analysis might suggest to him that "the analyst is a turd, a pompous old fart"; they might then colonize him completely and induce him to attack me with the same violent words. A timely interpretation to explain to him the purpose and nature of the "voices" would free him from the hallucinations and relieve him of the sense of guilt.

However, the patient's specific problem at this time was less the existence of an aggressive conflict with me than the form assumed by this conflict, under the sway of the "voices" and the destructive superego's attempt to conquer him and finally to assimilate him completely. By interpreting the conflict and the aims of the hallucinated voices to him, I was able to block the emergence of a destructive crime but not his subsequent susceptibility to persist with hallucination. For, until the work of rehumanization had reached an advanced stage through the analysis, it was impossible to detach the patient once and for all from the destructive and intimidatory power of the hallucinated world, which for a long time continued to resemble an invasive nucleus of violence.

The psychotic superego

The Old Testament tells how the rich, fortunate, and happy Job suddenly finds himself on a dung-heap. He loses all his wealth, his flocks are wiped out, his children are slain, and his body is covered with sore boils. Job carries on a lively discussion of his plight with his friends; he does not accept his fate, and protests his innocence before God. However, the answer he gets is disturbing. Blinded with wrath and haughtily insistent on His right to dispose of His creatures as He sees fit, God hurls himself upon Job and yells at this mere worm crawling in the dirt who dares to ask for explanations of His behaviour. Before such an arrogant and narcissistically touchy God, Job appears as a desperate and devout person; the violence of his words against God is dictated more by exasperation than by rebellion. Everything would be assuaged in him if he could only understand the link between sin and punishment.

The story of Job can, in my view, also be understood as the description of a relationship between the ego and the psychotic superego during the course of a psychotic breakdown, in which the protagonist, like my patient, finds himself expelled from the state of well being and flung on to a dung-heap, a prey to a destructive and accusing voice.

The psychotic superego bears a greater resemblance to the God of Job than to the primitive God of Abraham; even if the latter demands human sacrifices for offences or transgressions, He at least makes the link between the crime and the punishment explicit. The psychotic patient is more like Job: he has to confront a threatening world that is out to annihilate and terrify him rather than to make him feel guilty. The God of Job demands subjection without even allowing him to understand the reason for the wrath and the origin of the sin: the patient in this phase therefore has to face not so much guilt as terror.

Since there seems to be a relationship between primitive morality and intimidation, the term "primitive" suggests that conscience develops as a continuation of primal terroristic morality.

In her early work, Melanie Klein (e.g., 1929) maintains that the primitive superego, introjected in the earliest stages of development, is a basic factor in the appearance of the psychoses. During this phase, the superego punishes the ego for its destructiveness by mercilessly primitive means. This vision of the psychotic superego follows from the work on melancholia of Freud (1917e; Freud & Abraham, 1965) and Abraham (1924; Freud & Abraham, 1965), both of whom considered that the self-accusations of the melancholic, although stemming from a primitive superego, were substantially correct and indicative of an unconscious problem in so far as the patient "knew" that he was unable to love and was full of hate.

The Kleinian hypothesis of a cruel, merciless superego and of a primitive, murderous id has characterized the clinical work of every author who has engaged in the analytic therapy of psychosis. That is the theoretical frame of reference of Rosenfeld's (1965) studies of the therapy of psychotic patients. In his 1952 paper, in which he describes the therapy of an acute catatonic patient, Rosenfeld contends that the auditory hallucinations bombarding the patient during the session are nothing other than the punitive voice of the superego in response to death wishes towards the

analyst. From this point of view, the superego's cruelty and merci-
lessness are proportional to the destructiveness of the ego.

This model, based on a correlation between destructiveness and
persecutory guilt, was subsequently modified by new insights, in
particular by Melanie Klein towards the end of her career and by
Bion and Rosenfeld.

In one of her last contributions, Klein (1958) distinguishes the
primitive from the psychotic superego. The psychotic superego is
stated to be not so much a primitive and cruel superego (of the *lex
talionis* type) as a terrifying internal object that can be neither assimilated nor transformed. Whereas the primitive superego evolves
during the course of development and becomes integrated with
good experiences, its psychotic counterpart, which is destined not to
be transformed, is thrust down into ever deeper layers of the unconscious, where it becomes encysted and constitutes an omnipresent,
threatening nucleus of potential madness. She writes (*ibid.*, p. 243),
"I assume, however, that . . . terrifying figures in the deep layers of
the unconscious make themselves felt when internal or external
pressure is extreme". She goes on: ". . . we can see more clearly that
in [these patients] the super-ego becomes almost indistinguishable
from their destructive impulses and internal persecutors" (*ibid.*).

Bion (1962a, p. 97) discusses the relations between envy and the
superego. The envious object is an internal object without an
outside, an alimentary tract without a body, a SUPER-EGO (Bion
uses capital letters), which appears as a destructive activity tinged
with "moral qualities". In *Transformations* (1965, p. 38), he says that
the superego "appears to be developmentally prior to the ego and
to deny development and existence itself to the ego". Later (1967),
Bion writes that the mother's failure to introject the newborn's
projective identifications allows the formation of an internal object
endowed with devouring activity that wishes to introject the baby's
projective identifications with a view to destroying them. If the
infant identifies with this object, it becomes the "bad self", which
triumphs by destroying meaning and undermining the capacity to
learn from experience.

Rosenfeld, too (1971), in his theory of destructive narcissism,
equates the omnipotent narcissistic structure with a superego organization whose destructive nature is concealed from the patient: it
is this destructive and envious superego that makes the patient feel

guilty when he tries to improve and to detach himself from the destructive nucleus.

The terrorist nucleus

As this brief review shows, a conception emerges in which the psychotic superego forfeits every token of primitive morality ("an eye for an eye, a tooth for a tooth") and becomes a nucleus split off from the rest of the personality and possessing terroristic powers. The relationship between guilt and responsibility, between destructive accusations and persecution, becomes more complex. This theoretical perspective presupposes a destructive superego that colonizes and devastates the internal world, without any direct relation to the patient's guilt and responsibility; from this point of view, the submission of Job as a human being to the wrathful, arrogant God can be seen as one of the superego-related outcomes of psychosis.

In his contribution on bearable and unbearable guilt, Brenman (1987) points out that the judging object within these patients is made up of inflexible accusations, demands punishment without forgiveness, and insists on excommunication without extenuating circumstances. This superego deprives the subject of all his goodness, and nothing can redeem the sinner without grace. However, Brenman remarks that these patients are not only the victims of a superego of this kind, but are also dominated by their omnipotence, arrogance, and cannibalism. This view emphasizes the collusion between the patient's superego and his ego, reforges the link between the primitive and guilt, and re-establishes the connection between sin and punishment.

Bion (1992) points out that one of the difficulties facing a patient seeking to recover and reassemble the fragments of the destroyed personality is the appearance of an extremely destructive superego. The reparative process is therefore constantly hindered by a concomitant destructive trend.

My patient Alvise's dream of the naval captain seems to indicate the existence of this destructive threat, while the hallucinatory state perhaps corresponds to the action of the terrifying superego that accompanies the attempt at restoration.

Psychotic depression

It has long been known (Rosenfeld, 1952; Segal, 1956) that psychotic depressive feelings—an unbearable hotchpotch of guilt and cata-strophic anxiety—impede the process of recovery in the patient and represent a crucial obstacle that is difficult to overcome.

Bion (1957) writes that the psychotic is unable to restore his object or his ego because he has destroyed precisely the part of the personality that would be needed for their repair. Steiner (1991), with regard to the mechanisms used by psychotics to repair the ego and objects, points out that the attempt at repair is undertaken by violent and omnipotent means—that is, with the psychotic part of the personality—and is therefore doomed to failure.

Bearing in mind the ideas of Bion and Steiner, we can say that the anxiety stemming from the pain and perception of the impossi-bility of reparation leads to the fragmentation of psychic reality and potentiates the use of omnipotence. Note that this type of anxiety is not strictly depressive, because depressive anxiety concerns the loss of an object and the consequent sense of guilt at one's responsibil-ity for it. The much more severe psychotic anxiety stems, by contrast, not only from the perception of the destruction of the self and of one's internal world, but also from the awareness of the loss of the psychic instruments with which to attempt the repair. At some points in this process, the suffering is so acute that the patient attempts to escape from it by alteration of his mental state and by seeking mutilated forms of existence, or by taking refuge in psychic torpor.

At times of maximum difficulty and anxiety, Alvise would stay in bed in the mornings in order to put himself in a peaceful state of mind. By laying in supplies of food, coffee, and cigarettes, he managed to produce a mental state that gently cradled him and did not make him think. If this pleasurable state was excessively prolonged, he felt "scattered to the winds" and feared the loss of his identity. He would then need to make a great effort to leave the house to come to his session.

This explains why, at times of progress, the agonizing and unbearable perception of guilt at the catastrophe that has occurred can easily give rise to a relapse. The psychic reality is so painful that the patient produces an alternative one, or destroys the perceptual apparatus so as to evacuate it. Hallucinatory fragmentation is one of the seemingly paradoxical but effective defences used for this purpose.

The second phase of the analysis included a long period in which it was important to pay constant attention to the patient's painful mental state; it was a period in which thoughts yielded to the impact of intolerable realities and the emotional tensions resulting from insight caused the mind, as it were, to burst its banks.

Acceptance of loss

The gradual dawning of consciousness and the acceptance of the loss sustained paved the way for the transformation of the world of hallucinatory perception. We examined more closely the computer-like superego system that dominated him, the ferocious and disparaging attacks that emerged at times of discouragement, and the capacity to obtain pleasure through the creation of excited, "superior" states of mind (the patient told me that before his break-down, whereas his friends used narcotics, he could put himself into a mental state similar to that induced by cocaine by means of thought alone).

The psychotic breakdown, which had seemed like a sudden and unexpected explosion, could now be seen as the consequence of a gradual transformation of the personality to which the patient had devoted himself with all his energy for a very long time. Alvise had submitted to the dominion of the superego under the illusion, before the breakdown, of freeing himself from pain by recourse to the method of abolishing emotions and depending on mental sensual pleasure. Later, during the crisis, he found himself turned into a depersonalized automaton. With the progress of the psychotic state, a perverse system had developed in which the "truth" revealed by the "voices" was directed towards obtaining submission and not knowledge. The destructive superego that emerged in the psychotic state was a continuation of its pre-crisis counterpart and had gradually perfected the capacity to confuse the perception of emotions, increasingly developing the power of intimidation over vital aspects of the patient's personality.

In my view, the production of the hallucinatory state bore witness to the enormously wide crack that had opened up between the self and the rest of the world during the second period of analysis, when the hatred of reality had become more obvious. The patient's hallucinations changed and ultimately disappeared as he moved from a destructive and destructuring posture to one that was closer to the melancholic state, and passed in reverse order through the same positions that had transformed his personality before the breakdown.

CHAPTER SEVEN

Difficulties in therapy: relapses into psychosis

"Schizophrenia cannot be understood simply in terms of traumata and deprivation, no matter how grievous, inflicted by the outer world upon the helpless child. The patient himself, no matter how unwittingly, has an active part in the development and tenacious maintenance of the illness and only by making contact with this essentially assertive energy in him can one help him to become well"

(Searles, 1979, p. 22)

Spider

David Cronenberg's film *Spider*, which is based on Patrick McGrath's identically titled novel (McGrath, 1990), tells the story of a schizophrenic, nicknamed Spider by his mother, who is sent to a halfway house after being discharged from the psychiatric hospital where he has been a patient for twenty years. On leaving the hospital to return to normal life, Spider is fearful, withdrawn, and suspicious of the world around him; he moves about like a zombie, as if lacking any awareness of himself and others.

The halfway house where he is to live is situated in the district on the edge of town where he spent his infancy. So he is able to revisit the house where he lived as a child, the canal and the gasholder, the little garden, and the pub where his father was a regular. The reconstruction of his past is central to the unfolding of the film's plot. Everything Spider sees brings back memories of his infantile years.

Those memories tell us that he had a good mother, who was neglected and despised by his father. The father, having taken up with a prostitute, eventually kills his wife when she catches the pair together. After the murder, Spider has to live with his new stepmother, an aloof woman interested only in sex and drink, who treats him roughly. Spider "knows" that the father and his mistress have murdered his mother, and also fears for his own life. Hatred of this woman and the fear of meeting the same fate as his mother drive him to gas the stepmother to death.

The audience emotionally take the side of Spider, an orphan at grips with a stepmother and a violent and murderous father; they eventually conclude that the mental illness for which he was hospitalized might also be due to the trauma of the loss of his mother and his father's vile relationship with the prostitute. But it gradually becomes clear that the memory of the past has not re-established the truth, but instead led Spider to confuse it with fantasy: the landlady of the halfway house, a distant and authoritarian woman, assumes the stepmother's features and impels him to kill again.

The film ends with Spider on the point of killing the landlady in her sleep, but this project is frustrated when his victim suddenly wakes up. He then sees again the images from the past, which show that he himself had murdered his mother, whom he had seen as a stepmother. It is only at the end that the audience is able to understand that in the film the past—which the patient does not remember, but "sees"—has been presented to them in Spider's delusional version. The delusional imagination had transformed the mother into a persecutor to be eliminated, and it now becomes clear that the psychosis, modelled on the false memory of his adolescence, has re-invaded Spider's mind. Finally, the film's protagonist is re-admitted to hospital.

We can now attempt a reconstruction of Spider's actual history. He has committed a crime, killing his mother in a state of delusional confusion, spends twenty years in a psychiatric hospital, and is then discharged. He seems better; there has been a spontaneous remission, but the psychosis has remained untreated. Spider spent his infancy in a fantasy world, in a close and privileged relationship with his mother, who constantly drew his attention to her husband's deficiencies and thereby made him feel ideal. When the parents get back together—the father stops frequenting the pub and starts going out with his wife—Spider not only begins secretly to hate the parental couple but also transforms the mother into a bad, sexualized woman.

Until the moment when he kills his mother, Spider is a boy who has always dissociated aggression: he has never protested or quarrelled and has never had any friends. The dissociated aggression ultimately turns into criminal violence and drives Spider to commit homicide in a delusion of denial.

I have summarized the plot of Cronenberg's film because it exhibits amazing insight in its description of the reasons for the recurrence of a psychotic attack. Spider has been discharged by the medical staff because he is no longer delusional. He is not cured, but has merely *forgotten* (or dissociated) the episode. While "contained" in isolation in the mental hospital and having occupational therapy, he was, it may be surmised, kept away from delusional stimuli, so that productive symptoms were not in evidence. When he returns to his childhood haunts, the memories of the past—and of the previous episode—cause the delusion to resurface intact. Spider becomes psychotic again *precisely because he remembers*. He has no memory of himself; his personal past has been expropriated by his schizophrenia, which now causes the delusion to recur in the present.

Because the act of remembering is no different from that of reliving the crisis, the audience, too, is induced to see the delusional reality as true. At the peak of the delusion, the authoritarian landlady, associated with the bad mother of the past, reawakens the bad, poisonous spider in him. The film is at its most dramatic when the audience become clearly aware of the delusional nature of Spider's mental state. The recognition of the pathological state and the readmission to hospital put a stop—at least for the time being—to the devastating workings of Spider's deadly web of psychosis.

"Recovery"

Spider's story helps us to understand why recovery from psychosis is often only a seeming recovery. In the therapy of such patients, remissions, sometimes persisting for long periods, followed sooner or later by fresh psychotic episodes, are frequently observed. The reason for these relapses is unclear, but they are no doubt attributable to the form assumed by the remission. Once the acute episode is over, perhaps with the aid of drug therapy, the patient's mental functioning returns to its pre-illness form, often with some obvious limitations. However, all the conditions that facilitated the first breakdown are unchanged. The impression is gained that the clinical improvement occurred without any in-depth transformation of the patient's mental structure. The delusion carved out a path that remains open and which the patient will sooner or later embark upon again. In other words, although the psychosis has been halted, the causes of the patient's active tendency to fall ill again have not been eliminated. In order to "recover", the patient has reconstructed a psychic skin that keeps him seemingly whole, but he always remains a "two-dimensional" person who is liable to fall apart at any time under the pressure of specific emotional impacts.

To sum up, during a remission the illness is dissociated from consciousness and is put aside in a place where it lies *forgotten*. The psychosis re-emerges from this dissociated memory as soon as sufficient conditions for its recurrence are once again present. Upon its exhaustion, the psychotic episode in effect leaves behind a *matrix* that is able at any time to reproduce delusional representations similar to the original ones. The secondary aspects may vary, but the basic configuration of the delusion remains identical.

Return of psychosis

The analysis of a patient who has emerged from an acute psychotic episode may sometimes go well for a time. The breakdown seems to have been relegated to the past, the anxieties become similar in nature to those of a neurotic patient, and the analyst concentrates his attention on dreams, transference material, or problems in the patient's relational life. This picture is then suddenly disturbed by the onset of a fresh psychotic attack.

The analyst is now compelled to realize that the improvement was illusory and that therapist and patient have unconsciously colluded in "letting sleeping dogs lie": that is, in refraining from analysing the underlying psychotic functioning and exposing it to the light of day (one example among many is the case of Ada, described in Chapter Five). The signs that foreshadow a renewed breakdown will be more apparent to an analyst who is accustomed to treating psychotic patients and who might already have experience of therapeutic failure. Relapses have taught us not to underestimate the danger of a repetition of the psychotic episode, even when the clinical situation is seemingly under control.

My aim in this chapter is to address precisely the difficulty of working through the psychotic crisis once and for all. At the 41st Congress of the International Psychoanalytical Association in Santiago, Chile, García Badaracco drew attention to this difficulty by noting that very few cases of recovery from psychosis are reported in the analytic literature (García Badaracco & Mariotti, 2000). This well justified pessimism about the treatment of such patients should spur us on to augment our therapeutic arsenal and to learn also from our failures.

Alvise (continued)

In this section I shall present clinical material on two patients who relapsed into psychosis while in therapy. The first is Alvise, whose case was described in Chapter Six. I can now add some notes on the outcome of his therapy, which was not as successful as I had hoped at the time of the original publication. As stated, Alvise had been in analysis for about eight years after a serious psychotic episode that culminated in his attempting suicide while in a confused and delusional state. After the acute stage and a period of hospitalization, the patient had commenced drug treatment and psychotherapy, and had then, with the agreement of his attending psychiatrist, asked for analytic therapy.

The analytic reflections in my published paper had focused on the transformation that had taken place during the course of therapy in a particular psychopathological structure that trapped him in psychosis and seemed to be connected with the generation of hallucinations by a specific type of superego. I had attributed this hallucinatory system to a destructive superego structure, and felt that the analysis and the transformation of this pathological construction had enabled the patient to emerge from the psychotic state. The writing of my contribution coincided with a time of seemingly stable improvement in the patient, even though I did have some residual doubts about the permanence of the change.

After eight years of analysis, the patient's condition had improved to such an extent that his parents had persuaded him to complete his university studies, which had been in abeyance for a long time (he had just one more examination to take). Although reluctant to do this and intolerant of intellectual work, the patient had agreed to his parents' suggestion. In order to prepare his degree thesis, Alvise had had to reduce his number of sessions from four to two (to enable him to come to analysis four times a week in the first part of his therapy, he had rented a bedsit, as he lived a long way from Milan).

With only half the number of analytic sessions, Alvise was unable to cope with the tension of preparing his thesis and relapsed into psychosis during the summer holidays while separated from his analyst. This time the auditory hallucinations had been experienced not as a disturbance as in the case of the first episode, but as a special quality that made him unique, so much so that he believed the CIA was looking for him with the aim of kidnapping him to America and making him work for the US government. This made him feel persecuted.

Owing to the new psychotic episode, his readmission to hospital, and a series of adverse circumstances, it was not possible to analyse his idealization of madness, so that both Alvise and I were discouraged, and he stopped coming to his sessions. I heard that he was back in his home town living a very limited life as permitted by antipsychotic medication, not unlike other patients who have failed to emerge from psychosis.

Questions

I reflected long and hard on the outcome of this therapy, and doubts about my conduct of the treatment persisted for a long time in my mind. For me, the decisive fact remained that, by virtue of the work on the psychotic superego, the patient's internal world had undergone a positive transformation: Alvise had improved when systematic analysis of the psychopathological structure underlying the psychotic state had rid him of hallucinations and enabled him to tolerate the pain of the psychotic catastrophe that had taken place. During the therapy, however severe the psychotic pathology, I had always considered it favourable that, before he fell ill, Alvise had attained a good level of development: he had done well at school, had friends, and was a successful sportsman.

In other words, I had thought—and hoped—that basically, once he was out of the psychotic state, he would be able to maintain a sufficiently stable psychic world, as he had done before the onset of his illness. I had probably taken an excessively one-sided view of the patient's improvement and his emergence from his psychosis.

For the improvement had been followed by a fresh, serious relapse: the badlands of the psychotic experience had not been reclaimed at all. With the return of the psychosis, in the form of delusions of grandeur, I began to wonder if I had, in fact, delved, together with the patient, in sufficient depth into the origins of the previous psychotic episode. If we had not shared and together worked through the reasons for its occurrence, how could I have imagined that the crisis would not be repeated? In other words, I realized *only after the event* that the psychotic episode had, in many respects, remained like an inconvenient third element between us.

I also remembered that every time I had tried, in the analysis, to raise the issue of the psychotic episode for which he had been admitted to hospital, the patient had put up a stubborn resistance, quickly taking flight from the memory of what had happened or trivializing it. I had not undertaken a systematic, in-depth analysis of the first psychotic episode, but had concentrated instead on his need to repair the damage and on finding ways for him to recover his mental functioning.

The failure of this analysis helped me to adopt a new approach to the therapy of psychotic patients. I now consider that all the work we did ought to have been supported by a systematic analysis of how it was that Alvise was still liable to yield to the seductions of psychosis. Although this aspect of the therapy had by no means been neglected, we had not gone into it as deeply and systematically as I now consider necessary. My present view is that it is essential for the patient to confront this task and to devote himself to it strictly and on an ongoing basis if he is to learn to distrust and defend himself against psychotic functioning.

Precarious equilibrium

As a rule, once the psychotic episode is over, the patient tends to preserve the precarious equilibrium attained, even if it involves substantial limitations. He learns to keep away from potentially destabilizing emotional experiences and senses that there is a limit beyond which he cannot push himself. To this end he maintains tight control over relationships and affective cathexes that might trigger new psychotic processes.

When the patient smashes through his personal pillars of Hercules, catastrophe ensues: the relapse into psychosis is facilitated precisely by his having thrust himself forward while lacking a progress-sustaining structure. It is rather like adding a storey to a building constructed on inadequate foundations: the extra load causes the entire structure to collapse.

Something of the kind seems to have happened to Alvise. The fact of pushing himself to write his degree thesis, which for him stood for having to confront life, must have unleashed the crisis.

It is therefore important for symptomatic improvement in the patient during therapy to be paralleled by the development and strengthening of his personality structure. The increasing imbalance between symptomatic improvement and "structure" contributes to the onset of the crisis.

Giorgio

Let us now consider the case of Giorgio, which I supervised for a time. Here, too, the psychotic crisis occurring during the course of therapy is preceded by symptomatic improvement.

Giorgio is a young man of twenty-two who appears to have remained thoroughly immature. He lives at home with a father who dominates him psychically to such an extent that he has no personal identity of his own. His main reason for coming into therapy is anxiety, which prevents him from continuing his studies. The anxiety is so invasive that he loses control of reality. For instance, while driving his car he suddenly fears that he may have caused an accident and has to turn back to make sure he has not harmed anyone. In the preliminary interviews, he fails to mention the psychotic episode that overcame him some months earlier, which, however, he eventually describes in the first few months of his therapy.

The facts are as follows. In the previous summer he felt threatened by some men in a disco, where he claims a girl had offered him a drugged drink. Giorgio says that a few days after this episode, he drew the attention of the police to a suspicious car, and from then on the persecution by the criminals increased dramatically. The psychotic episode, however, remained limited owing to the intervention of his father, who had a relatively small dose of antipsychotic drugs prescribed for him by a psychiatrist.

Certain facts from his childhood seemed particularly significant to the therapist. Giorgio's mother died in a road accident when he was very small. The father reported that from then on he had great difficulty in feeding him. Giorgio has no memory of his mother; he knows only that after her death he did not want anyone in the family—his father or grandparents—to talk to him about her. He felt very ashamed not to have a mother like other children, but claims never to been aware of any pain at her loss.

As a child, the patient felt that he belonged to a special family (the father is a grandiose personality and a local notable), but he was very afraid of his coevals and of "criminals" in general. From an early age, the people he really related to were the police, whom he experienced as heroes and with whom he identified.

At the beginning of his analysis, he seriously proposed to become a policeman and the therapist feared that this decision was irreversible. The wish to become a policeman was dictated more by hate and fear of criminals than by an ideal of solidarity with the weak. This initial infantile structure, midway between grandiosity and persecution, was to serve as the foundation of Giorgio's subsequent delusional development.

When the therapy began, the therapist had seen the patient less as psychotic than as an immature and anxious boy who was always a prey to devastating insecurity feelings. The previous summer's psychotic episode, although mentioned at the beginning, seemed to him to be circumscribed and to bear no relation to the patient's present life.

The symptoms that had impressed the therapist most included masochistic fantasies, in which the patient was subjected to the attentions of a masculine, overpowering woman. Up to a certain point, the therapy took a favourable course: Giorgio's anxiety diminished and he found it easier to do his academic work and to relate to his fellow students.

In the second year of his therapy, the patient, who has never had a girlfriend and is afraid that this is precluded by his masochistic fantasies, meets a girl who is happy to enter into a relationship with him. When he asks to be introduced to her family, she refuses, because her father is strict and her brothers very possessive. The patient is offended and threatens to leave her. From then on, Giorgio builds up a delusional structure in which the girl's father and brothers appear as persecutors. The delusion gradually extends to many of the people he meets. In particular, the local police, whom he has always seen as protective figures, become part of the conspiracy. The therapist, too, is included among the persecutors, and the patient breaks off the treatment.

This fresh psychotic episode seems in many respects to be a repetition of the one that preceded the therapy, with the same dynamic and the same kind of persecution. The chance trigger is apparently the girl's refusal to introduce him to her family. Narcissistically wounded by this refusal, Giorgio constructs a fantasy conflict with the girl's parents, now seen as dangerous criminals, which escalates into a frontal attack. The delusional voice suggests to him that he is hated because he has defied them, so that his life is in peril.

I postulate that what paved the way for the new crisis is the failure to work through the previous psychotic episode, as might perhaps have been possible in the first part of the therapy, together with the neglect of the grandiose and aggressive aspects of the self (the hatred of the criminals and the wish to attack them had remained unchanged since infancy). During the episode itself, the therapist was rightly concerned at the virulence of the psychosis and tried to help the patient to distinguish the delusional fantasies from reality. The patient may perhaps, in the concreteness of his persecution feelings, have perceived the therapist to be denying his (delusional) reality and allying himself with his enemies. The development of the psychotic transference may have caused him to draw away from the therapy.

The original episode

In his book *Interpretation of Schizophrenia*, Arieti (1955, p. 678) writes:

> An important point to be considered is the relevance of the original episode. It is not just a precipitating event; it is a very important dynamic factor, without which the patient would have been able to check, or even compensate, his psychotic propensity.

In my view, not only the reasons for, and manner of, becoming psychotic, which are different for each patient, but also the infantile roots of the psychopathological structure that paves the way for the delusion are condensed in the initial psychotic attack. I am convinced that the adult psychotic illness stems from an infantile delusional nucleus that remains like badlands awaiting the possibility of being made good. As I shall explain at greater length later, an important part of the analytic work is the "deconstruction" of the delusion, involving identification of its structure and infantile roots.

While allowing for the difficulty of the patient's position and his precarious equilibrium, we must help him to understand the part that he himself has played, and continues to play, in the construction of the delusional state. Only in this way can he be enabled gradually to become aware of the dangers emanating from the psychotic nucleus in its constant attempts to reproduce itself.

The delusion often has its origins in pathological introjections of, or identifications with, grandiose aspects of the patient's adult care-givers in his infancy. This is the case with Giorgio, who was totally identified with his father's grandiosity. The primal nucleus of a grandiose identity eventually becomes part of the patient's personality and is destined to proliferate in the adult pathology.

Maria's secret delusion

It is very difficult to avoid psychotic episodes in the course of therapy where the analysand conceals the gestating delusional situation from the analyst.

In the early months of her analysis, Maria, who developed a delusional sexualized transference on to me, brought a dream that I was not able to understand until much later, in the light of subsequent events. In it, she left a group of people of her own age and got into a lift. Having gone up to a higher level, she noticed that she was no longer able to operate the buttons to leave the lift car and was imprisoned inside it.

When I heard her communication, nothing was further from my mind than my subsequent realization that the dream might be portraying the ascent towards psychosis—the state of exaltation of going up to a high level—and the impossibility of emerging from it. For a long time, in fact, my persistent analytic hypothesis was that, in view of Maria's aggressive and painful type of transference attachment, she was suffering from depression.

Her history was characterized by an infancy and adolescence tormented by the presence of an aggressive mother who often hurled abuse at her and her younger brother. Although I felt that the infantile experience was indeed traumatic, none of my attempts to put Maria in touch with her infantile suffering had elicited any emotional response. Perhaps the patient's megalomanic self could not tolerate my trying to put her in contact with infantile events experienced as humiliating.

At length the patient developed a delusional relationship with me, which became obvious when she announced her intention to marry me. Her plan had been kept secret—for instance, she would mention that she had had dreams but refuse to reveal their content—until it finally assumed concrete form in the imperious guise of the delusion. Whenever I tried to analyse her protestations, Maria would insist on not seeing her amorous delusion as a problem and would attack my attempt to interpret her love and the conviction that she could marry me as a symptom. She eventually became exasperated and told me that she intended to break off the analysis and embark on a new therapy with another analyst.

After talking to a woman analyst, whom she felt was in a better position to defend her against the complications that had arisen with me, she brought a dream: she was a guest in this analyst's garden and the atmosphere was wonderful and timeless, but then the whole thing was interrupted by a security man who had the presumption to lock the gate to the villa and put an end to the party.

It seemed clear to me that *I* was the security man whom the patient hated owing to my decision to expel her from the enchanted garden. However, the delusion was making its presence felt in the transference relationship with the proposed new therapist, too, who was experienced as more accepting than myself and hence more apt to revive the ideal fusion that had previously given rise to the illusion that she could marry me.

The dream also revealed that the magic garden corresponded to a real experience of her infancy that she had never told me about. At that time, her maternal grandmother used to take her to a country house where they would spend months on end together—just the two of them, withdrawn from the world—and she had then not wanted to go back to school and see her friends again. I believe that the seduction of this grandmother, who carried her away into an ideal, timeless atmosphere, had laid the foundations of her stubborn attempt to establish the same special but delusional condition with me (and with the new analyst).

I must confess that Maria had already communicated her propensity to succumb to the amorous delusion through her dream of going up in the lift, which she then found herself unable to leave. She did not bring any associations to the dream, and I had not been capable of understanding it. For a long time it remained like a "hole" in the analysis, as had the early death of Maria's father in her infancy when she was just eight months old. This absence had been obliterated from her memory and awareness. It did not seem to cause her any conscious pain. The void left by the perception of loss had been filled by the illusory, delusional, and grandiose fusion with the object, as in the privileged and timeless experience with the grandmother.

Implications

These catamnestic reflections have convinced me that, if the psychotic state is to be genuinely improved, it is essential not to lose sight of the primal delusional nucleus. It must be examined in each session, both in its past manifestations and in its tenacious and deceitful action in the present. Unless we can discover how the patient "creates" the psychotic state, the hallucinations, and the delusion, even the best of therapies may be unable to avert a relapse. Post-critical understanding of the delusional episode can give rise to the creation of areas of self-awareness, thus avoiding the situation in which patients *recover* in the only way they know: that is, by blotting out the psychotic episode and carrying on as if it had never happened.

Complex as this therapeutic approach might appear, it is essential to adopt it, because otherwise the defensive structures erected by splitting and denial of the illness will sooner or later crumble and the acute psychotic episode will recur.

CHAPTER EIGHT

Intuitive and delusional thought*

> "Delusional production positions itself in a space that is neither the inner space of the psyche, nor external space, and not even intermediate or transitional space . . .. Does this mean that delusional people are the inventors of a fourth space? It must be agreed that delusion cannot be limited to its manifest or latent meanings. Delusion has a way of placing itself in its own space—that is, of secreting a space of its own"
>
> (Racamier, 2000, p. 823–824, translated)

Mackey: How could you . . . a mathematician, a man devoted to reason and logical proof . . . how could you believe that extraterrestrials are sending you messages? How could you believe that you are being recruited by aliens to save the world? How could you . . .?

* This chapter is an expanded and reworked version of a paper originally published in the *International Journal of Psychoanalysis* (De Masi, 2003).

Nash: Because . . . the ideas I had about supernatural beings came to me the same way that my mathematical ideas did. So I took them seriously. [Nasar, 1998, p. 11]

The above passage is quoted from a conversation between Professor George Mackey of Harvard University and John Nash, a Nobel prizewinner and eminent mathematician who became psychotic, and whose disconcerting life was reconstructed in the film *A Beautiful Mind*. Although cast in the sickly-sweet Hollywood mould, this film, which has a certain fascination of its own, can help us to understand how delusional imagination and intuitive imagination seem identical to a person who experiences delusion.

In Nash's case, the capacity for scientific intuition and for delusion coexisted during the psychotic episode, without excessive mutual interference. The mathematician could therefore be in touch with the Martians and at the same time undertake important scientific research, but was unable to grasp the difference between the two situations.

The area of darkness

The formation of the delusional system remains a research issue that has hitherto been resolved neither by psychiatry, which has after all studied it tenaciously, nor by psychoanalysis, which has perhaps approached it too cautiously. The same areas and functions of our mind that make up subjective psychic experience are probably involved in the progressive construction of delusion, which appears when the capacity to distinguish between delusional and intuitive imagination is lost.

My clinical experience suggests that, in order to understand the psychotic state, we need fresh knowledge of the aspects and functions of the mind that have so far escaped systematic psychoanalytic investigation owing to their characteristics. The lack of this knowledge stands in the way of the clinical psychoanalyst who wishes to analyse a delusional adult. The alterations taking place in the patient's perceptual and emotional apparatus make him increasingly unaware of the process in operation, so that he finds himself more and more at the mercy of the delusion.

I pointed out in Chapter Four that the psychotic state blinds the intuitive and perceptual functions of the unconscious: that is, the functions of emotional perception and intrapsychic communication that are performed other than on the level of conscious awareness. Freud was unable systematically to investigate alterations in the normal functions of the operations on the non-conscious level that underlie the recognition of emotions and the understanding of psychic reality, although he had a clear idea of their importance:

> ... psycho-analysis has shown us that everyone possesses in his unconscious mental activity an apparatus which enables him to interpret other people's reactions, that is, to undo the distortions which other people have imposed on the expression of their feelings. [Freud, 1912–1913, p. 159]

The need to identify areas of inquiry and to find the appropriate analytic response on the basis of a precise hypothesis concerning the nature of the patient's suffering and disorder is the common task of every analysis, but becomes particularly acute in psychotic patients owing to the specific character of their psychopathology.

These introductory remarks are necessary in order to explain how certain aspects of the psychotic state can be analysed and transformed during analytic treatment.

In this chapter I discuss a patient who came to analysis after just one psychotic episode, and whose psychotic symptoms would certainly have worsened without appropriate therapy. On the basis of the clinical material, I shall also comment on the significance of the psychotic transference during the analytic process, for it is not uncommon in therapy for a psychotic transference or a transference psychosis to develop, and while these must be adequately worked through, they also prove useful for throwing light on the patient's psychotic functioning.

The pleasure of intuition

The mental state of a psychoanalyst and an analysand at work closely resembles that of an intuitive scientist, for the work done in the analyst's consulting room involves the use of operations of conscious and unconscious thought to identify, by means of intuition, a link between a set of sense data, images, memories, or emotions that were previously unconnected and apparently meaningless. Since the process is primarily unconscious, the path and the chain of associations that gave birth to a thought can be reconstructed only *a posteriori*. In order to be born, intuition needs a long incubation time.

Freud must take the credit for the insight that the free flow of thought and evenly suspended attention are essential to the genesis of a new idea; thus, he anticipated present-day intuitions concerning unconscious cognitive processes. Freud's recommendation that the analyst should be like an opaque screen, and Bion's injunction to be without memory or desire, indicate that analytic interpretation comes from the unconscious only when one has rid the unconscious of all mnemic images and conscious wishes. The functions of the unconscious in thought processes have also been identified by researchers working in fields far removed from psychoanalysis, who never cite Freud or invoke the unconscious described by him.

In studying the path that leads to the intuitive solution of a scientific problem, these workers have emphasized the non-conscious matrices of thought. In his scientific autobiography, Einstein (1949) writes, "For me it is not dubious that our thinking goes on for the most part without the use of signs . . . and beyond that to a considerable degree *unconsciously*" (p. 9, my emphasis). Another author who investigated the unconscious pathways of scientific discovery was the mathematician Jacques Hadamard (1945), who states that the unconscious possesses the important property of being multiple and that various, probably numerous, things can occur simultaneously in it. This contrasts with conscious ego, which is unitary. Discovery, says Hadamard (following Poincaré), is not purely a matter of chance.

Although intuition seems to arrive unexpectedly and by chance, in fact it is preceded by an unconscious process. An invention or discovery comes about through a combination of ideas: the number of such combinations is huge and only very few of them are useful; the majority are not. These combinations occur more readily in a state of evenly suspended attention. As Souriau (quoted by Hadamard, 1945, p. 48) states, "In order to invent, one must think aside."[1] This is, of course, reminiscent of Freud's *evenly suspended attention* and Bion's recommendation of being *without memory or desire*, as mentioned above. Creation, after all, consists precisely in not making useless combinations and in examining only the useful ones: invention involves discrimination and choice.

Poincaré (1908) writes that the unconscious ego is not purely automatic, but is also capable of discerning; it has tact and subtlety. It knows how to choose, and is better at guessing than the conscious ego because it succeeds where the latter fails.

A sense of pleasure in intuition arises when the magmatic field of phenomena and perceptions comes to be organized around a figure that emerges from a ground, a figure that arranges all the elements present within a higher, meaningful order. This is the moment of *illumination*, a triumph great or small that accompanies scientific discovery and, to a greater or lesser degree, always exalts the birth of ideas. The conclusion must be, therefore, that excessive dispersal of attention—i.e., consciousness—makes it impossible to think, while, on the other hand, forcing attention too much in one direction is equally damaging to intuition.

Intuition, the insight that leads to new discoveries, enlightens us and confers order and meaning on data that previously lacked these. Psychoanalytic interpretations and the understanding that comes in analysis are lucky events of this kind that happen in the specific field of psychoanalysis: that is, that of the emotions. Yet, the moment of insight is temporary, because immediately afterwards the horizon widens and there is something else to be intuited or a new problem to solve. Consequently, man can experience knowledge not as an aim achieved once and for all, but instead as an open horizon that allows oscillation in creative doubt.

The delusional imagination

The aspect I shall now address concerns the system that is altered in psychosis. This is the system that allows intuitive thought to develop in a dynamically selective manner and to perform its function of internal communication. Many observations have shown that severe disorders affect the intuitive and perceptual functions of the self and of emotional awareness that underlie psychic life. In the view of Fonagy and Target (1996), in patients with serious

personality disorders a particular aspect of the normal development of the mental processes—the reflective function—is inhibited,
so that they fail to respond flexibly and appropriately to the sym-
bolism and meaning of other people's behaviour; they also lack the
capacity for self-representation and awareness of their own
emotions.

Modern conceptions of infant development (e.g., Emde, Stern,
and workers in the field of infant research, as well the theories of
Fonagy and Target on the reflective function) increasingly emphasize the emotional competence of children, which may be either
confirmed or distorted by the maternal response. Certain forms of
environmental and other interference may undermine the intuitive
and emotional functions in early life, thus making for vulnerability
to illness in adulthood.

I have previously expressed my opinion that the psychotic state
blinds the "unaware" emotional and intuitive functions, so that the
patient totally lacks the capacity for self-observation and awareness
of his mental and emotional processes. Here, I distinguish between
consciousness and awareness, two concepts that are often deemed
equivalent. *Consciousness* is the capacity to register, memorize, and
remember a psychic event, while *awareness* has to do with the
meaning and understanding of that event and is linked to the presence or otherwise of the intuitive function and the capacity for
self-observation. The state of unawareness resulting from the
impossibility of practical utilization of the unconscious intuitive
function is extremely pronounced in the psychotic process. Conditions antithetical to the analytic method itself arise in the psychotic
state, because this method is based on the possibility of new acqui-
sitions on the level of awareness through associative work originating from the unconscious intuitive processes.

Difficulty arises with the use of the interpretative method in the
therapy of psychosis, owing to the lack of associative connections.
This is clearly expressed by García Badaracco, who writes,

> With regard to analytic interpretation, there is also the problem of
> interpreting hallucinatory manifestations and delusional contents.
> Here, however, unlike the situation with dreams, where the
> dreamer's associations reveal links between the manifest dream
> and its latent content, such links are apparently absent in the case
> of psychotic productions. [1983, p. 700, translated]

Giovanni's delusion

The system that is altered in psychosis is the one that normally permits dynamically selective learning from intuitive experience: the psychotic consequently denies dependence on reality, in the sense of the constant doubting exploration of our intuitions. Bion showed that psychotics suffer from a disturbance of the curiosity, which, if activated, might render the therapeutic process possible. He writes,

> Another feature obtrudes if the course of the analysis is favourable; problems which in sophisticated language are posed by the question "Why?" cannot be formulated. The patient appears to have no appreciation of causation and will complain of painful states of mind while persisting in courses of action calculated to produce them. [Bion, 1967, p. 108]

To demonstrate how the failure of intuitive thinking impedes the normal course of analytic work, I shall describe and comment on part of the analysis of Giovanni, a patient who functions psychotically. (Giovanni is the patient described previously in Chapter Four. Here, the case history is continued and later stages of his analysis are presented.) In this material, I shall concentrate on the analysis of the delusional construction.

Giovanni, aged twenty-six, has had a psychotic episode of a delusional nature while abroad. His symptoms have been partially silenced by antipsychotic medication. The persecutory delusion, which followed a period of megalomanic expansion, was triggered by a quarrel with a foreign colleague seen as the leader of a group of conspirators who had made attempts on his life. I meet Giovanni after a period of hospitalization and consultations with his psychiatrist. In our initial interviews, Giovanni tells me that he feels reassured by his return home and thinks he can recover the "affects" from which he has detached himself.

The first months of the relationship with this patient, whom I see once a week, help me to form a clearer picture of the psychotic episode and to assess whether the wish to embark on an analytic journey can mature in him. Eventually, the number of sessions is increased to two a week, and after a while he agrees to lie down on the couch. Later, despite his difficulty in admitting that he needs help, we have three and then four sessions.

However, I experience considerable emotional frigidity in the analytic relationship: I feel that I am seen as a potential intruder to be kept at a distance. I also notice that, by his impersonal style of speaking, the patient is slowly reproducing the suspicious, "interpreting" kind of atmosphere that may well plunge him back into delusion.

Although he is showing a partial improvement and has resumed work as a part-time consultant (he leaves home and meets people), he is functioning as though suspended between two contiguous psychic realities, one of which can suddenly usurp the other. He is also afraid of being poisoned in the bar where he takes his breaks; he sees the casual glance of a passer-by or a trivial nosebleed as a threatening signal and proof of the conspiracy against him. When a girl who attends the same gym as himself accidentally hurts herself and the instructor tells her to apply disinfectant to the wound, Giovanni interprets this as confirming the presence of toxic substances in the environment, used by the enemy to harm him.

Notwithstanding his relative improvement and the absence of overt psychosis, the patient feels threatened and forced to live an absolutely clandestine existence: whenever the veil of total anonymity is lifted, he suffers violent persecutory anxiety. At times he tells me that his persecutors constantly deploy diabolical instruments and sophisticated devices (microphones or television cameras) that monitor him and everything he says, so as to mark him out to his assigned killer.

I feel that the analytic consulting room, too, is being secretly scrutinized for the presence of microphones or bugs. I realize that the delusional atmosphere of the psychotic episode has been re-established, re-created by the power of the imagination.

The following sequence shows how the delusion is generated and exercises its power of attraction. While attending a meeting of an organization for the defence of Third World rights, the patient joins in the ovation that greets a speech by a vehement opponent of powerful international monopolies. He immediately senses an atmosphere of danger, which takes the concrete form of the perception that the owner of the restaurant where he has gone for a meal break with his companions in the interval wants to poison him: he sees strange actions being carried out while his food is being prepared. The patient thinks he is being singled out for homicide because he joined in the applause after the speech, thereby revealing his emotions and putting himself at the mercy of persecutors who now want to poison him. He is convinced that when he lets himself be "emotional" he exposes himself to terrifying retaliation.

In the session, I suggest that the vehement orator may also represent a part of himself that adopts an aggressive and polemical attitude towards the powerful organizations to which he is ideologically opposed. I point out that his "emotionality" is a mental state of rage and destructive violence against characters perceived as tyrannical. On this occasion we are able to make some connections with previous psychotic episodes of which the patient had not informed me: the one that occurred in the foreign country was not, in fact, the first. Before going abroad, while on holiday in southern Italy, he had also felt persecuted by the local Mafia, who he thought were going to kidnap or kill him. At that time, by self-idealization, he had begun to think that he could defeat the Mafia, seen as the incarnation of absolute evil, hence the persecution. During the psychotic crisis, he had imagined himself becoming the leader of a global organization that could eliminate injustice throughout the world, but then gradually came to identify with a greedy, power-hungry character.

The improvement has obviously plunged him back into the aggressive situation from which his delusion stemmed: he is evidently pervaded by a power-related conflict (embodied in the Mafia and the clan of foreigners) that causes him to imagine evil, destructive, and persecutory figures. He cannot distinguish his wish to assert himself from aggressive competition with a powerful character whose place he secretly wants to take. The problem for the analysis is how to help the patient to extricate himself from this melting-pot of explosive passions without giving up his essential life aggression. (A psychotic patient's state of persecution usually arises out of conflict with someone perceived as powerful and threatening, against whom he in turn reacts with defiant violence. This conflict gives rise to the ongoing perception of threats and conspiracies created by the patient's delusional imagination. In Giovanni's case, this delusional constellation, centred as it was on a conflict with an omnipotent figure, originates from the early infantile conflict with his father, who, on the one hand, encouraged him to be "extraordinary", while, on the other, humiliating him whenever he tried to compete with him. However, the patient is totally unaware of this conflict: in fact, he wants to be like this bullying father who is always the "winner". Instead of conflict, he has developed a pathological identification with the father that prevents him from acquiring a separate identity.)

The psychotic transference

I have already mentioned the unusual sense of alienation conveyed to me for a long time by this patient. From the beginning I notice that, in spite of the easy flow of verbal communication between us, he tries to avoid involvement in the relationship, and at times his presence in the consulting room is only physical. Throughout this time, however, the analytic space appears to remain neutral and sufficiently protected from persecution.

Yet, this "neutrality" is always precarious. For instance, if the patient mentions his doubts about moving out of his parents' flat, as his mother has suggested, I sense that whatever position I adopt might be subjected to special scrutiny. If I express doubts about whether he should leave the house immediately (after all, there he is more protected from persecution), he may see this as a confession of anxiety on my part, thereby confirming that he does indeed have enemies who wish to eliminate him. If I am aware of the danger, I may well be in cahoots with them. His mother's position, urging him to move away, is more reassuring to him.

One day I pass the patient as he sits in a bar near my consulting room, but fail to see him and therefore do not greet him. In the next session, making a great effort and overcoming considerable anxiety, he confesses that he saw me. I seemed to be running, no doubt towards a nearby little restaurant run by someone of the same nationality as his rival, which is the hideout of the persecutors who want him dead.

Such a communication is immediately of great concern to me. With hopes wavering that the analytic setting can remain free of persecution, I begin to fear that I, too, am included in the delusion and might lose my analytic function. However, I have to realize that my hopes do not coincide with the nature of the therapeutic process, which simply takes its course. Although worried, I feel that the psychotic transference will enable me to probe further into the secret scheming that has engulfed and transformed not only the figure of the analyst, but also the patient's psychic reality.

So I ask him how he can possibly imagine that I, as the person who cares for him, could ever think of betraying him by joining forces with whoever is persecuting him. He says that he knows nothing about me, that I am a stranger, and that I might betray him. For example, he adds, I might be frightened by his omnipotent persecutors or be attracted by the vast sums of money they could offer me. I now see that the patient regards me as someone so likely to succumb to terror or so fascinated by money as to obliterate any affective bond I might have with him. Giovanni explains that he does not trust anyone outside his family circle.

I wondered afterwards why I had not interpreted to the patient in that session that I had been transformed into a persecutor on account of his projections. I had obviously sensed that he was unable to understand or accept such an interpretation—a description of his projective identification—owing to the concrete nature of his thought. For this reason, I had in turn responded with a question that might help him to go back over and reflect on this psychotic transformation.

In subsequent sessions he repeats that he does not know me or anything about me: anyone except his parents could be bought by enemy power or brainwashed into destroying him. He admits to having been reticent precisely because he knows nothing about me and therefore does not trust me. The admission of his distrust helps me to gain a better impression of the significance of the emotional distance and the sense of alienation between us that I have had from the start. I can now also understand his difficulty in asking me questions or trying to find out about me, as well as his apparent lack of curiosity concerning myself.

The next few sessions enable us to start working through this situation. The patient begins to conceive that, if he was courageous enough to seek information about me, he might be able to think of me as a human being and thereby rid himself of the image suggested to him by an inner voice, of me as an affectless puppet that is utterly pliable in the hands of his enemies. This might help him to build up a good relationship with me that could serve as a stable experience in his internal world. (It is, in my view, very important to note that psychotic or other severely disturbed patients have great difficulty in wanting to learn about the person of the analyst. In such patients, curiosity is inhibited because it is felt to involve intense guilt or to constitute an invasive intrusion. As for Giovanni, he seems not to have wondered at all about the person of his analyst up to this point.)

I realize that the construction of the psychotic transference contains, in a nutshell, the same mechanism that structures the delusional system. When Giovanni experiences me as being under the sway of his powerful enemies, he is manifestly projecting past attitudes or anxieties of his own on to me: for instance, his being overwhelmed by power and wealth, or his submission to powerful individuals.

However, I am struck by his lack of empathy and his inability to understand the feelings of others, including mine in the analytic relationship. In this way, it does indeed seem as though he can obliterate the presence of any human relationship and feeling in the outside world, and make objects negative and dangerous.

Terror and imagination

Thomas Freeman (2001) notes that even when a patient has emerged from a psychotic episode, the "crisis" persists as a powerful destabilizing element. Terrified of having to relive it and of becoming psychotic again, the patient is frightened even to remember the circumstances, let alone the development, of the psychotic attack. However, this is not always the case. As will be explained in Chapter Fourteen, psychosis leaves behind such a pleasant memory of freedom and omnipotence that it is feared on account of its irresistible fascination. In both cases, the psychotic episode is like an uncleared minefield that any attempt at remediation might reactivate. Freeman considers that this fear is hard to overcome owing to the regressive potential of analytic treatment, which in itself tends to destabilize psychic structures. While agreeing with Freeman about the terror induced in patients by the possibility of a return of the psychotic episode, I do not regard the hypothesis of analytic regression as helpful for explaining their difficulty in working through the "crisis". In my opinion, there are many reasons for this, and some of them have nothing to do with the fact of being in analysis. In analytic work with someone who has had a psychotic breakdown, one comes into contact with the profound devastation it has wrought on their psyche. Even when overcome, the psychotic episode, with all its vicissitudes, remains as a terrible trauma experienced alone by its victim, destined *not to be forgotten* because it is unthinkable.

The patient's state of mind in relation to the past psychotic attack is dominated, even years later, by terror in case the delusional reality returns. Even chance words spoken in the analytic dialogue that trigger associations to the traumatic event arouse the patient's terror, owing to the sudden invasive feeling of not remembering the event but of reliving it in the present and, hence, of still being trapped in psychosis.

In this situation, any association to the trauma is immediately blotted out because it is connected with catastrophic anxiety and is therefore likely to reconstruct the delusion. That is why the analyst finds it extremely difficult to succeed in examining the past psychotic episode with the patient. Psychoanalytic studies of trauma indicate that memories and feelings connected with traumatic experiences are radically separated (dissociated) from the rest of the psyche because they are intolerable. However, by inhibiting perception of the event, the dissociative defence impedes the process of working through the trauma and perpetuates it.

Recent neuroscientific discoveries have shown that panic remains enclosed in the primitive circuit of fear, which involves the amygdala, instead of entering into the rational circuit that includes the cortex. Joseph LeDoux (1996) writes that unconscious memories of fear established by the amygdala seem to be branded on the brain. This might be one reason why traumatic experiences, including delusional ones, are so difficult to work through.

Traumatic terror

Delusion, therefore, persists as an indelibly fixed trauma that tends to be impossible to work through and can never be *forgotten*; a

smouldering fire that can flare up at any time if fanned by an association, a memory, or an allusion. The psychotic breakdown is not
"forgotten"; it does not become a memory, but remains looming
over the sufferer, and consequently cannot be understood or
worked through. In order to be understood and become the subject
of thought, an event must be forgotten; it must become *past* and be
accommodated in memory, where it can become thinkable because
it belongs to us but is not confused with us. In other words, it must
be seen, because it is situated in memory, as separate from the
perceiving ego.

My impression is that the psychotic experience escapes this
transformation and cannot be accommodated in memory like other
types of experience owing to its specific traumatic quality, which
prevents it from being placed at a distance and forgotten. According
to Bion (1962a, 1967), the unconscious is a metabolizer of psychic
experiences, so that if it malfunctions the mind cannot produce
thoughts. The unconscious furnishes the stock of symbols and
images that transform sensory experience into thought. Owing to
the excessive anxiety they involve, traumatic and psychotic experiences cannot enter the unconscious for transformation and can
therefore be neither repressed nor "forgotten". Even when the crisis
has been overcome, the psychotic nucleus, unworked through and
untransformed, remains *encysted* in the psyche in such a way as to
give rise to instability and the possibility of a return. This is perhaps
one reason why even a spontaneous improvement in the psychotic
state occurs in the form of a *recovery by default*, with limited integration of the personality.

The ghost in the closet

A useful case history is presented by Werbart & Levander (2005) in
their report on a programmed interview research project that seeks
to make explicit the therapist's and the patient's implicit theories
about the origins of the first psychotic episode.

Andrea, a twenty-nine-year-old Swede, made the acquaintance
of his therapist on discharge from a brief period in hospital, where
he had received drug treatment. The outbreak of the psychotic
episode occurred after a heated argument with his boss in a hotel

where he was staying for work reasons in Stockholm. He claimed to be convinced that, after the quarrel, he had been given an aperitif "poisoned with cocaine" at the bar. In the ensuing days he had felt persecuted by foreign secret agents.

Andrea said that it had all begun a few months before in Copenhagen, when his company had been sold to a competitor. At the same time he had discovered that his Danish girlfriend had been unfaithful to him with an older man who was working as a secret agent. In an interview conducted after about one year of therapy, Andrea said that the incident with the girlfriend was very important to him, but that he proposed to go on dealing with it using the "closet theory". Having discovered the girl's unfaithfulness, he said he had put everything out of his mind and "shut the ghost in the closet". The psychotic breakdown had occurred when he had, for incidental reasons, been unable to keep applying the weight of his body to the door: the ghost had escaped and captured him.

The therapy had ended after a further six months. Andrea told the interviewer that he was better, that he had no major problems except that he was unable to travel to southern Sweden, and that he considered the girlfriend incident to be over and done with.

At the same time, the therapist, too, thought that Andrea had no choice but to keep the ghost shut in the closet; he only hoped that in the future the patient would be in a better position to tackle the problem by himself, even if in his opinion other family issues had come up which it would have been useful to explore.

The theory implicitly espoused by both Andrea and his therapist had been that some of the patient's functions could be restored and the psychotic episode encapsulated. This strategy had permitted a symptomatic improvement, but had also left behind a sequela of terrifying experiences that remained incomprehensible.

The breakdown had been triggered by the girlfriend's unfaithfulness, and Andrea had felt persecuted by secret agents (imagining that this was his rival's occupation). Ironically, the Stockholm hotel where the patient had quarrelled with his boss was called the Broken Hearts Hotel.

The delusional construction had developed in a number of successive, linked phases: first, pain at the girlfriend's unfaithfulness; then hatred of his rival; and finally the persecutory state after a seemingly trivial incident. After the end of his therapy, Andrea confessed that he found it heart-breaking to set eyes on the strait that separated Sweden from Denmark.

It can be postulated that the memory of the Danish girl's unfaithfulness and the consequent delusion had remained unmodified, projected into certain places, and could overwhelm him again at any time. This thesis is borne out, for instance, by Andrea's inability to travel to Sweden's southern regions, the ones nearest to Denmark. The therapy had come to an end when Andrea and his therapist had convinced themselves that it was not a good plan to explore the "ghost in the closet" in case it leapt out again.

Working on the delusion

I do not accept the idea of "keeping the ghost shut in the closet", but consider that, to release the patient from the terrifying power of the psychotic nucleus, it must be confronted, albeit with due patience and sensitivity.

Since the danger area is specific to each patient, I suggest that we should carefully explore the nucleus around which the delusional ideation and traumatic anxiety are organized. My chosen approach with Giovanni was to share his perceptions of terror and connect them with past and present events so that the psychotic episode could become susceptible to reconstruction, reflection, and possible insight. For example, to defend against the panic anxiety emanating from the psychotic nucleus, Giovanni has to believe that he controls the whole of reality. Consequently, any unexpected event becomes an occasion for persecution. I believe that when he unexpectedly saw me outside the analytic setting, this triggered his anxiety because it abolished the spatial separation between the persecutory thought and the uncontaminated analytic figure.

After two years of analysis, my impression is that the analytic work done on the factors that led—and still lead—him towards persecutory terror has weakened the power of the psychotic nucleus to some extent. The badlands of the past now seem to have been at least relatively reclaimed, and it is possible to talk about them together with a view to eventually understanding them. In my opinion, his present anxiety has aspects that more closely

resemble panic or hypochondriacal ideation than a genuine delusional structure. (Phobias and panic attacks, too, are unleashed in
the imagination by persecutory objects. Whereas in a panic attack
the anxiety relates to the body [the fear of death], in the psychotic
experience it is transformed into terror at the possibility of being
killed by persecutors. Segal [1954] draws attention to similarities
between the two conditions.)

Here is an example. Giovanni has recently had to attend a
refresher course in order to find a job. This time, while no longer
denying the impact that every new experience has on him, he says
he is afraid that, when he meets people he does not know, his
psychosis will return in the same form as in the past. (During our
first summer break, the patient had totally denied his anxiety and
gone to a holiday club on a Mediterranean island, where the delusion had returned.) To avoid over-invasive anxieties, he imagines
keeping away from potentially *phobic* places such as the canteen,
and bringing his own food from home so as not to be persecuted by
the idea of being poisoned. As he explores this hypothesis, it occurs
to him that his precautions might be guessed at by possible persecutors, who might then think up further ways for poisoning him.
At one point he says that I, as his analyst, could unmask him to the
supposed enemies, thus rendering all his protection useless.

While showing him that his imagination is constantly developing catastrophic thoughts that expose him to panic, I also concentrate on the *psychotic contamination* of the transference. "Why," I ask
him, "should I, your analyst, be in the service of the persecutors?"
"Because anything is possible," he answers.

I reply that, even though I realize that this statement will collide
with his omnipotent thinking, some things are possible, some
improbable, and some impossible. Only in the world of his imagination is anything possible: there he can flout any rule and then be
absolutely free to think whatever he likes.

The patient answers, "When I came in I looked at you and asked
myself if you were good or an emissary of my persecutors. Now I
am really sorry I thought that." The patient's idea that "anything
is possible" foreshadows the mental chaos in which anything
is indeed possible: in the imagination that leads to psychosis,
there are multiple realities that never contradict each other. Every
new hypothesis is superimposed on its predecessor in a constantly

shifting perceptual constellation. (The falsification principle and the *a priori*s of time and space are absent from psychotic thought. For the patient, I can be not only his analyst, but also someone who sells him for money. The persecutors are abroad, in Italy, everywhere. As Popper might put it, psychotic thinking is not falsifiable.)

The patient's persecutor, too, can do what he likes, not only because he is persecuting him and wants to kill him (there is no limit, and no representative of the judicial system), but also because he has every possible facility, all the equipment needed, and an enormously powerful apparatus. The "anything is possible" type of thought reflects the exaltation of the prior delusional period. But now the perspective is reversed: whereas before everything that made for exaltation came to pass, now everything Giovanni fears actually happens.

The brief but significant analytic sequence described above sheds light on the development of the delusional experience that leads to the creation of the psychotic transference, which can be used as the starting point for together understanding how the patient constructs the delusion, whereby I am turned into the persecutor. In this patient, the state of delusional terror is equivalent to the creation of a dehumanized world in which dangerous feelings such as revenge, greed, and the wish to kill are perceived as real and omnipresent, while affective relations between people are totally absent, or, rather, obliterated. The persecutory development and the omnipotence with which the persecutors relentlessly harass Giovanni are credible for him because he himself has experienced as genuine and real the wish to dominate the world, in so doing destroying any perception of bonds of solidarity and friendship in himself. In the above sequence, he emerges from the delusion during the course of the session once he regains the perception of the human relationship between himself and me.

Dream-as-thought and dream-as-delusion

I am going to try to describe the impressions of a long illness which took place quite entirely within the mysteries of my soul: I don't know why I use the word "illness", for as far as my physical self was concerned, I never felt better. Sometimes I thought my strength

and energy were doubled. I seemed to know everything, understand everything. My imagination gave me infinite delights. In
recovering what men call reason, do I have to regret the loss of
these joys? [de Nerval, 1996, p. 4]

Here began what I shall call the overflowing of the dream into real
life. From that moment on, everything took on at times a double
aspect—and did so, too, without my powers of reasoning ever
losing their logic or my memory blurring the least details of what
happened to me. Only my actions were apparently insensate,
subject to what is called illusion, according to human reason . . .
[*ibid.*, p. 8]

With these words from "Aurélia", one of his most evocative works
and a faithful account of his psychotic crisis, Gérard de Nerval foreshadows and describes the onset and progressive establishment of
the dream-as-delusion that was to thrust him under the fascinating
dominion of madness. This quotation, in my view, tellingly
describes two aspects of the psychotic experience: the absence of
awareness and the fascination of the psychotic world. These two
points draw our attention to important questions about the quality
of the psychotic "dream" and the nature of delusional intuition, on
which I should like to reflect further.

One of Bion's original contributions was the idea that thought
originates from precursors and that, among these, the dream work
generated in the unconscious is intimately linked to waking
thought. According to Bion (1992), it is the *dream-work-alpha* (as
distinct from Freud's dream work) that elaborates psychic reality
and confers meaning on experience by means of an unconscious
process that is always active in the waking state. This ongoing
activity, which is subliminal and of which we are unaware, shows
us what is happening inside ourselves, enabling us to perceive the
continuity of our existence and personal identity, and to have a
perspective on the future. Waking thought and dream thought are
therefore closely connected and operate in co-ordination with each
other.

To be usable for the production of a dream, the perceptions of
an emotional experience must be transformed by the α-function
and acquire oneiric characteristics. Unlike the situation in the psychotic state, a non-psychotic subject *turns perceptual reality into a*

dream and thereby establishes its basis as subjective experience. In this sense, the capacity to "dream" becomes the prerequisite for the development of the specific imaginative function that permits the perception of one's own and others' emotions. This is the function that Bion calls "reverie": that is, the spontaneous capacity to use intuitive imagination to understand the emotions. The capacity for understanding ourselves and our links to objects stems from the continuity and mutual permeability of waking and dream thought. However, the way in which we know ourselves and become aware of psychic reality escapes even our own perception.

Here, I should like to mention the contribution of another particularly intuitive psychoanalyst, Christopher Bollas (1987, 1992). His concept of the "unthought known" denotes the existence of a type of thought of which we are unaware, which escapes representation and operates inside our very being. Bollas says that it is essential to acknowledge the part of the psyche that lives in a world without words. Put differently, we are unable to recognize certain mental areas and functions that contribute to the formation of subjective experience. These are the areas of both realistic and delusional intuition. A mysterious watershed separates the two attitudes: *dreaming for the purpose of intuiting* and *dreaming for the purpose of delusion*.

As to the use of visual images in dreams, Chianese writes,

> What distinguishes dreams from other formations of the unconscious is the visual element, but one with a singular constitution. What is seen in dreams cannot be confused with what is seen in the waking state. The visual element in a dream is both near and far, intense and elusive, within reach yet untouchable. The image is never a simple copy or reproduction of reality; it joins and combines figures far apart in time and space. The visible in a dream is close to the invisible that the work of a painter renders "visible". [2000, p. 326, translated]

A *dream-as-thought* (dreaming for the purpose of intuition) is a symbolic transcription of an emotional experience, and the dream images indicate the presence of thoughts in a language that seeks to integrate the dreamer's emotional history, defences, or unconscious fantasies.

In a *dream-as-delusion*, the visual element does not hark back to the invisible rendered visible by the painter, or to that which can be made comprehensible and discoverable by the intuitive function of the analyst and the analysand. Instead, as in the case of hallucination, the visual "kills" intuitive imagination and visual perception replaces representation. The psychotic state foreshadowed in the dream confers a concretely hallucinatory character on that dream, takes away space for intuition (insight), and interferes with the function of the dream-as-thought.

In analysing a psychotic patient, we must be careful to distinguish *dream-as-thought*, the expression of the normal function of dreams, from *dream-as-delusion*, which alerts us to how the patient's perceptual experience is being transformed, with the eventual result of manifest clinical psychosis. Bion would say that a psychotic cannot tell us about the difference between sleep and the waking state, between dream and non-dream, and that we, in turn, cannot distinguish between the patient's dreaming and his sleeping (James Grotstein, personal communication).

The hallucinatory fantasy

To demonstrate how an ongoing process of imaginative production resembling that of a dream takes place during the course of the psychotic process, I shall now present a fragment from the supervision of a young male analysand. He says:

"A thought came to me yesterday evening when I was half awake, a fantasy perhaps, but I don't know how far it really qualifies as a fantasy . . . I remember that after beginning analysis with you I came here one day when you were maybe not working but just seeing various people. You arrived shortly afterwards and were surprised to find the door open: you wondered if you had left it open by mistake or if someone had come in. I thought it might have been some youths looking for documents: you asked me to go and have a look and . . . I thought perhaps there was a room right at the back in a terrible mess but I didn't even notice . . . I thought I might have seen two boys running away as I came in, but I hadn't paid any attention and wouldn't have been able to recognize them . . . I felt inadequate, as though you had asked me for help and I had not been up to it . . ."

The patient has been in analysis for two years at four sessions a week on account of a prior delusional episode. I shall disregard the significance of the patient's delusional fantasy, the emergence of the figure of an analyst–parent as a mother incapable of defending herself and who demands a heroic performance from him, and his world replete with bad people, juvenile delinquents from infancy who have now grown into terrible criminals; all of these are important components of the delusional construction and are covered by the analyst's interpretation. Let us instead listen to the patient's comment following the intervention of the analyst, who can only remember having allowed him to come on an unofficial holiday and thinks that the entire sequence of events is a construction of the patient:

> "I realize that previously I had real things right under my nose that I did not see, while other things that I invented seemed real . . . Now I am less obsessed with the idea of having caused things that never happened; I am fairly sure that these were fantasies of mine, but I still keep creating more of them . . ."

In other words, the patient is beginning to realize that his imagination is ceaselessly at work falsifying the memory of events, and that this is beyond his conscious control.

Deconstructing the delusion

While resembling a sensory production analogous to a dream, a *dream-as-delusion* remains fixed in waking memory, and in the waking state continues to confer life on its characters, who impose their presence on the "dreamer". Hallucinations and delusions have a paradoxical element that is lacking in dreams: whereas dreams are mysterious because their meaning remains to be discovered, delusions are uncanny because their meaning is manifest. They are "dreams" that never end, unlike genuine dreams, which disappear when their communicative function is over. Delusion constantly seeks confirmation so as fully to maintain its assertive force.

If, for example, I try to show my patient Giovanni that his persecution might have originated from megalomania, and postulate that he may have found it unacceptable to be of no consequence to his foreign colleague—who destroyed his megalomanic sense of existence by stealing his girlfriend—and that, to defend against this humiliating perception, he fantasized an epic struggle with his rival, he says that he understands this hypothesis, which goes in one ear, and finds it useful. However, as soon as his session is over, it flies straight out of the other ear.

In other words, the delusional memory cannot be worked through until the patient can remove himself from the powerful image factory of his grandiose self and his true personal identity has fully developed. In the therapy of these patients, it is important to grasp the attractive force and the power of the delusional imagination, by identifying its underlying anxieties or omnipotent wishes, with a view to *deconstructing* it. I use the term *deconstruct* because the word "interpretation", which we use to denote our therapeutic instrument, seems unsuitable for tackling the clinical problems posed by the power of the delusional imagination.

My point is that analysand and analyst must be able to examine and to recognize gradually and in detail how the delusional experience is constructed and develops, by carefully perusing the present emotional situation and the remote roots of the delusion, and linking up the various scattered fragments that have appeared and continue to emerge during the analysis. This work must be done constantly, session by session, over a prolonged period.

Similarly, García Badaracco writes,

> Clinical experience has led us to believe that the intermediate links are in effect lacking, as if the process of therapeutic working through were in fact one of dismantling the psychotic productions so that the components can subsequently be recomposed in a different form by means of the therapeutic process itself. [1983, p. 700, translated]

In Giovanni's case, I gradually realized the importance of returning to the first delusional episode, which had characterized the patient's descent into the psychotic state, and of holding fast to this reference point for the possible working through of the delusion. It is only by containing the energy of the delusional fantasy and constantly seeking the present and past reasons for it that mental spaces useful for the development of thought and personal identity can be freed up.

A particular aspect of the process of analytic working through with this patient was the reconstruction of his infancy. After all, it was then that the seeds were sown of the idealization of the father and the confusion with his grandiose figure as one of the pathways leading to the delusion. Just as his father imposed his supremacy over his mother or the patient himself, so Giovanni constantly demanded acts of submission from his younger sister. He was fascinated by games of skill and was fanatical about records; he often sought confirmation from his mother that he was exceptional, and remembered her as watching him with ecstatic admiration.

For him, the game of being like his father was not a "game" but reality: he *was* his father, a pathological and confusing identification with a grandiose figure. In adolescence, he was so entrapped in fantasies in which he performed heroic deeds that his playmates had to prompt him to re-emerge from his exciting withdrawal. The "deconstruction", or dismantling of the force of the delusion, is accompanied by the acquisition of the functions of awareness that gradually allow the patient to "see". The maintenance of this capacity over time guarantees that if the delusional experience recurs, it can be recognized and made potentially transformable, thus preventing its automatic conquest of the mind. Similar considerations, albeit less dynamically complex, apply to the construction of a perverse system, panic attacks, or hypochondriacal experiences (De Masi, 2004).

As an example of this hoped-for progression, let us consider the analytic experience of Giovanni at the time when we were trying to gain a better understanding of the dynamics of the transition from the grandiose state to the persecutory delusion. On this occasion, the patient senses that, when his foreign colleague failed to give way and continued with his seduction of the girlfriend, he had attributed his own omnipotent mental state to him. The colleague had become his persecutor because he wanted to take revenge for the offence he had suffered when the patient tried to bar his way to omnipotent power. The ensuing conflict had been catastrophic because it had prevented the patient's grandiose self, which also contained his potential self, from continuing to live. The grandiose self, in projection, was now perceived as ultra-powerful and capable of doing whatever it liked to him.

In reality, the patient had used the competitive aspects of his colleague to see him as a suitable object for the projection of his own omnipotent, greedy parts, which were replete with wishes for domination and narcissistic triumph. In this way, the mad part of the patient, accommodated in his colleague, had begun to live an independent life—albeit one that was indissolubly bound to him as the effect of an omnipotent projective identification (cf. Klein, 1946).

My reason for presenting this sequence is that it is in my view one of the moments that may lead to the "deconstruction" of the delusional experience. Through this process, the delusion ceases to be a concrete mental state imprisoning the patient and becomes a psychic fact in which the delusional experience is "digested" and transformed. Analytic work of this kind has been possible only by virtue of the gradual re-establishment in the patient of the capacity for intuitive thought, which was for all practical purposes absent at the beginning of the analysis. (When working with psychotic patients, the analyst must be alert to moments when the intuitive imagination—i.e., the capacity to understand their own mental processes—begins to manifest itself through dreams or particular associations.)

The assertive energy of delusions

In my commentary on Giovanni's therapy I have attempted to demonstrate the difficulties encountered in an analysis when intuitive thought gives way to the development of its delusional counterpart. I have also drawn attention to the need to relive the psychotic episode—which may readily return during the analysis too—with the patient, so that it can be worked through progressively as intuitive thought becomes more possible. Owing to traumatic anxiety, which tends to keep the psychotic episode split off from the patient's awareness and may well generate further psychotic crises, this is anything but an easy undertaking.

The *assertive energy* (Searles, 1979) that sustains this patient's psychosis seems to involve the development of an ideational system in which grandiose imagination takes the place of the normal capacity to evaluate his own and other people's mental processes. From this point of view, the grandiose route taken by Giovanni can be seen as a defence against annihilation anxiety ("being nothing"), an illusory defence that wreaks yet more destruction on the possibility of the recovery of personal identity.

If it is a condition of a psychotic's existence that he has to transform his identity by altering his perceptual functions, he must at the same time shut down the system of emotional truth that permits mental growth and the understanding of emotional reality. For this reason, he is destined ultimately to plunge into chaos. In the psychotic system, the solitary imagination, which is like a film projected on to the mind with characters living lives of their own, takes on an essential, ongoing role. This cinematic production blocks the channels of the intuitive imagination necessary for the perception of psychic reality.

The complex nature of imagination

Whereas the theoretical references deployed by psychoanalytic thought for understanding delusional constructions—e.g., projective identification, omnipotent unconscious fantasy, or hallucinatory wish fulfilment—are still applicable to the psychotic state, they cannot, it seems, adequately account for a complex process of transformation as unstoppable and constantly shifting as that supported by the delusional imagination. In my view, the status and role of the delusional imagination therefore must be seen to a greater extent than hitherto in context. It will then be more readily distinguishable from other forms of imagination, such as daydreaming, withdrawal into a fantasy world, infantile fantasy and play, and even religious or artistic imagination, in which the aspects of defence, exploration, or construction are obvious. In other words, a distinction must be made between the positive forms of imagination necessary for keeping the future open or constructing new shared realities (*dream-as-thought*) on the one hand, and delusional falsifications (*dream-as-delusion*) on the other.

Although a product of imagination, a delusional construction is the antithesis of the development of thought. Paradoxically, however, thought, like delusion, arises in and is sustained by the imaginative capacity. As Freud pointed out in "Formulations on the two principles of mental functioning" (1911b), the pleasure principle, which pre-exists the reality principle, continues to operate even after the latter becomes established. Fantasying and dreaming are expressions of the pleasure principle and constitute a thought activity parallel to that inspired by the reality principle. In order to think, one must be able to imagine.

The imagination, or the capacity to dream, which permits the birth of thought, must never be extinguished if psychic life is to remain a potential space open to the future. Through imagination a child feels free to create, and knows that he is exploring a new reality that does not yet belong to him, with which he is not yet acquainted, and which he cannot yet understand. A child uses imagination to search for the not yet experienced reality inhabited by others. When he says "Let's pretend I'm . . .", he is in the fantasy area necessary for psychic life. However, in his infantile play, my patient Giovanni was *not pretending* to be his father, but *was* his father. Religion, too, belongs to the imaginary realm, one of whose functions is to keep open the space required for life. Its strength lies in the creation of a shared imaginative area. This is, at any rate, an open area, resembling children's play, which may be the subject not only of belief but also of doubt. Believers are not always convinced of the entire reality of the religious universe to which they belong

The characteristic feature of the psychotic state is not projection on to the world or curiosity, qualities typical of intuitive imagination, but psychic withdrawal and use of the organs of perception to construct artificial states of well being.

When imagination no longer has a potential relationship with reality, imagination itself becomes reality. As Husserl points out, thought is always anticipatory and moves by projecting itself in time and space. Delusion takes the form of an attack on thought because it destroys its anticipatory character. Owing to the constant creation of new realities projected outside himself, a psychotic person achieves the mental state attributed by man to God, who created the world out of nothing as a projection of his imagination alone. To become established, the delusional reality must therefore abolish the hypothetical or exploratory nature of thought, stripping it of any metaphorical element. (Artistic creation, although the contribution of an individual, calls forth new imaginative worlds and broadens psychic reality. These new worlds are progressively assimilated and shared, and the artist becomes a creator of new realities that anyone can use. Conversely, perverse fantasy shares

certain characteristics with psychotic constructions: although originating in the imagination, it has elements of concreteness, repeti-
tiveness, and exclusiveness that run counter to the openness and
novelty of an actual encounter. In this respect it resembles delusion
by virtue of its concrete fetishistic character.)

Words are stones

Delusional fantasy is not the expression of unconscious wishes or
conflicts. The strength of delusion stems from its vocation of
presenting itself as a higher reality: personal madness becomes
stronger than reality. In the psychotic state, a particular quality of
ideation fuelled by visual combinations, assonances, or linguistic
identities continuously cathected by the delusional meaning takes
the place of the subject's normal capacity for evaluating his mental
processes. Psychotic constructions are fed by "revelation", which
operates by manipulating thought and turning it into anti-thought,
and which constitutes an already saturated proposition that
demands that facts adapt to the "revelation" rather than the other
way round. Psychotic thought is essentially a sensory thought that
"sees" and "hears".

Sometimes Giovanni claims that enemy emissaries come into his
house to spy on him; at first he also suspected that this was the case
when he entered my consulting room. When I ask him why he
cannot find the microphones and bugging devices that he "knows"
have been installed to spy on him, the patient replies that these
objects are invisible to the naked eye. The objects of persecution do
indeed elude his vision, because he *"sees" or "hears" with the eyes of
the mind.* His mind operates like a sense organ that generates reality data that accumulate in the delusional memory and projects
them to the outside. The reality thereby produced becomes part of
this dissociated memory, in which the delusional memories are
stored in an archive from which they can be retrieved and reactivated on the slightest pretext.

And indeed, all that is necessary for the delusion to be rekindled
is a mere *associative connection*, whether verbal or visual, with past
delusional experiences. For instance, the words "polluted" or
"danger", casually uttered in conversation, reactivate the image of

the persecutors, and any chance connection with the characteristics of the group of foreign enemies—nationality, language, or physical features—bring back to life all the past events stored in the delusional memory and revives the patient's psychotic anxiety.

As the title of Carlo Levi's well-known novel has it, in the psychotic experience "words are stones"; in effect, concrete vehicles that trigger the sensory functioning of a mind incapable of thought.

Note

1. Translator's note: *"Pour inventer, il faut penser à côté"*: A more up-to-date translation might be: "To invent, one needs to think laterally".

CHAPTER NINE

Transference psychosis*

"I realize now that, in the past, I was like a man who, having at first denied the existence of light, made himself blind to the objects which it nevertheless illuminated. I have unfortunately had to realize that I experienced nearly all of my external life not as such, but as a film, or as a mirror of the film which my mind projected on to the screen of my unconscious"

(From a letter written by a psychotic patient after the end of his analysis)

Misunderstanding and the analytic impasse

A fundamental aspect of analytic work, in my view, is the patient's capacity to apprehend and explore the analyst's mental functioning and to interact with it. This experience

* An earlier version of this chapter was published as Chapter Eight of Nissim Momigliano and Robutti (1992, pp. 167–188).

may develop by way of correct perceptions or under the influence of past traumas or primitive objects that inevitably alter the image of the analyst. The two elements are often present simultaneously. When the analyst systematically distorts the patient's communications, this usually gives rise to a blockage in the analytic process, which is commonly referred to as an impasse. As a rule, the patient will signal his difficulty to the analyst soon after this situation arises, and it is essential for the analyst to accept this communication and turn it to account.

In "The elasticity of psycho-analytical technique", Ferenczi (1928, p. 90) describes analysis as a process of development rather than the work of an architect implementing a project. Thinking along the same lines, I wish to show how the analytic process can facilitate the development of vital relations and the acquisition of identity in the patient. This is particularly important in the case of patients whose emotional development was already blocked at the time of the very earliest experiences of dependence. A complex and often tacit relational network unites patient and therapist. Some seriously ill patients require the analyst to support their vital functions uninterruptedly for long periods and to protect them from the danger of physical or mental disintegration. An imbalance between the different aspects of this complex relational network can give rise to the disruption of the analytic process of development mentioned above. In some cases the patient reacts silently during the impasse, withdrawing physically or mentally from the analysis. This will now be illustrated by a clinical example.

This patient had commenced analysis at the age of twenty-four because she was depressed following the premature death of her mother. In the third year of her treatment a persistent and to me incomprehensible situation arose. Having become silent and unapproachable, she one day brought a dream that threw light on what was happening.

> She was in the kitchen and felt thirsty, but there was only a bottle with a broken neck. She could not drink because there might be glass splinters mixed up with the water. At one point she even felt that slivers of glass might be all around her. After a long silence, the patient said she was trying to understand what was happening to her, but could not. She wondered, for example, why she sometimes only got to her session when there were just five minutes of her time left.

When this patient had brought dreams in previous sessions, they had seldom been accompanied by associations, and I had interpreted the seemingly very clear material in terms of the transference relationship. In trying to understand the effect of my interpretations, the patient had once admitted with difficulty that she had felt "torn away": my words had made her feel "pulled to one side or the other, like a piece of chewing gum". In other words, she felt unable to think, but said at the same time that my attempt to help her was making things worse. I was forced to recognize that my interpretations, which seemed legitimate on the basis of the material, had failed to unblock the situation and to make it meaningful; and it remained meaningless until the patient eventually produced another dream. In it,

> a female friend returned four ice-cream bowls to her, but they were damaged; overcome by uncontrollable rage, the patient finally smashed them to pieces.

She associated the four bowls with the breast, and at that moment realized that she had at last understood a forgotten problem from the past involving her mother. She remembered that when she was a child there had been long periods in her relationship with her mother when she had felt incapable either of understanding her or of being understood, and she had never been able to tell whether this was her fault or her mother's.

These dreams had enabled the patient to represent her confused state in detail (the glass fragments mixed up with the water), and also to explain her self-destructive rage when she was not understood and held with perfect adhesion by the analyst (the bowls stood for her four sessions a week). The second dream also showed that this past problem, which had blocked her experience and confused her, was active in the present and unconsciously superimposed on the analytic situation, which it adversely affected.

This example illustrates a clinical situation not infrequently encountered in analytic work. The analytic process undergoes a temporary blockage without manifest dramatic effects. Eventually, in the symbolic language of a dream, the patient reveals the nature of the difficulties; the understanding of the dream marks a turning point, and the analytic process can resume.

Psychotic transference and transference psychosis

The situation is different in the case of certain patients with more serious pathologies, such as borderlines or psychotics, where such circumstánces may often result even in the traumatic breaking off of the therapy. What happens is the emergence in the analysis of a psychotic process centred on the analyst, a clinical condition called *transference psychosis*. When the analyst finds himself at the focus of the delusional process, he finds it difficult to maintain the balanced form of involvement that was preserved with the patient described above.

In another case, the swift and unsuspected onset of a transference psychosis that lasted for several months surprised me and put me severely to the test. At the same time, however, it stimulated me to pay particular attention to what was happening. My ideas developed in difficult circumstances, when the patient had ceased to co-operate and to communicate with me and my interpretations were distorted and rejected with hatred and violence.

Transference psychosis (Kernberg, 1968, 1975; Rosenfeld, 1978) is defined as the emergence of psychotic manifestations in the analytic relationship. In the past, a clear distinction was not drawn between *transference psychosis* and *psychotic transference*: the two conditions were considered to be equivalent.

Whereas the psychotic transference is an overall clinical manifestation that includes the figure of the analyst in the patient's delusional world, a transference psychosis is a *psychosis in the transference*. In the latter situation, it is only within the analytic situation that the patient develops delusional ideas, psychotic forms of behaviour, or hallucinations. The loss of the reality-testing capacity in the transference psychosis does not unduly interfere with the patient's life, which remains seemingly unchanged. He develops aggression and hatred only towards the analyst, who is perceived as a source of anxiety and terror and is feared and attacked in delusional fashion. Interpretations are misunderstood to such an extent that any communication proves impossible, and the analyst feels impotent, overwhelmed by the developing violence of the psychotic process that engulfs him.

There are two approaches to transference psychosis, due to Kernberg and Rosenfeld, respectively.

Kernberg's hypothesis

Kernberg (1975, p. 89) states that a transference psychosis can readily arise in the therapy of borderline or psychotic patients and can be useful in facilitating our understanding of the genesis and psychopathology of their condition. He enquires, "Does the transference psychosis also represent the reproduction of unconscious, pathogenic object relationships of the past, and thus provide further information about the patient's conflicts?" Again:

> Ego boundaries fail only in those areas in which projective identification and fusion with idealized objects take place, which is the case especially in the transference developments of these patients. This appears to be a fundamental reason why these patients develop a transference psychosis rather than a transference neurosis. [*ibid.*, p. 34]

For this reason, according to Kernberg, the development of a transference psychosis is inevitable in the analytic relationship with a borderline patient, since it satisfies primitive aggressive drives that constitute an obstacle to the transference. The patient repeats the unconscious pathogenic object relations of the past, and the confusion is due to the typical lack of ego boundaries in these conditions. For this reason, in Kernberg's view, the transference psychosis can be blocked by laying down rules or setting limits to the expression of the patient's aggression.

Rosenfeld's hypothesis

Rosenfeld (1978, 1979), on the other hand, distinguishes traumatized borderline patients, who are dominated by confusional anxieties and pathological splitting processes, from others who idealize destructive narcissism. What is specific to traumatized patients is confusion between libidinal and aggressive aspects of the self and between good and bad aspects of the object. Other confusions concern the difference between persecutory and depressive anxieties, between oral, anal, and genital impulses, and between the nipple and the penis. In this last case, patients are confused about their sexual identity.

Rosenfeld's hypothesis is based on the finding that traumatized borderline patients are unable to accept interpretations about the destructive aspects of the self owing to the presence of a highly sadistic superego. (I shall return to this hypothesis later and examine it in the light of my clinical material.) When this superego is projected on to the analyst, a transference psychosis develops: the patient is overcome by terrible anxiety, feeling that the analyst is telling him that he (the patient) is utterly bad. The anxiety has to do with the fear of disintegrating, of dying, of going completely mad, or of being driven mad by the analyst.

Rosenfeld suggests that the analyst can see the transference psychosis not only as a threat to break off the analysis, but also as an aid to understanding, as it may throw light on the patient's entire psychotic process. In this way, the understanding of this situation—which, while admittedly undesirable, need not be feared absolutely—can facilitate comprehension of the patient and his pathology.

Psychosis in the analyst's consulting room: Tullio

I shall now describe the development of a transference psychosis with a view to formulating some hypotheses as to its nature. In a supervision with Eric Brenman at the Milan Psychoanalysis Centre (some of the supervision sessions concerning this patient are described in Brenman, 2002b, pp. 113–134), I had learnt to see Tullio, a patient who had proved particularly demanding from the beginning, in a new way. The transference psychosis arose in the fifth year of the analysis—after the end of the group supervision—and took the form of a total breakdown in the analytic relationship. The crisis was particularly surprising to me because I was convinced that we had made a good start and that the progress achieved, both in the analysis and in the patient's external life, could now be deemed permanent.

Tullio, a man of about forty, was terrified that he might be "outed" and ridiculed as a homosexual, and this fear had made him avoid any homosexual experience. In fact, he not had any sexual experience at all: what particularly aroused his anxiety was the idea of contact with women and of an emotional, psychological relationship with them.

Since he had been unable at the beginning of the analysis to pro-vide sufficient information about his infantile experiences, I could reconstruct his history only *a posteriori*, on the basis of the transfer-ence or of hypotheses stemming from the clinical material. Tullio had two elder sisters and was born when his mother was in her forties. As he was growing up, his mother became depressed and increasingly withdrawn, and eventually committed suicide. The truth was concealed from Tullio, then twelve years old, as the suicide had occurred far away. Consciously, he thought she had died suddenly, of natural causes. In the first years of his life he had developed an idealized, fusional relationship with her, whereas his feelings for his authoritarian father, who was often away from home, were of hostility and physical repulsion.

Tullio had never formed any close relationships, particularly outside the family. Although he seemed a friendly person, his contacts with others were in fact exclusively formal. His secret homosexual fantasies were not only gratifying to him, but in his view essential to his survival. His masturbation fantasies, centred on his own body or parts of it, sent him into what was in effect a dream state, a special condition of pleasurable withdrawal from the world.

I shall not dwell on the paternal transference, which initially developed along negative and persecutory lines. For a certain period of the analysis, he saw me as a sadistic, cold, indifferent father, interested in the penis and in dominating him. I shall concentrate instead on his relationship with his mother. Once the patient had ceased to deny the reality of her suicide, this relation-ship was a source of extremely painful psychological experiences. This theme was to become central to the development of the trans-ference psychosis.

It was only at a certain point in the analysis that Tullio remem-bered that, as a child, he had distanced himself from his mother on the physical level, too, even refusing to see her for long periods. For this reason, the patient blamed himself for having been unable to save his mother, or even saw himself as solely responsible for her death. Her suicide had given rise to the concrete image of a mother unable to survive, who was often confused with myself.

Before any separation from me, the patient's anxiety centred on the fear that I might have sexual intercourse while we were apart, something he felt would put my life in danger. He would then be convinced that he had to think of me constantly in order to keep me alive, and that it was his responsibility to look after me. When, however, the separation finally occurred and he realized that he was not the centre of the world, he experienced violent hatred at the frustrating aspects of the relationship, as well as guilt and persecution for his attacks on me.

The oedipal experience was manifested in crude and primitive forms, and identification with the depressed mother who wanted to die was often his only available model. The image of the mother also re-emerged as a source of terror and persecution: sometimes the patient would abandon the session or get frightened if, in apprehending or repeating his words, I pronounced the word "mother". It was the same if I uttered the phrase "sexual intercourse".

I realize that, in my attempt to describe this case, I am failing to convey its intense emotional climate and complexity, as well as my misgivings at the fact that the patient seemed to stay confused in spite of all my efforts. However, even at the most difficult moments, Tullio had remained strongly attached to me and to his therapy, profoundly convinced as he was that in it lay his only chance of salvation. Yet, this trust had collapsed in the course of the transference psychosis. The sessions were now dominated by terror and a deadly hatred of me.

Violence in the transference

Tullio had become very hostile and verbally aggressive. After attacking me, he would order me to speak; but as soon as I said something, he would silence me or contradict me both in words and by his violent tone of voice. He yelled at me that I was damaging him, trying to alter his mind, and was a violent "communist". Since it was not clear who was attacking and who was being attacked, drawing his attention to the violence of his words only made the situation worse. He obviously saw me as a real threat to his physical and psychological integrity, and his aggression was manifestly a reaction to a destructive object. At times, he would exasperatedly shout at me that I had been tormenting him for twelve years (his mother had committed suicide when he was twelve). In this way, I came to realize that for Tullio I actually was a mother who was intruding into him so as to confuse him or drive him mad.

In my attempts to understand what past situation had been reactivated, I began to think of an infantile experience of his that had emerged some years earlier and must have been very traumatic. In his infancy, when his mother was clearly scared of killing herself, she had told her son about her death anxieties. She had often terrified him with macabre accounts of her death and the wicked stepmother who would replace her, and Tullio had eventually refused categorically to see her.

I wondered what in the analysis might have had such a traumatizing and confusing effect on the patient. My inner attention gradually came to focus on one recent session when the patient, who had a clerical job, had told me how he had wanted to help an old lady in his office. His description had been full of scorn and defiance towards his workmates, who had not helped this person but instead made fun of her. I remembered that in that session I had taken verbal note of his wish to help, but also emphasized his need to feel that only he could provide this help. On a deeper level, however, I had felt disturbed by what I felt to be a mere show of kindness.

The patient now remembered my tone of voice in that session, which had frightened him and made him feel threatened. He said that this situation had arisen on other occasions, too: he thought that I was a violent "communist", that my calm exterior was a sham, and that I was seething with violence inside.

I was aware that the patient was then still talking about his mother: seemingly calm and good, she had subsequently become violent and committed suicide. For the patient, I had repeated the behaviour of the psychotic mother. I remembered that in one of my interpretations I had used the word "Nazi" with a negative implication. "What do you have against Hitler?" he had shouted, "Don't you know he was slandered by Stalin about the business with the Jews?"

Sometimes he could not bring himself to come to his session and would write me a letter, saying that he would not return until I changed my attitude towards him. Even when we succeeded in clarifying something, he would come to the next session in a confused, drunken, or drugged state, and talk about the previous session in delusional terms. On these occasions I felt impotent and worried about him.

At other times, however, he was aware of the delusional aspect of this fear of myself and his fear of dying. When calmer and more lucid, he said he felt desperate at his inability to achieve any personal experience in his life (in Tullio's language, he would "never have any private property"), because I, as "a communist", prevented him from doing so. The problem that aroused his anxiety was his inability to use destructive measures to ward off a threatening danger that terrified him. I began to think of "communism" as something that belonged, in the patient's mind, to his mother or to himself, and that this might be what he was confused about: there was something that frightened him, which he hated, and hated in me. That might explain the confusion between himself and me, his sense of terror, his fear of going mad, and also the fury of his onslaught on me.

Areas of confusion

I realized more clearly how important it was for him that I should notice his attempt to express—perhaps for the first time—feelings of solidarity and sympathy for the old depressed mother (the old lady in the office). This was extremely important, considering his former persistent contempt for women, in particular his mother, seeing them as "empty, needy, and bloody whores". In his external life he had always admired and chosen as his friends men who succeeded in possessing and also despising women. The wish to fuse with such men was one of the psychological aspects of his homosexuality.

In the transference, he had sought to establish such a relationship with me, and this had become a central aspect of our work. I felt that my failure to understand this new element had had a devastating effect on the patient, owing precisely to the difficulty he had experienced in reaching and maintaining this position. Tullio had felt rejected just when, inside himself, he was separating out the good aspects from the contemptuous ones, the latter for the moment projected on to his workmates. That is why I had become for him a "communist" who dominated his life, prevented him from living, and deprived him of his self-esteem. Hence, his stubborn hatred of me.

The same problem had probably arisen on other occasions, too, but had not been expressed because Tullio had been afraid to address it for fear of conflict. Hence, the vindictive nature of his projections and his need to strike and beat me, so as to pay me back for the other times when he had felt attacked by me.

I postulate, therefore, that any failure on my part to grasp positive manifestations in him thrust him violently into a sadomasochistic kind of relationship: Tullio was the masochistic victim and I in effect was someone who had to face his own sadism.

I had now begun to work with him on this level and we had attempted to identify the points where such misunderstandings had arisen. Tullio had progressively plucked up the courage to re-examine some remote episodes that had seemingly been passed over in silence.

Yet, I was convinced that the situation was more complex and that we needed to discover what was making him so confused about his ability to live and to respect himself; I had to try to connect the pathological interaction of the transference psychosis with the areas of internal confusion.

As trust returned and the climate of tension relaxed, Tullio began to talk to me about his "communism". In his mind, a "communist" was someone who entered into a house or a person with a view to causing devastation inside. "Communism" was a state of total wretchedness and greed. In this situation, the state of deprivation fuelled destructive voracity, and envy of anyone who "possessed something" gave rise to uncontainable hate. It was this deprived and destructive self, confused with the depressed, suicidal mother, that the patient was attacking in terror when he yelled at me, "What about you, De Masi: have you or have you not any cash in your pocket?"

Tullio had then brought a sadistic fantasy: he as the "communist" entered his mother's body, removed her breasts, and attached them to himself, so that the two persons merged with each other. In effect, he could only have anything for himself by killing; and after he had done this, Stalin and the "communists" immediately did the same to him. Tullio had added, too, that communists had terrified him all his life: whenever there was a trade union demonstration, he would shut himself in his house and not set foot outside. Given the political climate prevailing during his infancy, he was afraid they would kill his father, who was a vehement anti-communist. Tullio felt—and this seemed a key experience—the depressed mother to be inside him, and when the "communist" mother, depressed and hungry, manifested herself to him, he felt threatened from inside. He would then draw the mother into a sexual relationship and, in a state of masturbatory excitation, throttle her with his urethra (I have already mentioned the importance of the body— in this case, the musculature—in the patient's fantasies).

The cruelty of the relationship with the depressed internal mother who was asking him for help had now become clear, as well as the reason why sexuality had such terrifying connotations for him. The sadistic, murderous fantasies had been brought about by the terrible sensation of hunger or the anxiety of being left to die. In the patient's mind, the internal depressed mother, empty and hungry, kept herself alive by voracious sexuality. In this state, Tullio did not know whether the child or the mother, or both, were about to die, a prey to their voracity. It was then possible to understand the masturbatory or homosexual fantasies (for example, of appropriating the penis so as to suck it, or of being penetrated anally) as also constituting a defence against terror. Tullio had placed his madness—his hated greedy, murderous self—inside the external object he called "communism", and the transference psychosis had revealed the terrifying nature of this object. The fear of no longer being able to split off and project on to the external object made him utterly confused, and the risk was that he might turn the destructive impulses against himself. The danger of self-harm was present throughout the period when I was perceived as a wretched, destructive mother. Tullio was confused with this mother, who did not help him to live and who chose death. Fusion with her seemed to be the only solution.

Projection of murderous parts

Let us now consider this greedy, murderous part, which the patient describes as "communist". In the paper mentioned earlier,

Rosenfeld (1978) describes in detail the basic anxieties of borderline patients with traumatic infantile experiences. He notes that these patients are unable to accept interpretations about the destructive aspects of their self owing to the presence of a highly sadistic superego: when this superego is projected on to the analyst, a transference psychosis arises.

My own view is slightly different from Rosenfeld's because, in my experience, it is not so much the interpretation of the destructive aspects of the self that proves intolerable and triggers this process, as *an interpretation based on a misunderstanding of the patient's level and position at the time*. Interpretation of the destructive aspects of the self is perceived as devastating if the timing is wrong: that is, while the patient remains under the sway of a sadomasochistic universe used as a defensive weapon for survival. I fully agree with Rosenfeld on the character of these patients' superego, which is particularly applicable to my patient, but I believe that what is projected is not so much the superego as the greedy, murderous part, which, once projected, threatens the patient with death and madness. The same dynamic underlies the fear of dying or of being killed that these patients experience in the transference psychosis.

Unbearable guilt

In my patient's case, the delusional projection had been facilitated by my misunderstanding of his reparative experience. I had therefore been seen as a destructive mother, envious of her child's well-being and mental growth. Projection had also been the only way of disposing of intolerable guilt. That is why Tullio told me, "If you are a communist, De Masi, I'll dump my communism on you and get rid of it." In other words: "If you don't recognize my good aspects and help me to tell them apart from the murderous bits, then my guilt is unbearable. I'll rid myself of this terrible, murderous relationship with my mother by dumping it inside you. You are the one who kills; you are Stalin, and Hitler is innocent!" The projection rid the patient of his guilt ("I'll dump communism on you . . ."), but only for a moment, for immediately afterwards he was persecuted anew. The transference psychosis in this case took the form of a defence against guilt, plunging the patient into a terrifying sadomasochistic relationship in which he was totally identified with the sadistic superego and the analyst was identified with the murderous part, which was feared and attacked.

Once the transference psychosis had been overcome, Tullio had been able to explain that when I drew his attention to his aggressive tone towards me, his confusion had increased. Now, at last, he realized that he was in reality attacking not me, but a hated part of himself, which was projected and confused with me. From then on, it was easier to help him to discern this tangled experience of hunger and explosive hatred into which he had plunged.

As stated earlier, when the patient felt hunger pangs, he turned to the mother, but in his internal world it was the mother who leapt on to him and greedily invaded him. My attempts to help him understand the confusion between himself and the depressed mother, between the mother and the analyst, between the hate and the desperate calls for help, might have resulted in further misunderstandings. I might also have been over-hasty in my attempts to help him, thus arousing his anxiety about my capacity to understand him and to accept the means at his disposal for communicating the problem. When he tried to silence me, or failed to come to his session, he was asking me to think long and hard before opening my mouth and to understand his situation properly. The attacks on the depressed, hungry mother were an expression of his hate and contempt for a needy, hungry ("communist") part of himself: he found it difficult to distinguish hate and contempt for the depressed mother from the attacks used to defend against the danger of invasion by the psychotic mother. Internally, the patient was confused about the meaning of his greed, which compelled him to intrude and to empty out the object in order to survive; it had been important to discover why he had felt forced to steal so as to survive and not to starve to death. The fact of penetrating greedily into the object as the only possible way of feeding underlay Tullio's confusion between his libidinal and aggressive aspects.

The primal emotional trauma

In a Rome seminar in 1979, Rosenfeld said that a common feature of all borderlines was probably disturbances of internal origin, but more commonly ones of *external origin* (my emphasis), which prevented the normal working through of primary anxieties (i.e., Melanie Klein's paranoid–schizoid position).

My experience with this patient confirms the importance of early emotional trauma in the development of psychopathology. The transference psychosis arises at the point when the image of the analyst coincides with the internal image of the pathological parent, thus rekindling the primal trauma. The working through of the transference psychosis enabled us to identify the specific zone of pathological interaction between myself and the patient's areas of confusion.

Bion writes that if the mother cannot tolerate the child's projection of suffering and confusion, the child resorts to constant projections of increasing violence. The violence strips the projection of meaning, so that the projection is reintrojected with equal violence. The child then introjects an object that deprives it of any understanding and is likely to cause it to starve to death. This dramatic situation is, in my view, reproduced in the transference psychosis and constitutes what the patient allows us to observe, albeit not as privileged observers protected from the drama unfolding before us.

I agree with Rosenfeld (1978) that only a detailed analysis of the psychotic transference relationship makes it possible to re-establish the continuity of the analytic process. The working through of this situation, which is conditional on the analyst's being able to recognize any misunderstandings, helps the patient to introject a non-omnipotent analytic object endowed with reparative capacity. Apart from analysis of any pathological interaction in the analytic couple, I consider it equally important to identify the areas of internal confusion that underlie the process.

In Tullio's case, I felt that the interaction, the internal relationship, and the confusion with a pathological parent imposed a heavy burden on his entire psychic organization and rendered any improvement in the analysis precarious. It was essential to determine with the patient what past experience of his might have distorted the development of normal infantile dependence in his case.

With borderline or psychotic patients, it is, in my view, of paramount importance to analyse the delusional psychopathological nuclei, often originating in infancy, that lead to confusion between self and object or between parts of the self. If this is not done, the analysis, especially of the destructive aspects, is likely to be completely distorted by the patient's internal experience.

A new object

It is widely considered that transformations in analysis largely depend on the possibility of introjecting new objects, even if, as Brenman (1980) points out, the old objects often tend to remain alive alongside the new ones and could re-emerge at times of crisis. It is my firm conviction that patients can distance themselves from the old pathological objects only when the in-depth experience of a good analytic relationship has been internalized. In patients who are more seriously ill, such as Tullio, the introjection of new experiences is often particularly difficult owing to the presence of psychopathological constructions formed in the course of the first relations of dependence. In analytic treatment, we may observe oscillations between the presence of new experiences and the reappearance of the old delusional constructions; these confuse the patient as to the nature of his experience and cause him to lose contact with reality.

One of Tullio's psychopathological structures was masturbatory withdrawal into his body and confusion between its parts. Sexualization and confusion between the penis and the nipple—the "ferocious mixing up of external food and the subject's body"—gave rise in him to complicated perceptual distortions that made the analytic relationship totally incomprehensible to him. In the last period of the analysis, at the moment of change and emergence from confusion—"coming out the other side, into the light of reality"—Tullio realized that he had to "resymbolize everything", and confessed that, to "understand the difference" between masturbation and feeding, he had to masturbate and drink milk simultaneously.

I maintain that it is only the internal experience of the analyst, who keeps him alive and in turn stays alive and capable of thought, that reduces the patient's recourse to fantasies of theft or compulsion to intrude into the object in order to survive. In my view, the enormous psychological dependence developed by such patients in the analytic relationship can be explained by their extreme need to rid themselves of areas of confusion, which they unconsciously experience as dangerously likely to plunge them into madness.

Let me now return to the intensity of Tullio's relationship with me, which had increasingly taken on the characteristics of a new real experience. I felt that one reason why his attitude to me was so tempestuous was his need to fill the voids of the past. In this connection, I should add that the transference psychosis reappeared, albeit in a weaker form, at the very end of the analysis, when I again became a "communist" for him. This was a brief episode, lasting only a few days, which the patient himself resolved and understood.

In the final months of the therapy, Tullio kept asking to meet me outside the setting of the sessions, to discover whether I saw him as a friend or a son. I confess that I was somewhat disturbed by the resumption of these greedy demands; I thought I had already supplied him with enough proof of sympathy and solidarity and that I had sometimes deployed the last ounce of my resources in working with him, so I was surprised at his inability to hold this as a stable experience inside himself.

In our attempt to understand why I had become the "communist" for him again, Tullio had recognized that, for a part of him, my resistance to his demands had meant that he could no longer "think of me" as a parent. My refusal, he said, might well thrust him back; it might force him to devour again in order to survive, and to be unable to preserve the image of me inside him without the fear of being accused of theft. Tullio was asking me to be a completely new object, with whom he could have an experience that he had never had before, without which he would not have been able to grow emotionally; he needed constantly to test my real capacity to receive him and to keep him alive inside me. This experience was the prerequisite for his personal development and for his capacity to keep the links with me alive once the analysis was over.

CHAPTER TEN

The fate of the transference in psychosis

"If it is to be possible for an analyst or a mental hospital to cure a schizophrenic patient it must certainly be possible for a mother to do so while the infant is right at the beginning, and the logical conclusion is that the mother often prevents schizophrenia by ordinary good management"

(Winnicott, 1987, p. 45)

As we know, Freud considered that psychotic patients were not amenable to psychoanalytic treatment because they were unable to develop a transference. Abraham (1912), on the other hand, was convinced that the transference existed even in schizophrenia. Other analysts, too (among others, Ferenczi, Federn, Sechehaye, Sullivan, Fromm-Reichmann, Searles, Rosenfeld, Aulagnier, and Benedetti), have expressed the conviction that conditions useful for the therapeutic process can be created even with psychotic patients.

In Abraham's view, the need, in cases of narcissistic neurosis (i.e., schizophrenia), is to seek actively to maintain a relationship with the patient by taking advantage of the positive transference; if the transference were to be analysed, as in the therapy of neurotic patients, the analytic process would be disturbed.

Abraham's position—that the transference should be left alone—is greatly at variance with analytic technique, which suggests that it is precisely the transference that should be the focus of analytic work, so that the conflictual part can be analysed and transformed. Freud, after all, called the fundamental process of analytic treatment the *transference neurosis*.

The various models of transference

Transference is a polysemic concept, whose meaning is strictly bound up with the theories espoused by each individual analyst. In brief, the transference as described in the analytic literature might be: the manifestation of infantile drives (Freud and the ego psychologists); an indication of the state of the internal objects and the object relationship (Kleinian theory); or the expression of the dyadic interaction constructed by the patient and the analyst (relational theories).

It is well known that Freud at first saw the transference as a kind of *contaminating influence* that gave rise to a resistance to the analytic method. He later realized that the transference expressed the drive-based forces of the infantile world, which kept the individual bound to his neurosis. This intuition led him to theorize the clinical importance of the transference neurosis (Freud, 1912b), whereby the primal infantile situation was manifested in the present. The neurosis could be worked through precisely because the infantile conflict re-emerged from the unconscious and was expressed in the transference. The working through of the transference, which acted as a resistance to recovery of the memory, helped the patient to distinguish past from present. Therapy enabled the patient to move on from repeating the past to remembering (from acting out to thinking); interpretation of the transference, which was necessary for the recovery of the repressed past, was fundamental to this type of transformation.

In Kleinian technique, the transference is seen as the expression of the patient's unconscious fantasy, constructed with the projections of his internal world. Since the distortion of reality also involves the perception of the past, transference interpretation (interpretation of the here and now) is essential to the acquisition of insight. Recovery of the split-off parts in turn permits integration of the personality.

The importance attached to transference analysis thus varies in accordance with the theoretical model of mental disturbance adopted. In the Freudian model, an idea or drive complex is repressed during the course of development because it gives rise to conflicts. The Kleinian model, on the other hand, postulates that parts of the personality are split off and projected into the object and that these split-off parts, both good and bad, become sources of suffering. The transference is seen as an indication of the persistence of a conflict or pathogenic unconscious fantasy, and it is only by analysing these that the conflict can be worked through and the split healed.

Hence, the clinical importance of the transference and its interpretation depends on the analyst's individual pathogenetic hypothesis.

Transference and the analytic relationship

For a clearer view of the use of the transference in the analysis of psychotic patients, it is, in my view, helpful to distinguish the *transference from the emotional relationship between the analyst and the analysand*. Put simply, whereas the *transference* results from the patient's projections, his split-off aspects, or his infantile past, the *analytic relationship* can be regarded as the fruit of the meeting of the receptive parts of the analysand and the analyst, which develops by the contribution of both. In particular, the character of the analytic relationship depends on the analyst's interpretative capacity: that is, on his receptivity and on his responding appropriately to the patient's communications.

Since they constantly overlap, it is not easy to distinguish the transference from the analytic relationship. After all, the same subjective elements that make up the analytic relationship influence the manner in which the transference is manifested. In its specific manifestations, the transference depends not only on the patient's projections, but also on the conscious and unconscious responses of the analyst, whose emotional attitude influences the projections of the patient's internal world, facilitating, inhibiting, or transforming them. Notwithstanding these difficulties, it is in my opinion important to make this distinction when studying the problems that arise in the analytic treatment of psychotic patients.

The psychotic transference

In the previous chapter, I distinguished the *psychotic transference* from *transference psychosis*. I stated that, unlike the psychotic transference, transference psychosis included a traumatic element, which was reactivated in the transference. Therefore, it contained a nucleus of truth bound up with the past. The psychotic transference, on the other hand, corresponded to a delusional contamination of the transference caused by the invasive workings of the delusional imagination.

This difference indicates that, whereas the transference psychosis, like any analytic impasse, can be worked through, the psychotic transference must be "deconstructed" in the same way as any delusional construction. The psychotic transference includes the figure of the analyst in the patient's delusional world, whereas transference psychosis corresponds to *a psychosis concentrated exclusively on the figure of the analyst.*

Yet, it is not always possible to distinguish clearly between the two situations. It is insufficient to maintain that, in the transference psychosis, the loss of contact concerns only the figure of the analyst and does not interfere with the patient's life, which remains seemingly unaffected. There are psychotic transferences—for instance, those which assume a sexualized form—that are initially confined to the figure of the analyst, but then expand into a full-blown delusional structure. According to Rosenfeld (1997), the development of a psychotic transference must be understood from the beginning in order to prevent the concealed delusional part from rapidly colonizing the healthy part and triggering a psychotic episode.

A useful reference for distinguishing the neurotic from the psychotic transference is Bion (1965) and his concept of rigid-motion transformation and hyperbolic transformation. In Bion's view, the neurotic transference resembles the *rigid-motion transformation* of geometry, in which the figures, although modified, retain certain unvarying constants; it involves a transformation of past infantile experience that preserves a correspondence with the parent figures. The psychotic transference, on the other hand, is, in effect, a *hyperbolic transformation*, in which the projective mechanism makes the original figure unrecognizable. (In addition to these two forms, there is transformation in hallucinosis, in which the mental event is transformed into sense impressions of pleasure or pain [Bion, 1970].)

The analogical transposition of past relationships into the present therefore applies, according to this view, only to the neurotic transference, whereas the psychotic transference involves a radical transformation in which the relationship with the original object is completely lost (Fornaro, 1990). In other words, the neurotic transference arises out of the dynamic unconscious, which has its roots in infancy, whereas its psychotic counterpart stems from psychotic functioning and bears no relation to the infantile past. In a psychotic patient, the experiences of the past do not enter into the construction of the transference because either they have not been mentalized or else they have been transformed.

Unlike the neurotic form, the psychotic transference is a dangerous event *because it undermines the foundations of the analytic relationship*, without which the therapeutic process cannot take place. It must be identified at an early stage, otherwise the contamination of the analytic field and the endangerment of the setting may become irreversible. It will be easier to contain the psychotic transference in good time if the patient does not conceal the activity of his delusional imagination from the analyst.

Although the appearance of a psychotic transference is, in my view, always a perilous event, if it is understood and worked through the patient can be helped to become aware of his tendency to distort reality in a delusional manner.

Should the transference be interpreted?

With regard to the possibility of interpreting the transference in the therapy of a psychotic patient, we must consider the more general question of the usefulness of interpretation in the psychotic state.

I have already mentioned Abraham's view that caution should be exercised in the making of transference interpretations. Another author who has expressed an opinion on this matter is Federn (1952), who contends that therapeutic work with psychotic patients cannot avail itself of interpretations of content because these patients are invaded by an excess of meaning. In other words, Federn considers that, since psychoanalytic interpretations concern understanding of the latent meaning (i.e., the symbolic content) concealed behind the manifest content, they are perfectly legitimate in the case of repressed contents, whereas psychotic patients are unable to symbolize or to use repression because the normal line of separation between conscious and unconscious is lacking in their case. With these patients, symbolic interpretations are not only unsuitable, but could prove harmful, because they will merely add to their confusion.

In the psychotic state, symbolic interpretations do indeed have the effect of stimulating the delusional perception and contributing to the loss of the sense of reality. They are construed as revelations of a new version of concrete reality and not as relating to an emotional reality concealed in the unconscious.

As an example of this situation, here is a fragment from the therapy of a psychotic patient reported by Benedetti (1980, p. 65).

The analyst had attempted to show the patient that her behaviour with a male friend corresponded to the childhood relationship she had experienced with her father. The patient had responded to this interpretation with intense anxiety, adding that she felt *she had deceived her friend by mixing him up with her father*. The interpretation of the past, which had been intended to demonstrate to her how she formed her emotional relationships, had not been understood by the patient, but had had the effect of confusing her and making her feel guilty.

In the therapy of psychotic patients, extreme caution is necessary with transference interpretations because they may be premature or even positively wrong. Whereas a neurotic patient can ignore an incorrect interpretation, or instinctively repress it for subsequent retrieval, borderline and psychotic patients, who are totally dependent on the analyst's mental functioning, are confused by imprecise or mistaken interpretations. In my opinion, the need, in the analytic therapy of psychosis, is not so much to concentrate on the transference—which must obviously be interpreted where it exists—as *to preserve the analytic relationship*, thereby providing the patient with the experience of being helped to understand the functioning that causes him to be psychotic.

Both Abraham and Federn counselled caution with regard to transference interpretations because they understood that psychotic fantasies are not unconscious experiences of which the patient can be made aware by symbolic interpretation. They had the insight that the central problem in the treatment of psychotic patients is to develop the sense of identity, which is so severely compromised by the excess of fantasies that alter the perception of psychic reality. My own belief is that, in the therapy of these patients, it is not possible to work analytically with the transference until an advanced stage of the analysis, when the patient is able to make use of symbolic thought and has re-established the perception of his own psychic reality. It is only at this point that the analyst begins to appear in dreams as the representative of both the present and the past relationship.

This will now be illustrated by a clinical case, accompanied by comments of my own. The material, presented by a colleague (Dr Thomas Müller, of Hanau) at a public seminar (the symposium "Psychoanalysis and Psychosis" held in Heidelberg on 28–29 September 2003), is a good demonstration of the gradual appearance of a transference connected with an infantile emotional trauma relived in the analytic relationship.

Franz

It is only now, thanks to the progress achieved in therapy, that I am able to give some biographical information about this patient, whom I shall call Franz. His mother died of chronic alcoholism when he was eighteen years old. He remembers his schooldays as characterized by a sense of alienation and of being closed to the world; he saw himself as fat and badly dressed. He was ashamed of his mother's illness, in consequence of which she often attacked his brother, whom he had to defend. The latter, two years younger than himself, had begun to use drugs in late adolescence and was now HIV-positive.

Because the mother was repeatedly admitted to hospital, the two brothers were often entrusted to outside families and always had to "manage by themselves". The patient also recalls that, until his adolescence, he had shared a bed with his mother, who was often drunk. The father, an office worker always in conflict with the authorities, merely exacerbated the chaos and disorder that prevailed in the family.

Franz had had his first psychotic breakdown at the age of nineteen, shortly before leaving school. He had received a bad assessment from his German teacher. Since another teacher had been of the same opinion as the first, Franz began to think that there was a conspiracy against him. He stopped eating for fear of being poisoned and began to wander about aimlessly.

He was admitted to hospital and treated with drugs; once discharged, he succeeded in remaining relatively stable and in learning a trade. He married at the age of twenty-seven, and two sons were born a year apart. Although improved, he continued to hear hallucinatory voices that belittled or ridiculed him and suggested that he kill himself. Alongside these negative voices, there were others that exalted him and told him he had saved the world by making important inventions.

It was not long before his marriage proved very unhappy: feeling sad and not understood, he began to drink and to despise his wife. At the age of thirty-two, he fell in love with the "woman of his dreams". He abandoned his family and stopped taking his medication. He lived with this woman for six months without hearing hallucinatory voices and, although slightly hypomanic, was able to continue working.

Meanwhile, his sons had been entrusted to their mother and Franz had washed his hands of them. His new girlfriend soon left him because she could not endure his manic states and felt suffocated by him. He started drinking again, and was readmitted to hospital, this time to a medical ward, where he had a hallucinatory paranoid episode. His family refused to see him again. When he began therapy with me, he had lost his job and was living on welfare.

This excellent and very clear account enables us to follow the progression of a serious illness. The therapist points out that it has only recently become possible to reconstruct the patient's infantile history. This is not a chance comment. A psychotic patient does not register emotions and is not usually aware of his infancy or adolescence. In deciding to take a psychotic patient into therapy, one should, if possible from the beginning, have information about his past. This can sometimes be obtained only from family members, if and when they are able to provide it.

This patient was brought up in a violent, chaotic environment. His father was an isolated person with a character disorder, while the mother suffered from alcoholism and was subject to violent fits of rage. With such an environment, the prerequisites for normal emotional growth are clearly lacking. Despite all his efforts, Franz was bound to break down upon entering into adult life. And indeed, he had his first psychotic episode at the age of nineteen. An additional traumatic element, admittedly, might have been his mother's death, a year earlier.

The chance trigger of the psychotic crisis was the negative opinion of two teachers, which presumably impinged on an underlying megalomanic nucleus in the patient. The frustration-induced narcissistic hatred made him cut himself off completely from the world of human beings. I postulate that, in the absence of genuine help from his parents, Franz grew up with a megalomanic self that perhaps supported him and impelled him to defend his younger brother. His conviction that there was a deadly conspiracy against him expressed the underlying experience of an unwanted, hated child. When the crisis was over, the psychosis continued to operate beneath the seeming improvement: the seductive, denigratory voices marked the transition from the megalomanic to the destructive self.

A second psychotic episode occurred when his girlfriend left him. He seems, in effect, to have swung between mania and depression, and the failure of the relationship evidently unleashed a persecutory, self-destructive superego. This patient was not only unable to tolerate frustration; he also had a megalomanic self that became destructive at times of crisis. After all, his illness began after his failure at school, and the psychosis re-emerged after the abandonment by his girlfriend, which, for him, represented another failure.

On the first few occasions when I saw him, I was struck by his shabby clothing and the stink he left behind in my consulting room. He always wore the same suit, which he never changed. In the first few sessions, he was very silent; I felt that, if I had not spoken, the entire hour would have passed without a word. When Franz did speak, I noticed the disorder of his thought; any subject he broached was twisted and tangled. He gave the impression of moving slowly through a maze. I was often unable to understand what he was talking about, but it was clear that he had completely lost the sense of his life. He seemed to be scattered in the void. The most serious problem lay in the "voices" that told him that he was a social parasite, an impostor, and ought to kill himself. Alongside these, there were also positive voices, which suggested to him that the analyst was Pan Tau (a character on children's television), who was with him all day.

He also talked about his feeling of having been cheated, and mentioned "common experiences", which I had not understood. He was afraid of being made fun of—something that was "normal" for him.

Gradually the cognitive disorder diminished, his communications became more coherent, the domineering voices were less obvious, and his relationship with his (female) psychiatrist assumed greater continuity. As he became more lucid, he began to think of his past differently; he criticized himself sharply for having been unable to foresee the abandonment by his girlfriend. He blamed her for betraying him, and also blamed his wife, who, in his view, refused to acknowledge that he was ill. At one point he even asked me to persuade at least one of the two women to come back to him, since he could not be regarded as responsible for his actions.

At the beginning of the therapy, Franz seemed to be non-existent: the specificity of this patient was to be nothing, to have no significance. A pitiless superego that would not allow him to understand his state of suffering made him feel a complete failure and demanded his elimination. Another seductive voice, on the other hand, caused him to feel special, destined to save the world. It would be interesting to know whether, in his infancy, his mother had swung between aggression and pleasurable seduction. The "voices" might have corresponded to the introjection of a mother who was, at one and the same time, mad, seductive, and accusing. I presume that the dangerous moment for the patient came when he was entirely colonized by the destructive voice that urged him to take his own life. Perhaps the alcohol, which he might have used as antidepressive therapy, ultimately intensified his guilt and self-destructive impulses. The presence of the analyst, who became an idealized protective figure (Pan Tau), helped him to arrive at a better organization of his thought and stimulated the development of his ability to communicate.

The first two years (two sessions per week, face to face) were quite a fruitful period: the patient seemed, within limits, to be getting the better of his confusion and suicidal thoughts. However, he never mentioned the past psychotic episodes and his emotions were on the whole flat: in his sessions, he only reported facts from his daily life. Even when he started drinking again, it was impossible to return to this subject, just as it was impossible to understand his reactions to losses or separations (from his children, from significant figures, from me during holidays, and so on).

I should now like to speak at length about the latest period of the therapy. I must say that I had felt worried as the last autumn holidays approached. Although the patient had not mentioned this, I was afraid of a return of the accusing voices. After the holidays, Franz did not show up for the whole of the first week, and also missed the first session of the second. I learned that he had been readmitted to hospital from a "friend" of his, who had been in the hospital with him and who conveyed his regards.

In the first part of the therapeutic process, there had been an improvement, but without any significant emotional interaction between analyst and patient. In this initial period, the patient was obviously trying to regain his equilibrium and to maintain the symptomatic improvement. He did not mention the prior psychotic episodes, perhaps because he was afraid that, if he did so, they might recur. But there may also have been another reason for this omission. In the past, referring to "common experiences", the patient had wondered whether the analyst, towards whom he had expressed distrust, was genuinely capable of understanding his psychotic experience. The patient's laconic mode of speaking may also have had to do with the fear that the analyst might not be able to understand his psychotic world. By the second year of therapy, it had not been possible to work through the patient's psychotic structure, and for this reason, during the last break in the analysis, a fresh episode had occurred, leading to his admission to hospital.

When he arrived for his session on the following day, Franz seemed to me to have slowed down and to have lost a lot of weight. He did not at first mention his hospitalization, his friend, or the lost sessions. I gradually understood that he had been discharged from hospital ten days before and that it had obviously been impossible for him to come to his sessions. His speech was so disordered that I was unsure of the reality of what he was saying. He told me about an apartment and a faulty car that someone had taken on his behalf, which had perhaps been cancelled or been undeliverable. He then asked me for a town plan of Hanau and enquired where he might find some cash. He mentioned a meeting that had failed because of certain complications, as well as "voices" that had been involved in the failure. At one point he confessed that he was very bad and was unable to get out of bed in the mornings; he really seemed to be torturing himself because he had not been able to stop himself having another breakdown.

At this point I felt that it was possible for him to understand that this fresh episode had been due to the separation, and I said this to him. He did not listen to me, and went on talking about a television programme in which some genetically cloned individuals had been forced to commit criminal acts, but were now beginning to defend themselves. He again said that he needed a map of the town. Then he fell silent, far away from me and casting fleeting glances in my direction.

On resuming his sessions, the patient appeared drained and confused; he hesitated to return to therapy and asked the analyst for a map. His communications seem to mean that he trusted someone who disorientated him, giving him an apartment that was wrong and a faulty car. He mentioned a TV programme in which clones were forced to commit criminal acts. My impression is that he was describing the activity of the delusional part (the faulty car that disappointed him), which had cloned his mind in the absence of the analyst. For this reason, he needed a map to guide him.

In retrospect, the intuition of the analyst, who had felt worried before the holidays, proved correct. His absence triggered a catastrophe, because an object that had protected the patient from psychotic functioning was no longer there. The delusional part— probably the part that had given him the false information—had taken the place of the analyst and instilled in him the illusion that he could get better in a hurry, without the therapy. So, the separation had not given rise to unpleasure, but caused a further loss of structure. In the analyst's absence, omnipotent functioning had severed the analytic link and dashed the hope of success in the therapy.

During this same session, I felt an urge to speak, a sensation I had in fact often had at other times in the therapy when Franz was unable to express himself coherently and his silences were becoming really stubborn. On this occasion, too, I felt that interpretations of the here and now were totally fruitless or that what I was saying was wrong. I understood that in any case I myself ought to have brought the patient back to reality and that it was entirely up to me to do all the work necessary to maintain the relationship between us. On the other hand, I felt that I should have left him time to "come down to earth"; he was so fragile that nothing could be demanded of him. I also felt irritated with the psychiatrist who had been unable to prevent him from relapsing.

I told the patient that coming to my consulting room must have cost him enormous effort: he must have been full of blockages and confusion inside. I added that, although I had returned from the holidays and was back at my post, I no doubt seemed unreliable in his eyes. Perhaps his silence meant that he had had to confront everything all by himself during the holidays. He now experienced me as unavailable for providing "information", perhaps as "faulty", and as not having a home for him. When I said this, he pricked up his ears, but prevented me from finishing the sentence, instead embarking on a kind of parallel communication. He complained about his wife, who was unable to understand his illness and had taken everything away from him, leaving him with nothing. His voice began to tremble: his brother had asked him for help, which he had been unable to give. He had had another feverish attack, had lost his job again, and had returned to the parental home. He again blamed himself for his stupidity in trusting the woman who had left him. He went on talking about his brother, whom the parents were not prepared to help: it was now his turn to do this. At this point, he became genuinely depressed.

I told him that, on the one hand, he was convinced that only he could have helped his brother and that, on the other, he thought that this was an impossible task; he felt compelled to do it, but was full of desperation. Maybe he had felt lost during the holidays, just as his brother might have felt during the feverish attack; but perhaps, at the same time, he had thought that I felt the same as he felt with his brother: invaded by demands and at the same time enraged.

After the psychotic episode, the patient was passive and drained; he apparently stayed huddled in bed all day. So, all the work was entrusted to the analyst, who attempted to make the patient realize that the separation might have made him feel that he was "nothing", and homeless. These repeated interpretations succeeded in getting the patient moving: he complained of having felt like an aborted foetus when he was abandoned first by his wife and then by his girlfriend, but then seemed unable to allow the perception of the analyst's absence to emerge in him. It was, in my view, the patient himself who had evacuated the analyst and fled elsewhere, without any sense of unpleasure or need. The patient evidently saw nothing useful in such interpretations and failed to understand them.

The constant presence of the analyst and the sessions had served to maintain his equilibrium before the holidays, but Franz was apparently unaware of the use he had made of the analyst's presence. Now the catastrophe had supervened, and he again saw himself as a failure. On the other hand, the patient was very moved by his brother, for whom he felt solely responsible, as he had been in his adolescence.

> He interrupted me and began praising a lecture by Professor X that he had once attended. He did not mention the fact that this professor had come out publicly against analytic therapy, but said only that his parents had arranged for him to have an appointment with him. He then talked about "something" to do with the machinations of secret agents whom he called not V (*verdeckte*, meaning "secret" in German), but HIV agents. These HIV agents seemed at the same time to be in league with the terrorists. Other agents, who were law-abiding, were therefore faced with an impossible task. Still others (or perhaps the same ones?) seemed to have abandoned their duties and were engaging in projects for their own account. He also mentioned agents linked to terrorists, who were fighting against the government and were totally out of control. They were battling against each other.

> I told him that his description reminded me of what he had said to me about the insuperable problems that had arisen with the social security system (on other occasions, he had talked like this about the welfare institutions: social security, medical or psychiatric institutions, and social workers were all fighting against each other and causing him enormous difficulties). Who on earth could ever overcome such difficulties? This time he agreed, saying that everything was "out of control".

> I added that, during the holidays, there had been many experiences that had confused him, and that, precisely for this reason, he had perhaps had to face lots of problems by himself, including the different therapies and the opinions of Professor X. The session ended with a prolonged silence.

He arrived late for the next session, sleepy and drained. He said he would not have got up at all had it not been for his appointment with me. It was impossible to consider this communication in depth owing to his resigned, passive mode of thought.

Next day he came on time and began to talk about his parents. They had promised him that, if he were evicted (he had not paid the rent for months), he could have a room in their apartment; he said he would have liked to accept. But, because his brother was living there too, it was doubtful whether this was feasible. He was worried because he could not sleep: he was afraid of thieves (in the previous session he had said that, during his adolescence, he had been unable to get to sleep because he could see thieves walking up and down in his room). He also mentioned his fear of the lift: he had to use the stairs because he was terrified that the floor of the lift car might suddenly give way. His main difficulty concerned driving and filling his car up with petrol. Some weeks before, a filling station had blown up. He said that, as a child, he had been unable to travel in a car with his mother or father. The mother was confused and had ruined the gearbox, causing serious damage to his father's car. His wife could not drive either; only his former girlfriend could do so, and she was also familiar with the technical side of cars.

I now told him that, during the break, he had lost my help and, thinking that I had gone away forever, had experienced my departure as a betrayal (the HIV agents had become treacherous and no one could be sure of their real intentions). A part of him had perhaps been unable to understand the meaning of separation; it had felt confused and that is why it had got "out of control". In this situation, the "room" was no longer available. He looked at me in amazement and rejected what I had just said. He said that now he was only afraid, and was unable to add anything else. In my countertransference, I felt resigned to believing that the holidays had caused the "invasion" or "fault" (the German word *Einbruch*—break-in—also means "invasion" or "collapse"). I repeated once more that he was really afraid of the possibility of invasions or intrusions.

When the patient talked about HIV agents working in secret, or other agents who combined with the terrorists instead of offering protection, he was referring to the psychotic confusion. When the good object is transformed into a bad one, a psychotic patient loses the ability to make sense of the experience. Even the institutions looking after the patient could change and fight against each other.

In other words, in the absence of the analyst things could change, people could get mixed up with each other, and—a very important point—could become transformed and fight against each other. Franz here seemed to be alluding to his internal struggle between believing Professor X and remaining bound to his analyst.

The situation in which the patient had felt immersed during the holidays was a repetition of the chaotic family experience: the parents constantly fighting, the mother with her sudden changes, whose behaviour it was impossible to understand, and good and bad mixed up together in one and the same person. The interpretations that proved useful in this case were those that described the chaotic state that had arisen during the analyst's absence. There were holes in the protective cover of the self, from which there emerged threatening figures (the thieves), the fear of infinite falling (the lift without a floor), or the terror of exploding and being smashed to pieces (like the petrol station). His parents failed to protect him in infancy, his mother mixed up the gears, and his father's car was faulty throughout.

Once again, the transference interpretation centring on the holiday abandonment was not understood by the patient, who insisted on the real fear that his body would lose its protective cover, fall into the void, or explode. The dangerous, intrusive, and violent objects appeared to refer to the experience of the infantile past with an alcoholic, explosive, and enraged mother. Something had arisen inside him; mad thoughts had invaded his mind, like the HIV viruses that had invaded his brother's body, resulting in subversion and destruction.

> After a while, Franz began to talk about his time in hospital. He had witnessed the violent restraint of a patient in a bed near his own, who had put up a determined fight against being tied up, but had eventually been subdued, suffocated with a pillow. (The experience of being floored and suffocated with a pillow in his face had been very significant in his life. When he was younger, because of his impulsive behaviour his parents had called in an uncle, who had pressed his face into a pillow to restrain him. According to the patient, the experience of receiving the bad assessment at school had been like such a suffocation.) This was conveyed with enormous rage; then he mentioned the domineering voices that had greeted this repressive action with approval. Next there was something about people who were HIV-positive, which

I did not understand. He remembered a dream: "I was shut up in a room with other patients and everyone was compelled to have an injection. They were all yelling and running away, but there was no way out . . ." I now mentioned the positive aspect of being able to communicate the dangerous experiences he had had in the hospital. I added that he perhaps felt pushed into and suffocated by the pillow by me, too, not only because of my holidays, but also when I seemed to disagree with him about his fear of driving, of the lift, of filling up with petrol, and of the thieves. My aim had been to offer him a different point of view— that is, to understand his fears as expressions of his internal world. However, he may have had the impression that I wanted to intrude into his mind with a view to cancelling out his perception of the facts, or indeed his very existence.

He looked at me, and after a while talked about the psychotic episode of two-and-a-half years earlier, which had occurred after his girlfriend left him. Terrified, he had run away to seek refuge in a church, and a man of sombre appearance had sat down beside him. He had realized that it was the Devil. The Devil had stolen his soul and he had become a "mere nothing". He then told me a dream he had had while in hospital: "I ran into the street and fell over. While I was on the ground, a flame came out of my head and a man standing nearby swallowed it. The flame was my soul."

I told him that it must have been a terrible experience to see good things turning bad and dangerous. What could he believe in? This might have led him to seek refuge in withdrawal, whereas he was now trying to open up in his therapy. He remained silent, and I had the impression that he had understood.

In the next session, he spoke with desperation about the separation from his children. He felt like "shitting and puking" on his girlfriend and his wife, and blowing up the court and the female judge who dictated when he was entitled to see his children. Eventually he fell silent again and looked in my direction. I then noticed his fingers, browned and yellowed by cigarettes, and smelt the stink of smoke that clung to him. He went on to say that he had to take at least two baths a day to warm himself up and that he would wander through the house smoking one cigarette after another. I gathered from what he said that he was drinking and hardly eating. He did indeed seem to me to be lost and desperate. I spoke to him about the separation from myself and from his children, but I was not sure that he had understood what I was trying to convey.

Again he started inveighing against "those people". He accused them of using dirty tricks to exert their power. When I asked him about his time in hospital, he said that, while there, he had taken part in a cognitive training course. The task to be performed had been to invite a reluctant woman to dinner. If he did not succeed, he would have lost. His invitation had been rejected by the woman and he had collapsed on the floor in tears. The course leader had concluded that he had failed because of his inability to control his emotions.

I told him that he had been faced with an impossible situation, and added that one reason why he had not managed to fight against this "bullshit" was that he had adopted the viewpoint of the course leader. I said, too, that his admired Professor X set very great store by cognitive training, and I was unable to hide a certain satisfaction as I did so. The patient did not react directly to my attack, but said that his parents had complained to the head of the clinic because "it had done nothing for me". I connected this with his disappointment over my holidays and with the paradoxical situation in which he had been left. He added that he was now disappointed with the medication he had been taking, because he had hoped to improve "quickly" with these drugs.

In these sessions, the patient brought an aggressive dream associated with his real infantile experience when no one could calm him down except by force. Here, Dr Müller aptly interpreted not only the violence during the patient's infancy, but also his experience of being intruded upon when the analyst failed to understand. The analyst was, in my view, right to emphasize the devastating effect on the patient of interpretations that did not confer meaning on his experience. The patient's communications referred partly to the violence experienced during his hospitalization, but also partly to the emotion aroused in him by some of the analyst's interpretations. When he was wrong, the analyst was experienced as someone suffocating him with pillow-type interpretations. On these occasions, the patient experienced the therapy as a disturbing action that left him no time to emerge from the state of confusion and did not help him to understand his thoughts. He felt only that the analyst wanted to force his own thoughts into him, and to obliterate his self and his entire existence. All this was clearly explained by the analyst.

Next time I had had to extend the previous patient's session by about five minutes; I had finished just in time to begin the new session with

Franz without taking my usual break between patients. I had not heard the bell and had therefore thought he was late. When I went into the waiting room after about a quarter of an hour, I saw that Franz was sitting there, waiting. Approaching him, I observed that he was paralysed and agitated at one and the same time.

In the session, we managed to reconstruct what had happened. On his arrival, another resident in the block had opened the outside gate. He had come in without ringing the bell and sat down in the waiting room just at the moment when the previous patient, whom he saw for the first time, was leaving my consulting room. He had sat down to wait without indicating that he was there. It had been so unusual for him to have to wait for his session that he had begun to wonder whether he had come at the right time or on the right day. He told me he was convinced that the man had left the consulting room to test him, to see how he, the patient, would react, and would then report back to me. Although later doubting the reality of this idea, in the end he repeated that he was absolutely convinced that I wanted to test him.

I answered that a part of him thought that the therapy consisted in confusing and testing him; so I was like those HIV agents that had "got out of control". This omnipotent, propagandistic part was able to change good things into bad, to pervert reality and confuse him about the therapy, offering him suicide or drink as solutions. I added that this part of him had been very active during my absence.

In response to my words, he seemed calmer and more thoughtful; he then mentioned his brother, who was in trouble because he was short of money and had nowhere to live. How could he help him? His brother would soon be dead. The patient now seemed really moved and overcome with emotion. He said that his brother intended to go to America for treatment with expensive drugs. Franz had offered his parents his inheritance should they wish to advance the money to him. After a pause, he went on to mention a visit on the previous evening by a friend who had had an "affective disturbance", but had made a good recovery. After the friend had left, Franz had felt demoralized. Comparing himself with the friend, he had felt that he had lost everything—his children, his job, and himself. He had felt that "something in my head had gone numb". He had tried to take his mind off these thoughts by watching skiing on television. The event location reminded him of a village where his family had spent their holidays a few times and where he and his brother had been happy. Looking at some old photographs, he had found this little village on the map. While perusing the photographs, he had not felt any emotion, and this had frightened him. He was convinced that he had lost his vitality for ever. His life had slipped by: not only had he lost his past, but his future had also disappeared.

As I listened to him, I felt that I shared his anxiety for his dying brother and for the dying part of himself. I thought at this point that the patient might have perceived that I, too, had been unable to tolerate his pain and had reacted only with logical explanations or polemics against Professor X. As I reflected on these matters, he began to talk about the voice that was telling him: "Have a drink, and then go to sleep for a bit." This voice had such a powerful seductive effect that it was irresistible; after a few months on the wagon, it had urged him to start drinking again, and then he had spent two days in bed. I told him that he was unhappy and worried in case I was unable to understand his feelings of despair at the wretched condition of his dying self. I also emphasized his efforts to stay in touch with his emotional experience, while another part of him was attempting to seduce him into drinking and going to sleep. Perhaps this had been the propaganda that had had such a concrete effect when the Devil had stolen his soul. His anxieties stemmed from his growing awareness of the action of this devilish part inside him.

The next session began with a dream: "I am trying to telephone you, but my phone is faulty; I fly into a rage, hurl it on to the floor and smash it to pieces. I then manage to get through to your secretary, but she says I can't speak to you because you are busy treating other patients. After a while I call again, and the secretary again refuses to put me through. When I protest, she laughs at me, makes fun of me, and tells me she will do everything in her power to prevent me from talking to you." The patient associated the dream with my holiday and with what had happened in the waiting room in the previous session. He then fell silent and seemed moved. I suggested that the dream might refer to the holidays, when he had experienced my absence not by missing me, but as a contemptuous rejection. If this was a plausible theory, the dream suggested to him how he had experienced the separation from me. I continued to insist on the difference between his dream and the experiences of me that he had mentioned in the previous session. He listened calmly and with keen attention. In subsequent sessions, he began to tell me about his psychotic episodes, dwelling in particular on the latest one. For the first time, he seemed interested in understanding the reasons for his breakdown. He told me, too, that he identified me with the Devil who took away his soul because he did not think he was "good enough".

Let me end by saying that Franz lately seems to have developed a certain reflective attitude and to be more capable of understanding what is happening in the therapeutic relationship. At times, however, he has "relapsed" into drinking, and on these occasions the domineering voices have come back to life. At the same time, he has become more aware of how he swings between different states, and more interested and active in the therapy.

Patients like Franz desperately try to understand their emotions by using the analyst's emotional intuition. For this reason, to be useful, interpretations must clearly describe their perceptions and internal world. Any lack of receptivity in this respect is experienced as a violent act by the analyst against the patient, equivalent to killing off his self.

The analyst here performed this receptive function well, describing as he did the various conflicting parts of the patient (the part in emotional contact and the devilish part that sought to make him drink and to take him far away). He also succeeded in explaining to the patient the content of the past delusional experience (a deadly part of himself had taken away his soul). During the psychotic episode, the analyst, too, had been perceived as someone who killed his soul, as a psychotic superego convinced that he was utterly bad and wanting to kill him, or as someone who annihilated him with contempt. From then on, the relationship with the patient became more alive, and sense-conferring analytic communication gained the upper hand. The analyst's contributions were linked to the patient's internal experience and his feeling of confusion that resulted from the warring parts mentioned above.

The progress achieved has enabled the patient to make an initial introjection of the analyst as a human figure. Previously, the analyst did not exist as an internal object. This transition was facilitated by the analytic understanding of the fantasies and emotions arising out of the misunderstanding that occurred while the patient was waiting. He had suspected that the analyst was a cold scientist, interested in experimenting on him (the figure of the cold scientist might at this time also have been connected with the father in the transference). In addition, perception of the emotional relationship linking him to the analyst enabled the patient to make contact with the feelings and hopes of his infancy. He succeeded in very painfully understanding the destruction wrought by the psychotic illness and the extent to which the seductive voice urging him to drink ("Have a drink, and then go to sleep!", which, I think, was like his mother's voice) contributed to shutting down his emotions and withdrawing him from life. Here, the analyst's interpretations became truly apt, as he described to the patient his submission to the distorting propaganda of the psychotic nucleus. These sessions witnessed the seeds of the internal experience of the analyst as a receptive object—an experience that the patient had never had before.

This important transition occurred because the analyst was working on the patient's internal world. This made it possible to observe and explain the action of the seductive, confusing internal voice. It was this internal clarification that gave rise to the dream in which the figure of the analyst appeared for the first time as the object of a difficult experience of dependence. In the dream, the patient expressed the difficulty of communicating his emotions (he has a faulty telephone), as well as the presence of an unreceptive human object (originally, the parents). The part of him that was alive became enraged and smashed the faulty telephone to pieces. The dream described not so much the analytic separation as the establishment of a meaningful relationship of affective dependence and the traumatic experience that might then ensue.

The patient's vitality was expressed with rage and protest. The rage was probably directed less at the absent analyst during separations than at the analyst present in the session when he failed to understand the patient's *faulty* communications. The patient's wish for a dependence that could be used for development emerged clearly, whereas his shutting himself off in a separate world (the faulty telephone) was attacked with rage.

In the dream, Franz described what happened when his affective, libidinal part awoke and opposed his emotional deprivation, as had occurred in the past. The good results were, in my view, attributable to the fact of having first worked on the psychopathological structure (for instance, on the voice that lulled him to sleep and on his psychotic functioning), rather than on the transference. Whereas the transference interpretations proved to be relatively useless because they were premature, the analyst's comprehension of the patient's mental state enabled the patient to begin to understand himself. By working on the structure, i.e., on the psychopathological nucleus, the analyst helped him to understand how he himself contributed to the construction of the psychotic prison inside which he had incarcerated himself.

Such work is never finished once and for all. In psychotic patients, insights do not give rise to stable transformations; often, any improvement is quickly cancelled out, and the old methods of denying and transforming psychic reality are always present. The last few sentences of the analyst's account also give some indication, alongside the progress achieved, of the complexity of the route that must be travelled in order to achieve a stable improvement.

CHAPTER ELEVEN

Psychotic withdrawal and jeopardization of the sense of reality*

"Oblomov's face suddenly flushed with happiness: his dream was so vivid, so distinct, and so poetical that he at once buried his face in the pillow. . . . His obliging imagination carried him lightly and freely into the far-away future

(Goncharov, 1858, pp. 81 and 82)

"Once Chuang Chou dreamed that he was a butterfly. He fluttered about happily, quite pleased with the state he was in, and knew nothing about Chuang Chou. Presently he awoke and found that he was very much Chuang Chou again. Now, did Chou dream he was a butterfly or was the butterfly now dreaming that he was Chou?"

(Chuang-tzu, quoted in Blechner, 2001, p. 239, in the chapter entitled "Knowing what we know in waking and dreaming", and also in Borges, 1976)

---

* An earlier version of this chapter was published in the *International Journal of Psychoanalysis* (De Masi, 2006).

This tale is a good introduction to some considerations on the nature of delusion, the central core around which the therapy of psychosis revolves. In the waking state, how can we know whether we are perceiving something real or instead creating an object with our imagination? What helps us to differentiate reality from fantasy creations? A clinical vignette drawn from the initial interview with a twenty-five-year-old patient who used soft drugs will be useful for illustrating the clinical problem I wish to discuss.

Having broken off his university studies and split up with a girl of his own age, this patient has been living at home in a withdrawn state for months. He was a solitary child, perhaps overprotected by a depressed mother, who was also withdrawn from the world. He recalls that, as a child and then as an adolescent, he cultivated a fantasy world, but this daydreaming tendency has now become so invasive that it cuts him off almost completely from contact with the world. He lies on his bed for hours on end dreaming of taking his exams, getting his degree, being successful with women, being very rich, and travelling the world; he even sees himself as a successful television personality. He realizes that the "lie" of which he is the victim presents itself to him as "another world", a powerfully attractive force that distances him from relational life. He falsifies his perceptions to such an extent that he believes the world he has created to be true, and reality, which he painfully has to come to terms with, to be false.

The Chinese tale quoted at the beginning of this chapter seems to reflect this patient's experience: it tells of the daydream flowing into consciousness, of the confusion between the imaginary (the butterfly) perceived as real, on the one hand, and reality (Chuang Chou) seen in the manner of a dream, on the other. The sense organs of both Chuang Chou and the patient are, as it were, so greatly deceived that they can no longer distinguish between what is perceived and what is created in fantasy, "subjective" and "objective" being confused.

Psychic reality

One of the contributions of psychoanalysis to *how* the world is known is the discovery of the existence of psychic reality (an internal world) that is largely independent of the external, material reality in which we are immersed. When Freud abandoned the hypothesis of sexual trauma in favour of that of fantasy as the engine of illness (i.e., the intuition that the hysterical patient's sexual trauma never occurred), he gave birth to the idea that what really happens differs from what is only imagined. In other words, what is imagined can become real for the patient and will then constitute his psychic reality. So, psychic reality has an eminently subjective quality. What may be real for an individual might not be true. Truth, in order to be such, must be shareable with others; but not even this condition is entirely satisfactory. Psychoanalysis has revealed not only the existence of internal (subjective) reality, but also possible ways of understanding and sharing it.

By their very nature, psychic facts have an individual quality and can be understood only in shared subjectivity. The criteria that are valid for defining the perception of an external object do not work when psychic reality is examined, because, expressing as it does the affects and emotions that shape its representations, this reality is subject to constant change and not readily predictable. The beauty of nature—for example, a glorious sunset—may arouse a sense of astonished wonder in some people and painful melancholy in others. Moreover, the response may vary in one and the same subject. For instance, the same glorious sunset may have different emotional significance according to whether it is shared with a loved person or whether one is in mourning.

Another psychoanalytic intuition is that the psychic world is influenced by powerful forces that are at work in all of us. Freud discovered that we can defend against unpleasant emotions by disavowing or transforming them. In other words, unconscious emotional reality does not correspond to the reality of which we are aware. For Freud, the process of recovery coincides with the acquisition of truth about ourselves, the unconscious truth that was repressed because it was unpleasurable. With regard to our personal identity, it can be difficult to distinguish true and false in our representations. After all, many of our beliefs, while real to ourselves and useful for our existence, can be denied by others. Our very identity may often be partly imaginary.

Observation of infant development shows that, up to the age of two years, a child does not acquire a stable perception of himself as a separate individual and is not yet able to use the first-person pronoun (I) or the personal possessive adjective (my) to refer to himself. Until that age, a young child speaks of himself in the third person, as though indicating that he lives in the minds of adults—in particular, his mother's.

We all have this experience to some extent, otherwise criticisms or negative opinions of ourselves would not give rise to resentment. At the same time, however, being in someone else's mind only as an ideal object is a falsification that prevents mental growth. This raises the complex issue of determining how much of our personality is constructed in fantasy and how much is acquired as real identity.

The internal world

Psychoanalysis has shown that different, antithetical beliefs can coexist in the internal world. Freud maintained, for example, that the idea of personal death, even if present on a conscious level, can be unconsciously denied: we all try to imagine that death is something that concerns others, while denying it for ourselves.

Money-Kyrle (1971) holds that the human psyche tends to transform reality, and sees the aim of psychoanalysis as helping the patient to overcome the obstacles to consciousness of his innate knowledge. This implies that a region of the psyche retains the full unconscious perception of the truth despite the defensive distortion. While accurately describing the dynamics of the repression of psychic truth in normal or neurotic individuals, this conception of psychic functioning is inapplicable to the psychotic situation. After all, a psychotic delusion is not a lie that refers to something else; it does not correspond to the masking of an underlying emotional reality, but extends beyond unconscious falsification (that of the psychic reality of hysterical patients) and conscious falsification (a liar's lie). In delusion, not only external but also internal reality is altered and, with the latter, the sense of personal identity. Delusion can be seen as a falsification of which one is unaware, but which imposes itself on consciousness, causing a progressive alteration of the sense of reality.

The sense of reality lost in the delusional construction is sometimes preserved in dreams, as described in Chapter Five. The

unconscious awareness that appears in certain dreams is not understood by the patient and can be integrated at a conscious level only
after complex and difficult analytic work.

An analogous process takes place in a part of the patient's
observing ego that persists during the entire psychotic process but
is paralysed and helpless: a particular clinical difficulty to be overcome in the therapy of psychotic patients is their passive acceptance
of their entrapment in the psychotic world. Their subjection to the
psychotic nucleus is one of the most serious obstacles to therapeutic progress.

Dissociated reality

In "Dreaming, fantasying, and living", Winnicott (1971) postulates
a divergence between fantasies, on the one hand, and dreaming and
reality, on the other, in the lives of some patients. In this connection
he describes a patient who, from the age of two, had drawn a clear
line of separation between fantasies and relations with real objects.
Winnicott portrays her as a girl who, while playing other people's
games, is constantly engaged in fantasying. Her attraction to the
world of fantasy had prevented her from becoming a whole person
and drained her life of meaning:

> Gradually she became one of the many who do not feel that they
> exist in their own right as whole human beings. . . . while she was
> at school and later at work, there was another life going on in terms
> of the part that was dissociated. [The main part of her] was living
> in what became an organized sequence of fantasying. [Winnicott,
> 1971, p. 29]

At a certain point in the analysis, the patient seems to realize that
her withdrawal into the world of fantasy might result in her spending her whole life incarcerated in a psychiatric hospital, inactive
and immobile, while at the same time keeping up a continuous
fantasy activity allowing omnipotence to be retained and wonderful things to be achieved in this dissociated condition.

Commenting on this mental state, Winnicott notes that, while
fantasying and daydreaming are of the same order, dreaming
and living in reality belong to another. On the basis of different

theoretical premises and in the context of drives, Laplanche and Pontalis (2003, p. 133) place the origins of fantasy in autoerotism:

> Fantasy, however, is not the object of desire, but its setting. In fantasy the subject does not pursue the object or its sign: he appears caught up himself in the sequence of images. He forms no representation of the desired object, but is himself represented as participating in the scene although, in the earliest forms of fantasy, he cannot be assigned any fixed place in it . . .. As a result, the subject, although always present in the fantasy, may be so in a desubjectivized form, that is to say, in the very syntax of the sequence in question.

A dream is in contact with emotional reality: "Dream fits into object-relating in the living world, and living in the real world fits into the dream-world . . ." (Winnicott, p. 26), whereas "fantasying remains an isolated phenomenon, absorbing energy but not contributing—in either to dreaming or to living" (*ibid.*).

While dreams and real-life experiences tend to be repressed, this is not the case with fantasying: "Inaccessibility of fantasying is associated with dissociation rather than with repression" (*ibid.*, p. 27).

The dissociation from reality described by Winnicott is, in my view, a process that proceeds in parallel with that of projective identification (splitting off and projection of parts of the self into the object) outlined by Melanie Klein. Winnicott describes a dissociated mental state (withdrawal into fantasy) which obliterates the dream function and continuously creates imaginary characters, while Klein is referring to a dynamic process that ultimately produces a falsified identity because the projective identification gives rise to confusion between the self and the object into which the projection has been effected (see also Chapter Twelve).

Two realities

The dissociated nature of the delusional fantasy and its substantial irreconcilability with emotional reality find important confirmation in certain philosophical reflections. Husserl (see Ghiron, 2001), for example, holds that a clear distinction exists between an intuited object and a fantasized object. The field of action of fantasy, in his view, is quite separate from that of perception, to such an extent that no one can contemplate the field of perception and that of fantasy simultaneously. As soon attention is directed to the perceptual object, the fantasy field dissolves.

A fantasy image is not rooted in the current reality of the present. For this reason, there is a clear line of separation between the world of perception and that of fantasy. They are two distinct worlds that cannot be integrated with each other. (According to Husserl [Ghiron, 2001], the context of the perceptual field belongs within a space–time continuum. It is precisely consciousness of this space–time continuum that maintains the coherence of waking experience, as opposed to the arbitrary episodicity of fantasy consciousness. This guarantees the distinction between the real and the unreal, the true and the illusory. When the perceptual world, with its space–time continuum, is completely lost, the subject falls victim to hallucinations: fantasy then assumes the character of belief rather than of "as if" as in the consciousness of appearance.)

If, as I do, we accept Husserl's view of the radical irreconcilability between withdrawal into fantasy and thought activity, the problem is to determine whether delusional fantasy can be integrated or, if it cannot, whether it must remain an experience "apart". This problem reminds us of the conflict between *unitary* and *specific* psychoanalytic theories of psychosis (London, 1973). Unitary theories tend to attribute psychotic behaviour to intrapsychic conflicts, similar in nature to those of neurotic patients. Specific theories, on the other hand, are such because they hypothesize the existence of a particular disorder that does not concern the repressed unconscious.

For the former, the delusional experience stems from a psychic conflict, and therefore belongs on the level of the unconscious functions that govern the mental life of neurotic patients and normal subjects. For instance, Caper (1998) considers that delusional unconscious fantasy can be gradually transformed into normal unconscious fantasy. (This, incidentally, also seems to have been the view of Winnicott, as expressed in Winnicott [1971].) Conversely, specific theories postulate a sharp line of distinction between neurosis and psychosis, and contend that withdrawal is a dissociated experience that can be neither integrated nor transformed in the psychic world: even where the patient seemingly has some degree of awareness, this never extends to the delusional belief.

A clear example of the dissociation of judgement for the purpose of preserving the delusion can be found in the memoirs of Senatspräsident Schreber. Although able to comprehend other patients' mental states, he has no understanding of his own. He writes,

> I am fully aware that other people may be tempted to think that I am pathologically conceited; I know very well that this very tendency to relate everything to oneself, to bring everything that happens into connection with one's own person, is a common phenomenon among mental patients. . . . But in my case the very reverse obtains. Since God entered into nerve-contact with me exclusively, I became in a way for God the only human being, or simply the human being around whom everything turns, to whom everything that happens must be related and who therefore, from his point of view, must also relate all things to himself. [Schreber, 1903, p. 197]

Brentano (1874), Husserl's mentor, draws attention to the role of *unconscious consciousness*: that is, the presence in consciousness of parts of which the subject is unaware. (Unconscious consciousness is a concept very similar to the "unthought known" of Bollas [1987], which denotes a thought activity that fails to reach the level of awareness.) In his view, whenever a psychic act occurs, it is accompanied by a knowledge; the act contains not only the relationship with the primary object, but also itself in so far as it is represented and known. The unconscious consciousness described by Brentano corresponds, in my opinion, to the function, of which we are unaware, of *observing our own psychic processes*, which enables us to grasp the subjective quality of our psychic experience. I believe that this self-observing capacity is lost in the delusional state and that its absence prevents the subjective representation and awareness of what is experienced. Bion (1967) notes that psychotic patients have inhibited and indeed totally abolished the function that ought to arouse curiosity in them, so that the very capacity to put questions to themselves is non-existent.

It seems to me that the inhibition of curiosity about the external world and the subject's own sensations results from prolonged withdrawal into fantasy. Fantasy production replaces the relation to the world and destroys curiosity about one's own psychic development. The incapacity for self-observation reaches its peak in delusion, which, for precisely this reason, proves to be a concrete event that is neither representable nor comprehensible at symbolic level.

In analytic treatment of the delusional area, symbolic interpretation proves to be not only useless, but also misleading; this finding should convince us that delusion is not the expression of a repressed unconscious content, but a new psychopathological construction that dominates the patient's mind and alters his sense of reality. Hence, the need to *deconstruct* the delusion rather than to interpret it symbolically. Clinical examples of the work of deconstruction enabling the patient to emerge from delusional withdrawal are given in Chapter Eight, and in the material presented later in this chapter.

Withdrawal into fantasy

So far, I have attempted to demonstrate the need to distinguish the world of fantasy and imagination from that of *withdrawal into fantasy*, and have referred in particular to Winnicott, owing to his exemplary description of one way of becoming psychotic. His observations are especially important considering the difficulty of identifying the conditions of vulnerability to psychosis in infancy. Children predisposed to psychotic development are often ignored by their parents, who fail to distinguish between infantile fantasying and the construction of a world dissociated from reality, which they tend to mistake for a state of tranquillity. As Winnicott points out, the former coincides with the capacity to play, to create, or to share collective myths, while the latter takes the concrete form of *withdrawal* from psychic reality. It is an operation of opposite sign to that of creativity, or, as Bion puts it, it is $-K$.

The dissociation from psychic reality that underlies the future delusional proliferation occurs in this withdrawal, which begins in infancy. This mental state is particularly obvious in small children, who readily bring the world of dissociated fantasy to their sessions, as is clear from the following material concerning a nine-year-old girl in therapy at two sessions a week. (This patient's material was brought to me in supervision by Dr Manuela Moriggia.)

Anna, as she is called, has a twin sister who is very different from her: whereas the twin is endowed with aggressive vitality, Anna is inhibited and withdrawn and performs badly at school. From the beginning of her treatment, Anna invades the sessions with a constant flow of fantastic stories and games inspired by a television cartoon series, which are developed *ad infinitum*. This is the world that she inhabits.

> Patient: I want to tell you some more about the cartoon babies: you know that in one story there's Daffy, who gets frightened at night of the shadows of the toys in the bedroom because they look like monsters (she describes them and laughs).

> Analyst: You're telling me that Daffy is like you: you are also afraid of all the things you meet up with every day; you don't recognize them and then you mix them up with things that frighten you.

> Anna now pretends to be a monster and encourages the therapist to portray one too. As the therapist begins to use her voice to create an atmosphere of expectation, Anna urges her to go on even though she is frightened.

> Analyst: See, you're afraid because your mind ends up turning me into something else. I really could become a monster for you.

> Patient: In the same story, there's Petunia watching television and, when Melissa asks her what she's doing, she answers that she's playing with her best friends. At first Melissa doesn't understand, but then she comes closer and tells her that it's bad for her to watch all those stories on television and that imagination can be dangerous.

> She turns off Petunia's television, but along comes Lola and tells her to leave her in peace . . . Who is right?

> Analyst: You are Petunia, wanting to play with imagined stories all the time, but you know that Melissa is right, that it can be dangerous; but you would often like a Lola to come along and tell her to leave you alone in your world . . . after all, there might be monsters outside.

> Patient: Then Melissa turns off the electricity and Petunia is frightened . . .

> Analyst: But why do you think she is frightened?

Patient [thinks for a moment]:   She thought it was a nightmare . . .

Analyst: She must have thought—and I think maybe it happens to you—that her head had been turned off, that there weren't any more thoughts . . .

Patient: Oh yes . . . so all her friends decide to put on a pretend television show for her, a sort of play they all have fun in. Even Petunia joins in, so when the electricity comes back again she realizes it's better to do things than watch them and she stays there playing with them.

Analyst: I think her friends are very fond of Petunia: they don't want her to be in danger of staying withdrawn inside the television; but in the end even Petunia gives up watching something that attracts her a lot so she can play with her friends; it can't have been easy for her . . .

Patient: Yes, but I haven't got any friends at home who want to play with me.

Vulnerability to psychosis

In describing his patient, Winnicott (1971) states that, from infancy on, this dissociated world impoverishes her personality and is accompanied by a sense of futility and insubstantiality. He has the insight that withdrawal into fantasy represents a place where a mental state of pleasure can be achieved; in other words, the dissociated state of omnipotence offers a pleasure that creates dependence. Caught up in withdrawal, such a child derives no satisfaction from relationships with others and cannot learn from emotional experience. Even if not yet manifestly ill, he is destined not to know himself and not to understand others' emotional reactions, as well as to fear relational experience, which he does not wish for or understand, and which makes him anxious. The mental operations occurring in withdrawal are not subject to the laws of normal psychic functioning; they can be neither repressed nor "dreamed" in order to be transformed into thoughts. (This gives rise to specific problems for therapists working with psychotic patients. Withdrawal is the forge in which the psychosis is constructed and forms part of the patient's dissociated life. It is not described to the analyst because the patient himself is unaware of the danger it presents and fails to understand its meaning. For this reason, communication through dreams is particularly valuable, because here the withdrawal and the colonizing action of the psychotic part are often described uncamouflaged.)

The destruction of meaning that takes place in withdrawal increasingly distances these children from the possibility of learning from emotional experience mediated by the maternal object, and generates a dependence on an omnipotent system based on false constructions. Even if certain modes of functioning enable such a child seemingly to adapt to reality, these give rise to a void in his emotional development that will progressively increase until it devastates his entire personality. In effect, there is here a psychotic nucleus of the personality, because a silent process, destined to expand without encountering obstacles, has thereby been established.

In the therapy of adult psychotics, we can often reconstruct the state of infantile withdrawal and understand how their dissociation from reality was ignored or unwittingly encouraged by their parents. After all, the parents' influence in facilitating vulnerability to psychosis is not expressed solely by their intrusion into the child's mind, but also by their absence. The result of this absence is a failure of structuring of the child's mind. Children who eventually become psychotic enter into the dissociated world not only as a defence against anxiety, but also for the pleasure of experiencing gratifying, illusory self-sufficiency and omnipotence.

Dario

A patient of mine, whom I shall call Dario, comes for analysis (four sessions a week) following a persecutory delusional episode. In the initial interviews, he describes his parents as marvellous people who enabled him to have a happy childhood. In reality, as I gradually discover, the parents were indeed good, but completely absent psychologically. The "freedom" he enjoyed in his infancy coincided with their emotional absence and their implicit invitation to him to immerse himself in a fantasy world dissociated from real experience. Dario felt himself to be a special child, and was convinced from an early age that he would become an exceptional person. He accustomed himself to living in fantasized withdrawal, in a world peopled with heroes, in which he was the protagonist of great deeds. In adolescence, he continued to cultivate the illusion of being special. Having some expressive ability, he devoted himself to the theatre and was convinced that he could become famous, like Laurence Olivier. The most serious crisis in this defensive organization occurred at the end of his studies, when a symbiotic relationship with a friend from his adolescence was broken off and he found himself having to face life alone. After achieving some professional success, he began to develop a delusional, grandiose perception of himself, which was followed by a psychotic state of persecution.

I shall now briefly describe the probable infantile antecedents of his childhood withdrawal. During his analysis Dario learns from an uncle and aunt that, when unable to sleep, he would approach his father and tell him of his fears; his father would then answer: "No, no, you are a great warrior, you can't be afraid." This short sequence may serve as a trace that can help us to understand how he was indirectly impelled, as a child, to escape progressively from reality: the patient seems to have learnt from his father that psychic reality can be denied and transformed.

There follows a small fragment from the analysis of Dario, who is now clinically free of the acute psychotic state and capable of often surprising intuitive observations. Here is a recent dream of his:

> I am at the cinema with some acquaintances. Suddenly I need to defecate and do so with great naturalness and pleasure on my seat. The film comes to an end and my acquaintances are about to leave, but some of them comment on the pong in the cinema. They mention the intense stink in general terms.

I am struck by the description of how naturally the patient defecated, like a little child, and as I think this, Dario comments that for him what was significant in the dream was that none of his acquaintances referred explicitly to what he had done; everyone only mentioned it allusively and indirectly. No one had asked him, "Why did you do it?", or said, "One doesn't do things like that!" For this reason, the atmosphere of the dream was very odd. The patient adds that now he understands that in the dream he has described his parents' behaviour: to avoid conflict with him, they

never spoke to him directly and never confronted him with his res-
ponsibilities. Through this behaviour, they failed to endow him
with a mental structure.

It seems to me that precisely this type of emotional "absence"
did not offer any kind of containment for Dario's omnipotence, thus
favouring his withdrawal into fantasy by not enabling him to
distinguish between the psychotic and healthy parts of himself. I
am convinced, too, that his withdrawal into fantasy and his parents'
lack of emotional response helped to make the patient incapable of
deciphering his own and others' psychic reality. For Dario, there is
always an "other" reality, which he does not understand and which
worries him, something that happens behind the visible world,
which he can only sense indirectly. His delusional construction
includes silent persons spying on his behaviour or intentions.

I am not claiming that the absent but intrusive parents—the
patient says they are unable to ask him direct questions, but are
nevertheless very curious to know about him—are the objects of the
persecutory delusion (the enemies who plant bugs to listen in on
him, spy on him with TV cameras, or tap his phone); but I do
believe that the parents' inscrutable attitude could have contributed
to the patient's conviction that, concealed behind the apparent reality, there is another that is apprehended by hypothetical and imaginary intuitions. This is one of the patient's "paranoid" notions, one
that comes up constantly in the analysis and is also reflected in the
transference.

Withdrawal as a psychopathological structure

John Steiner's stimulating book *Psychic Retreats* (1993) describes a
wide range of mechanisms for creating psychic states to protect the
subject from anxiety and pain. These retreats are mental places to
which the patient flees after severing contact with the analyst. In
Steiner's view, these retreats correspond to pathological organizations of the personality, conceived both as groups of defences and
as systems of powerfully structured object relationships that serve
to avoid contact with others and with reality.

A psychic retreat, whose purpose is to defend against paranoid–
schizoid and depressive anxieties, may assume various guises,

ranging from withdrawal into a romantic, fairy-tale world where everything is idealized, to masturbatory withdrawal characterized by pornographic excitation. For this author, pathological personality organizations act as medication for an ego damaged by the insults of reality and incapable of engaging in genuine reparative processes. While the pathological organization serves as a defence against anxiety, at the same time it protects the subject from depressive pain, allowing the experience of loss to be avoided. In particular, psychotic personality organizations act as a defence against the fragmentation anxiety that threatens a psychotic patient. The catastrophic nature of the anxiety is, in his view, the cause of the patient's extreme dependence on the pathological organization.

For Steiner (following Bion, 1967), the psychotic patient, in attempting to rid himself of a hated and feared reality, attacks the perceiving ego, the part of the psyche that has to do with the perception of psychic reality. This attack gives rise to fragmentation of the ego and of objects; the anxiety and confusion are so strong that the only means of opposing them is the psychotic organization, which is based on delusional and omnipotent forces.

Steiner also invokes Freud (1911c, 1924b) in his contention that psychosis is the consequence of an internal catastrophe whose outcome is disruption of the relationship between the ego and reality. The delusional psychotic retreat is thus seen as an extreme attempt to defend against this mental catastrophe. The patient idealizes the delusional world and represents it as a pleasant place, so that he can accept it as a refuge from the psychotic terror of disintegration and annihilation. The patient, says Steiner, can recognize that the retreat thus created is a mad one, a cruel and persecutory construction, but nevertheless prefers it to the anxiety he would experience outside. Indeed: "It is as if the patient has become accustomed and even addicted to the state of affairs in the retreat and gains a kind of perverse gratification from it" (Steiner, 1993, p. 12).

Steiner, it seems, is suggesting that psychosis is a two-stage process, involving, first, the ego catastrophe resulting from an attack on thought, followed by fragmentation anxiety; and, second, the attempt to construct a delusionally based retreat. My own view, however, is that psychotic withdrawal is a primitive event, established in early infancy when a child loses emotional contact with the mother. (Nacht and Racamier [1958] hold that, as children, these patients live in a world characterized by *artificiality*. Their families are often very formal. The child moulds himself to this relational pattern and develops a fantasy activity that absorbs not only his instinctual but also, and in particular, his emotional energies. Thus, he becomes a social automaton with a life that lacks genuine object relations.) Such children lack an experience capable of structuring the mind. As stated earlier, the psychological absence of the parents encourages withdrawal into an omnipotent world that becomes the forge in which the delusional structure is shaped, and this structure develops only later in all its grandiose and persecutory sequences. As contact with emotional and relational reality is progressively lost, withdrawal not only banishes the perception of the parental abandonment and emotional absence, but also creates a state of pleasure. Catastrophic anxiety appears later, when the pleasure of omnipotence has torn asunder the functions of thought.

Whereas Steiner suggests that the patient's isolation in the retreat is secondary to the psychotic catastrophe, I postulate that withdrawal, which begins in infancy, is, in fact, the condition that paves the way for the psychotic explosion. Psychosis is fuelled by the emotional detachment and dissociation from psychic reality in which the patient has lived for a prolonged period. Withdrawal is not only a measure adopted for protection from anxiety—from meaninglessness and the relational void—but also, and in particular, a place of pleasure in which the patient feels like a god who can create his own objects out of nothing. To ensure his continued existence, he must see that this place is kept secret, initially from his parents and, in analysis, from the analyst.

In withdrawal, psychic reality can be transformed at will, even into its opposite. By altering the order of perceptions, the patient can condition his senses so as to modify reality. (The psychotic patient who creates an omnipotent reality in which he can do anything he likes strongly resembles the perverted subject, who brings forth a world in which he can subvert the organization of human relations. In the same way as psychosis, the perverse transgression subverts the order of the internal affective world, giving rise to sexualized pleasure [De Masi, 1999].) Sooner or later, this seemingly pleasurable exercise, which resembles a mental drug, proves (self-) destructive and catastrophic because it triggers a mental explosion that overwhelms the patient himself: the urge to do violence to the mind by the drugged pursuit of pleasure ultimately attains a pitch of disruption from which there can be no return. Psychotic anxiety then emerges in all its intensity.

This diphasic process is tellingly illustrated by the case of Philippe, reported by Piera Aulagnier, as described below.

Philippe

In her book on the "apprentice historian and the master sorcerer", Aulagnier (1984) movingly describes the analytic treatment of Philippe, a patient who fled Paris and his two affectless parents and went to Peru, where he had an acute psychotic breakdown. Just before leaving, he had begun to use hallucinogenic drugs, which no doubt facilitated the onset of the psychotic episode.

Philippe's infantile withdrawal manifested itself very early on: at the age of four or five he took refuge in the attic, where he lay huddled under a camp bed, as though in a tunnel or cave, and where he was overcome from time to time with the fear of dying or of disappearing into the void. He spent the rest of his infancy secluded in his garden, having fantasies about one day becoming like butterflies, fascinated as he was by the lightness of their flight.

By making emotional facts incomprehensible to him, Philippe's family contributed enormously to his withdrawal. After Philippe reached the age of six, his father was repeatedly admitted to a psychiatric hospital and would then disappear from the family. His mother would never explain to her children where their father would end up, and in any case they never asked. In this way, a ban was imposed on understanding or interpreting what went on in the minds of adults.

Philippe had never thought of leaving France, but one day he met a young Peruvian and immediately became absolutely convinced that he must drop everything and go to Peru. Of his psychotic episode, he remembers the suffering inflicted by the "voices" that ordered him to kill himself, to make a dangerous leap that only a monkey could have successfully accomplished, and bundled him into a car that would "smash his bones to smithereens".

Philippe was quite unable to understand why all this happened; nor could he even be sure that the gods, whose intentions were conveyed by the voices, were taking some pleasure in it. The crisis occurred at Pucallpa, not far from Lima.

The patient tells the analyst that even now he hears a voice urging him to do away with himself. This voice, which rose to a peak of intensity at Pucallpa, continues to torment him. It is a delusional voice, which seeks to persuade him that if he plunges from a great height he will become immortal, like a Satan with wings. Philippe says he cannot remember why he ate a cactus called St Peter. He had gone searching for that plant and, picking a fruit, had covered his body with its sap and eaten the inside. This had caused his thoughts to disintegrate.

Aulagnier refers with great sensitivity to Philippe's wish to take the place of the saint who holds the keys to Paradise. The patient recognizes that by eating the cactus he wanted to ingest something that would make him like God, but, having also eaten the stone and covered his body with sap, he ended up with his head burst asunder.

The reader of Aulagnier's account will be struck by the delicacy with which she addresses Philippe, how she waits for him to trust her, how she tolerates his silences and mental absences, and, in particular, how she accepts his profound doubts about ever being able to make sense of his life. She accompanies him session by session as she seeks to confer intelligibility on the chaos resulting from his omnipotent exaltation (wanting to be like God) and his consequent lapse into destructive accusation.

This period of the analysis culminates in a dream, perhaps the first of the entire therapy, which is seemingly a precise description of the patient's recognition that the analyst has been capable of entering with him into the psychotic withdrawal and helped him to emerge from it. I shall report this dream in full.

> I don't know where I am, but probably it is Pucallpa. My elder sister arrives to take me back to France. I open the door of the place where we are and it opens on to a green space, half-garden and half-forest, in which every blade of grass, every leaf, every stem is topped by a little light of a wonderful colour. My sister stops, fascinated by the sight, and I read in her eyes that she now knows that I am right, that the world is exactly as I see it. But this doesn't stop her making me leave this marvellous place and return to France with her [or rather, Philippe adds, "to reality"].

Aulagnier asks Philippe what this dream might mean. He answers: "For the first time my sister could see my hallucinations with me. At the end of the day, I don't know if that's what they should be called, but she could see that it was my reality, which deserved to be seen." He now reports another image from the dream, in which he picks up from the ground a vaguely S-shaped object that one has to hold in front of one's eyes so as to see the tiny lights that illuminate the blades of grass, and lends this mini-instrument to his sister (Aulagnier, 1984, p. 134–135).

My own comment on Philippe's case would be as follows. I think that, mid-way between the dimension of a true dream and that of hallucination, in this dream Philippe is describing the exalted sensory fascination of his withdrawal. By allowing his sister to see his hallucinatory reality, an idealized, seductive reality that she, too, might not be able to resist, Philippe is enabling the analyst to enter his hallucinatory retreat. This might help him to develop a partial awareness of the nature of the delusional retreat. It is important that the analyst has, together with him, seen the other face of reality, without allowing herself to be dazzled in turn by the delusional fascination, but instead remaining capable of emerging from the hallucinatory withdrawal.

The dream transcribed above reminds me of something else that Philippe said right at the beginning of his therapy: "People believe in just one reality, but that's wrong. I know that there's another reality—the one that people don't want to see" (*ibid.*, p. 120–121, translated). It is essential for the patient to reach the point where he can *see* the psychotic construction: this dream material offers a precise description of psychotic functioning and its exciting and confusing power to overthrow the patient's mental health, but also a possible way out.

I have commented on Philippe's dream in order to emphasize that a patient can be analysed only if he is progressively made aware of his imprisonment in the delusional structure. The parts that have remained outside the system must be supported; they must be prevented from being attracted by the system, and helped to *see*. This is possible only at certain moments in the analysis, when the patient lets the analyst share his perceptions. Hence, the importance of steering the analytic work towards creating an awareness of the meaning of the psychotic organization, which tends to engulf the patient's self and destroy the sense of reality. The dismantling of the delusional retreat is, however, a long and complex process, owing to the tenacity with which the pathological organization constantly re-emerges and weaves its web anew.

Self-deception

According to one analytic theory of emotional trauma, the mother's inability to facilitate the child's development leaves areas of non-integration and fault lines in the construction of the self. The analyst should pay close attention to the patient's emotional problems so as to provide him with the necessary supporting environment for resumption of the "natural" developmental processes. Clinical experience shows that a halt in psychic development not only produces a void that needs to be filled, but also creates psycho-pathological structures.

I have increasingly come to believe that, in seriously ill patients, an essential element for analytic reflection is afforded by the study of the psychopathological structures, which are specific to each type of patient, that develop in the area which led to the faults in personal identity. One of these psychopathological structures is psychotic withdrawal. It can be postulated that, when the mother projects anxieties or wishes into a child's mind, he must defend against the intrusion by creating an inaccessible place. This retreat then becomes the only reality in which the child can feel free and protected from adult intrusions. Parental psychic absence and intrusiveness alike stimulate the child to remain in the retreat, cutting him off from the contact with emotional reality that is structured by constant receptive exchanges with significant adults. In extreme cases, withdrawal into the psychotic retreat becomes the only reality in which the patient can live.

Patients' anxiety is often aroused by the possibility that too rapid an approach to psychic reality—represented by the analyst—might deprive them of their world of fantasy, the only inhabitable world. The analytic process should contribute to restoring the consciousness of reality and creating the conditions for emergence from psychotic withdrawal (as in the case of Philippe described by Aulagnier).

Conceptualization of the withdrawal as self-deception which is conscious but of which the patient is unaware, implies that the analyst can potentially reach the patient in his psychotic withdrawal. This psychopathological construction, although linked to the character of the primary objects and their relationship with the patient, develops early and autonomously. In the course of analytic therapy, it must be identified and its genesis must be understood, so as to enable the patient to free himself from its sway.

CHAPTER TWELVE

Disturbance of identity in the psychotic process

> "A man who wants to lose his self discovers, indeed, the possibilities of human existence, which are infinite, as infinite as is creation. But the recovering of a new personality is as difficult—and as hopeless—as a new creation of the world"
>
> (Arendt, 1943, p. 63)

In this chapter I shall consider one of the fundamental aspects of the psychotic process: the transformation of identity that takes place during the course of the illness. This transformation has particular characteristics. The patient perceives that he has a new identity, with in some cases ideal, and in others frightening, traits, or that he has become someone else—a character of his own fantasy—but is unaware that he himself is responsible for this transformation. The new delusional identity appears to him as a revelation, as an incontrovertible truth that casts new light not only on the present but also on the past, which is revisited and adapted to match the new version of the facts.

Yet, this statement is only partially true, as a psychotic patient partly retains the perception of his lost identity. It is rather like Gregor Samsa in Kafka's "Metamorphosis", who perceives that he has been transformed into a monstrous insect, but "knows" that he is still Gregor Samsa.

Philip K. Dick

As a mature adult, Philip Dick, the famous American science fiction writer, has a psychotic episode. Having spent years immersed in the construction of extraterrestrial worlds, Dick is ultimately projected into that universe and his own characters. He himself puts it as follows:

> My God, my life—which is to say my 2–74/3–74 experience [the period of onset of the psychotic episode]—is exactly like the plot of any one of ten of my novels or stories. Even down to the fake memories & identity. I'm a protagonist from one of PKD's books . . . [Dick, quoted by Sutin, 1989, p. 234]

(I cannot here go into other aspects of Dick's delusional production or other possible contributory causes of the psychotic episode, such as the abuse of narcotic drugs, Pentothal, and vitamins.)

The psychotic episode takes the following form. Philip Dick has been suffering for some days after a tooth extraction. When the effect of Pentothal wears off, he telephones his doctor for a prescription for an oral painkiller. The medicine is delivered to his home by a woman wearing a necklace with a fish-shaped golden pendant. Dick is hypnotized by the sight of the golden fish. In his eyes, it represents a code that banishes oblivion and allows his intuition to unveil reality. Dick senses that the young woman is a secret Christian who has been sent to reveal his true identity to him, that of a Christian believer persecuted by the Roman emperor. Like many characters in his novels who believe they are living a life but discover that they belong to different civilizations, Dick feels that he is tearing asunder the veil that clouds the consciousness of men. He is living in the year 70 AD, and that is the truth. He must not defend himself with reassuring explanations; for instance, that what is happening to him is a hallucination. The danger stems from the agents of the Evil Empire who are trying to unmask him as a secret Christian so that they can persecute him.

In his books, Dick refers to the psychosis as his "anamnesis" and describes it as an unforgettable fact. To understand and rationalize it, he transposes it directly into his literary production, as in his book *Valis* (Dick, 1981). The works of his last period, which narrate his psychotic experience in the third person, show how the hallucinatory visions have become indelibly imprinted on his mind, forming a complex, protean amalgam in which true and false, perceptions and hallucinations merge into each other without boundaries. Dick has, in fact, thrust himself so far into unreality that he can no longer turn back and distinguish psychosis from reality.

Before the onset of the psychotic episode, the writer had planned a novel in which the truth was as perceived by Senatspräsident Schreber, whereas Freud, who attempted to interpret the madness of that perception, appeared as a mere reductive hack (Carrère, 1993). This idea, while artistically felicitous, betrays his fascination with psychosis even before his own experience of that state.

The unconscious roots of identity

To understand the transformations of identity that occur in the psychotic process, we need to know what factors keep the perception of personal identity constant in the normal situation. After all, we perceive our individuality as stable in time. Notwithstanding the changes and new experiences that constantly pervade our lives, we know that we are always the same. The functions that allow us to see ourselves as identical even in different contexts and at different times remain as yet unexplained. (Inquiring into the sense of identity and the perception of the continuity of existence, philosophers have reached widely differing conclusions. Certain basic positions can be discerned [Di Francesco, 1998; Sparti, 2000]. The first is naturalistic [Descartes], and perceives personal identity as a substance. According to the second, identity consists in psychological continuity [Locke]. The third [Hume] maintains that personal identity is indeterminate because it is composed of an unstable

238 VULNERABILITY TO PSYCHOSIS

connection between subjective experiences. The fourth perspective [Kant] traces identity back to a transcendental property of human beings. Finally, Wittgenstein and the linguists postulate an identity constructed through language. This last line of thought suggests the hypothesis that the psychotic process alters the linguistic structures, of which we are unaware, that underlie the sense of identity, which consequently becomes susceptible to transformation.) Psycho-analysts use terms such as the ego (Freud) or the self (Winnicott) to describe the structure that enables us to recognize ourselves as specific individuals. Winnicott (1965) was the first analyst to propose a genetic hypothesis of the self and to invoke an innate potential that develops in parallel with the mental functions. According to this hypothesis, at birth a child is endowed with a potential space from which the perception and awareness of the self will arise in favourable circumstances. The foundation of the self guarantees the sense of continuity and cohesion of the person: everything changes, but the internal thread that binds us together as ourselves remains the same. It may be postulated, therefore, that the foundations of individual consciousness are laid even before the birth of representation and of verbal thought, that is, prior to, and outside of, awareness.

Cohesion of the self

The constancy of the sense of reality, which underlies our security and mental well being, is based on the earliest relations with an adult capable of recognizing us and feeding back to us the meaning of our personal specificity. Fonagy, Target, Gergely, Allen, and Bate-man (2003) hold that the internalization of the parent's affective response enables a child to develop representations of his own mental state, and consequently to structure the nucleus of his own self as an intentional agent. In order to develop, a child needs a mind capable of accurately registering his feelings and intentions without invading him (especially where negative affective states are concerned). The mother must reflect the child's emotion and return it to him in such a way that he can internalize his emotional state, now enriched with meaning. It is important for the communication to take place in a way that signals to the child that what he is seeing is a reflection of his own feelings and not of the mother's. The parent's capacity to attribute intentionality to the child—to regard him as endowed with thoughts and wishes—is stated by these authors to be central to the establishment of the sense of identity.

These observations can be placed alongside the findings of the neuroscientists, who tell us that awareness depends on unconscious cognitive processes. In this connection, the neurosciences invoke *implicit aspects of the self*—aspects of what we are, which are unavailable to consciousness and by their nature inaccessible. The implicit or unconscious aspects of the self play an important part in giving shape to what we are and do. Implicit and explicit knowledge combine to form the perception of the unity of the self, which is never fixed once and for all. (The neurosciences postulate that brain activity is organized in a number of sub-systems which work together to perform a specific function. The products of these sub-systems, like the objects of perceptions and emotions, do not converge in specific cerebral locations. A particular site dedicated to conscious experience of the self has not been identified. As a result, many neuroscientists have concluded that the sense of self is a mere "illusion", and that *identity* is to the brain as the waveform is to seawater.) In other words, the emotional functions that permit the development of identity arise at the beginning of life, when the child's implicit emotional communications are understood and appropriately returned by the mother. The subject himself remains unaware of these processes, which contribute to the establishment of emotional symbolization and of a language suitable for signalling the affective states of the self. Where appropriate conditions for the constitution of these processes that lay the foundations of the self are lacking, the result is the development of pseudo-identities, imitative identities, or psychopathological structures destined to become manifest in later life (as illustrated in Chapter Eleven).

Disturbances of identity

Disturbances of personal identity differ in nature and gravity. It is important to distinguish a temporary lack of cohesion of the self due to trauma or the episodic emergence of unconscious anxieties, which can lead to transitory states of depersonalization, from the *identity disturbances present in severe pathologies*, in which the *conscious* sense of personal identity presents discontinuities and fractures. In many cases, the confusion extends also to the perception of the subject's sexual identity.

In the psychotic state, the change of identity develops in parallel with perceptual distortions that alter the subject's relationship with reality. Unlike the situation in an episode of depersonalization or derealization, once triggered, the alteration of perception escalates until the patient becomes the prisoner of his own story, which is projected into his virtual world. The perceptual change is tumultuous and unstoppable. The patient, like a sorcerer's apprentice, can no longer control the mechanism he has set in motion: the psychosis bombards his perceptual organs, giving rise to perceptions and visions that are felt to be revelations of reality and alter his sense of identity.

Eva, a patient aged about thirty, requests analysis. She describes her first psychotic episode, which occurred when she was eighteen. A highly intelligent and able pupil at school, she progressively distanced herself from her schoolmates and allowed herself to be taken over by a "dream", whose protagonist was a hit singer. Full of anxiety at the idea of a life without him, she spent all her time searching for him. The image of this singer became so utterly painful that she came to feel desperate and empty. The next step was that she herself became the singer she loved and worshipped. At this point she was admitted to hospital, diagnosed as suffering from a "dissociative syndrome".

This example shows that, by virtue of the mad wish to unite with an idealized fantasy companion, Eva ultimately exchanges her own identity for that of the idolized character. Perhaps she has never, in fact, had a personal identity, and has always lived in a virtual dimension. The delusional transformation of identity occurs when the imagination invades psychic reality and confuses the patient.

Projective identification

The process of alteration of identity in the psychotic state was first described by Melanie Klein (1946). In her view, a psychotic patient transforms his identity by projecting unwanted parts of his self into the object and identifying omnipotently with the envied aspects of the person on to whom the projection has been made.

On the basis of a story by Julien Green (1947), Klein (1955) tells how Fabien, who is depressed and unhappy, makes a pact with the Devil to enable him to transform himself into a different person. Before changing into his college president, a wealthy and seemingly happy old man, Fabien notes down the address of the house where he lives with his mother. He is worried at the possibility of total loss of his former identity, and of not being able to go back.

Having transformed himself into the college president, he notices that he has acquired not only the desirable but also the negative characteristics of this person: he has become an old man. So, he decides to exchange identities with an athletic youngster he meets in a bar, but always takes the precaution of slipping the address into his pocket before effecting the transformation. As he progressively enters into other admired and envied characters, Fabien realizes that he is increasingly losing the perception of his original identity, and becomes aware of the risk of finding himself permanently trapped in one of the persons into whom he has penetrated. This perception arouses anxiety when he discovers that the last young man whose identity he has assumed is a murderer who has killed his female partner. To escape arrest, he again becomes a different person, but begins to feel more and more uncomfortable and acutely claustrophobic. In order to recover his own lost identity, he must embark on a backward odyssey, returning in reverse order through the characters with whom he has exchanged identities. After a difficult experience of reconquest and integration of his self, in the end he recognizes his house, where he comes to from a faint, watched over by the mother from whom he has never separated.

Through the vicissitudes of Fabien, Melanie Klein describes the transformations of identity that take place in psychosis and their underlying mechanisms. The prime mover is envy of the admired qualities of the object and the wish to appropriate them for oneself in fantasy. The projection of parts of the self into the object impoverishes the personality, which may even be totally lost.

In Klein's view, the areas of psychic death observed in serious pathologies result from processes of emptying out and loss due to the massive use of the mechanism of projective identification. It seems to me, however, that the projective identification described by Klein is only one part of a more complex phenomenon of trans-formation at work in psychosis, for, in the delusional development, the *projective identification* (i.e., the transformation of identity) is not with real objects, even if these are only idealized or envied, but *with omnipotent characters created in fantasy*. At the time of onset of the psychosis, the patient has already long been immersed in a retreat populated with characters created in fantasy, with whom the pro-jective identification is successively undertaken. Where only projec-tive identification with an idealized or envied object is involved, the result is the formation of a false self, as actually occurs in the con-struction of the premorbid personalities of many patients who will eventually become psychotic. For the identity of a psychotic patient before he falls ill is constructed on imitative foundations, that is to say, by "stealing" parts of the personality of others.

The imaginary twin: Paolo (second part)

This situation is clearly illustrated by the case of Paolo, the patient described in Chapter Four. Long ago, Paolo created an imaginary twin called Peter, the musician with whom he is engaged in a perpetual dialogue. Peter has everything that Paolo aspires to: artis-tic success, the admiration of others ("a rock star"), and women and beer to his heart's content: a state of total pleasure. At first he invokes this figure from his illusory world in a seemingly separate dimension; subsequently, however, he becomes fascinated by the idea of being able to transform himself into his imaginary twin, thereby effecting a radical change of identity.

For the patient, Peter is a "vision" that fascinates and seduces him, a representation of omnipotence and pleasure. The projective identification is made not with a real person, but with this omnipo-tent fantasy figure constructed through the alteration of perceptual reality. By becoming Peter, Paolo ceases to be the poor lad who has seen his musical dream collapse and finds himself isolated from his mates, but turns into a figure ecstatically happy at his own success. On a certain level, the patient "knows" that complete iden-tification with Peter would be tantamount to going mad. By totally transforming his identity, he would lose his healthy self once and for all, but the attraction of this mental state is irresistible.

The other world: Chiara

As noted in the previous chapter, some children who lack a structuring emotional experience withdraw early on into an omnipotent fantasy world in which, adopting a new imaginary identity, they abolish their emotional competence, the competence that would enable them to understand psychic reality and thereby to re-establish contact with the world around them. The psychotic progression that leads to the transformation of identity is a process that develops in stages. In the first, the lack of a true self permits withdrawal into the world of fantasy, while, in the second, the patient is transformed into one of the characters he has created. In the absence of an identity of his own, the patient takes flight into a false identity, which subsequently proves to be a prison from which it is difficult to escape. Emergence from the delusion involves a disproportionate amount of suffering and anxiety owing to the void that has been created.

Chiara is a young girl who comes for an analytic consultation at the age of fifteen. (This material was brought to me in supervision by Dr Anna Migliozzi.) She is receiving medication following the onset of a psychotic illness more than a year ago, characterized by serious self-harm and the risk of suicide. Because she is obviously suffering from a psychological illness, her teachers have been compelled to recommend her removal from school. She feels an irresistible impulse to cut herself when she does not see herself as psychically alive, and to leap out of an upper-floor window when she imagines that other people are talking about her catastrophic identity. A pathological identification with a damaged, destructive figure underlies her self-harming impulses.

The psychotic breakdown is in fact only the last act of a withdrawal that has been ongoing for many years. In her first interview with her therapist, to whom she presents herself wearing a wide-brimmed hat and a pair of spectacles that obviously serve to mask and protect her, she unexpectedly opens up and talks about her sense of ill-being and the "other world in which she lives". In this fantasy world, in which she has spent much of her days for the last eight years, she is twenty-three years old, married, and has a twin brother and two children; the marriage having proved unhappy, she has separated from her husband and is currently living in England. This secret existence has gradually taken over as the difficulties of her life have made relations with others increasingly problematic. Even at home at mealtimes, she gets up from the table, leaves the room, and "goes off into the other world".

While telling the analyst this, Chiara is visibly terrified. The analyst tells her that she (the patient) is afraid of being robbed of her thoughts and her secret world, and adds that this fantasy world is responsible for distancing her from reality, something that has happened without anyone noticing it. Chiara corrects the therapist, saying that, for her, that world is her real life. She, Chiara, has never had a life. She has always felt abused and ill-treated, prepared to accept anything if only she is loved by someone. In subsequent interviews, she says she has always felt bad, inferior to other people. Yet, her mother keeps telling her that she was a happy, sociable child and fell ill only two years ago. This is one of the many points of disagreement with her mother, which depress her.

At the beginning of the therapy, Chiara brings along her diaries to the analyst, and in one session happens to read out a page on which she refers to the "other world": in it, she can use a secret language that is not accessible to her mother's intrusive curiosity, and it is only there that her life is truly her own. The idea of reading the diaries together with the therapist seems to be an act of trust on Chiara's part in the new analytic relationship. The therapist can thus share an experience excluded from the patient's communication with her parents, and analyst and patient can together understand how she came to immerse herself in a world separate from other people. After a few months' work, conditions whereby the patient can think of emerging from her retreat have been created.

I shall now present some clinical material to demonstrate the dramatic nature of emergence from psychotic withdrawal; it shows that the collapse of her secret world exposes Chiara to anxiety at the lack of an identity and the consequent impossibility of living in the real world. This session dates from eight months after the beginning of the therapy (at four sessions per week).

Patient: Hello; sorry, but I haven't even put on any make-up . . . The thing is, I'm crying all the time and there is no point . . . I can't get it together . . . I can't go on . . . I'm always thinking of this . . .

Analyst: Tell me . . .

Patient: . . . what I told you about on the phone . . . what shall I do . . . I'm all washed up, what shall I do . . .? As I said, I don't know what to do any more; I don't feel like becoming a cartoonist any longer [the patient spent a long time drawing cartoons] . . . I'm having terrible nightmares . . . in one of them, I was actually in an old hospital and talking to a boy who told me . . . well, I'll leave out the details . . . because it's too long . . .

Analyst: No, no . . . tell me the dream as calmly as you can.

Patient: Well . . . I don't know . . . I was in an old hospital and there was a boy who was telling me that he drew Japanese comics . . . and my parents were coming to see me . . . and I was talking, saying something to him, and then we chased each other over a stream and were flying . . . and I was stuck there, and then he taught me to fly . . . but what am I to do now . . .? What shall I do . . .? I used to think I would become a *manga* cartoonist, but now I don't know if it suits me . . . I don't know anything any more, and then I'm also fond of my family, I don't want to leave them . . . whereas before, I would have gone to Japan and not cared about them . . . and because I didn't feel anything for them, I would have managed the separation like this . . . zap! . . . But now, without my family . . . I don't know . . . how I can manage to go to Japan . . . I mean, I can't be a *mangaka* without going to Japan . . . I can't draw Sanshiro Square[1] without having seen it . . .

Analyst: Perhaps you mean that you feel more human if you miss your parents . . . Perhaps things don't seem as easy to you now as they were before in the fantasy world, or in your dream, where you can fly and you are far away from your parents. I think you're frightened by this new sensation now; you're terrified and feel you can't cope . . . as the dream shows, it's easy to fly . . . but then, if you notice it, you're in a hospital . . .

Patient (laughing):   Oh yes, that's right, but what kind of work shall I do? You must tell me what kind of job I should get; what shall I do, I haven't got a degree or a diploma . . . no, no way, I don't want to be a shop assistant . . . for heaven's sake, I respect what they do but it's not for me . . . I couldn't . . . no, for heaven's sake . . . I don't want to be a secretary . . . all the things I don't like . . . I can't follow the film . . . I went to see *Secret Window*—it's great . . . oh yes, I can't follow the film . . . it's half-way between *A Beautiful Mind* and *The Sixth Sense* . . . fantastic . . . it tells the story of someone who is a writer who gets into the plot of a book he is writing and then discovers that it's himself and that he has a split personality . . .

Analyst: I think you are obsessed with terror about not managing to lead a different life without the front you have erected for yourself; you feel naked and terrified . . . you've had to hide your reality from everyone from an early age, thinking you were a happy little girl who didn't cause problems and pleased everyone. You took shelter in your secret world, where you led all the lives you wanted to . . . like the writer who finds himself in the plot of the novel he is writing. That world was magic . . . now you feel full of anxiety and discouraged . . .

Patient (crying)   . . . I know I've always had to falsify everything, but . . . I was certain; now I don't like drawing any more . . . I'm fed up, a failure . . . what shall I do without a degree . . . what shall I do? You tell me . . .

Analyst: I think you want to slip right away into something that will shelter you from everything.

Patient (after a silence):   You see, I'm also afraid of disappointing you, because you're the only one who thinks I'm intelligent, and then if I don't succeed . . .

Analyst: You think I won't be able to stay near you when you are in difficulties . . . You seem to believe that success is the only road to being loved . . .

Patient: So I shouldn't hang myself after all . . .? That's impossible, but my only hope is that I won't wake up in the morning . . . every night I pray for it to be my last . . . before, at least I used to think I would work in Japan for 24 or 25 hours a day and have no time to think . . . if you make a mistake, you're done for.

Analyst: Just because you are dominated by a voice that tells you that mistakes are catastrophic and irreparable, you don't think you have anything you can build on.

Patient: You see, I think that if I had got into the world of comics, that would have allowed me not to think about real life, which frightens me, or about relationships . . . but what am I to do now instead? Do I have to learn all these things . . .?

I have reproduced this sequence from a session in full because it clearly shows the pain that accompanies the perception of psychic reality on emergence from delusional withdrawal. A difficult point in the analytic process comes when a psychotic patient eventually finds himself in a position to emerge from his delusional retreat and to confront psychic reality, but does not possess the appropriate instruments for doing so. To defend against depressive pain, the patient may be compelled to relapse into his former condition.

In this connection, what is particularly telling is the material of this session in which Chiara directly addresses the problems resulting from the collapse of her delusional world. When the delusional world loses its force, it is succeeded by anxiety at the possibility of falling into the void and the fear that there is no alternative to the delusion. In the dream, the patient, who is now out of the omnipotent world (flying far away from the parents or the fantasy idea of living inside the Japanese comic), sees herself as a psychotic little girl without parents, who has been admitted to an old hospital. To emerge from her confusional state, Chiara must be helped, among other things, to distinguish the mad from the healthy aspects of her personality. For instance, advantage could be taken of her skill and enthusiasm for drawing, but the patient does not want to start drawing again, for fear of relapsing into delusion. She is then persecuted by anxiety; she can neither "dream" nor project herself positively into the future. Chiara's therapy appears as a complex journey of reconstruction of her emotional world, with the aim of supplying a new foundation for the perception of her personal identity and its underlying functions.

Deficient awareness of reality

Bion points out that, by constructing his delusion, a psychotic patient at the same time deprives himself of the means of escaping from it. He writes,

> The patient feels imprisoned in the state of mind he has achieved, and unable to escape from it because he feels he lacks the apparatus of awareness of reality which is both the key to escape and the freedom itself to which he would escape. [1967, p. 51]

In other words, a psychotic patient becomes the prisoner of the false identities he has constructed because he no longer possesses the apparatus of awareness of reality, which is the only thing that could help him to construct a real identity.

The loss of the delusional identity leaves behind an anxiety-ridden void; emergence from psychotic withdrawal to confront psychic reality is experienced as catastrophic. Unlike dreams, in which it is possible to compare two simultaneous perceptions, conscious and unconscious, delusion obliterates unconscious knowledge. That is why the patient, having emerged from the delusion, is faced with severe depression. Because delusion destroys the roots of thought, he becomes incapable of understanding psychic reality. The painful realization of the self-deception in which he has lived for so long gives rise to a disorientation that pushes him back. For this reason, the analyst at work must be able to maintain within himself, and to convey proportionately and realistically to the psychotic patient, the hope that for him too a potential route to healthy development exists.

Note

1. Translator's note: There is a double meaning here: Sanshiro is an omnipotent Japanese fantasy character, but San Siro is a district of Milan where an important football stadium is located.

CHAPTER THIRTEEN

Trauma and psychosis

> "The aetiology common to the onset of a psychoneurosis and
> of a psychosis always remains the same. It consists in a frus-
> tration, a non-fulfilment, of one of those childhood wishes
> which are for ever undefeated and which are so deeply
> rooted in our phylogenetically determined organization"
>
> (Freud, 1924b, p. 151)

This chapter is concerned with the complex relationship between trauma and the psychotic state. After examining infantile emotional trauma as an experience conducive to the onset of illness in adult life, I shall discuss the traumatic effect of psychosis on the psyche, and, last, describe the inability to tolerate frustration in the psychotic state.

Emotional trauma

Maternal violence

Piera Aulagnier (1975) links psychotic illness to *maternal violence,* the violence practised in normal circumstances by a mother on her child to structure his reality sense. In the case of a psychotic patient, excessive violence has the effect of an intrusive action that creates an object with the same characteristics in the child's mind. To rid himself of the pressure of the intrusive object, the child must construct a self-representation contrary to the mother's will by violent methods. The violence inflicted by one mind on another is repeated in the analytic process: the patient feels compelled to believe in his delusion, and the analyst likewise feels invaded by a distorted and alien kind of thinking.

Aulagnier's considerations are consistent with the many observations of unwitting parental manipulation, where parents use their children as parts of themselves and thereby do violence to the infantile psyche. A possible hypothesis is that the persecutory delusion is rooted in the early experience of a child who finds that his conflictual emotions can emotionally destabilize a parent, who consequently turns on him with hate. The fact that the father or mother reacts with rage to the child's violent protests may give rise to a persecutory resonance of which he is unaware; in such a case, the conflict arouses the expectation of a vengeful response, as is observed in the persecutory delusion of the psychotic state. In this way, the parents' intentionality, whether conscious or unconscious, affects the child's growth, undermining his potential development.

The likely conditioning factor responsible for psychopathology will in this case be *emotional trauma*. In addition, the pathogenic parent–child relationship facilitates the formation of psychopathological structures or objects that continue to function as parts of the self or of the object.

To distinguish this traumatic action from an acute trauma such as, for example, sexual abuse, Anna Freud (1967) uses the term "psychopathological situation". However, *emotional trauma* is, in my view, a more appropriate description, because it defines as traumatic precisely the type of psychological violence that interferes with the early experiences out of which the perception of the self will be constructed. In patients whose mental structures are more developed and who are capable of representing infantile emotional traumas, these situations are often revealed in dreams in which the analyst appears as the traumatic object of the past. Although seemingly transference dreams, in fact they provide an excellent description of the nature of the relationship with the primary object.

Balint (1968), the Hungarian psychoanalyst who was a pupil of Ferenczi, describes in detail the early establishment of a traumatic action in the child and defines it as the *basic fault*—something that happens in the very first months of life and remains unintegrated in mental growth. The distorted mother–child situation is incorporated early on and begins to influence the child's psychological development.

Memory without awareness

Sandler and Sandler (1987) describe a *past unconscious* that contains events of which the subject is unaware and which cannot be recovered in memory. According to these authors, the *present unconscious*, which is structured later on the basis of emotional experiences that have been represented and subsequently repressed or forgotten, is that which is knowable through analytic experience. On the basis of this distinction, the concept of infantile amnesia which Freud invokes to explain the absence of memories of the first two or three years of life must be reconsidered. What is not and cannot be remembered precedes the appearance of repression; remembering is possible only after the development of the capacity to represent and register the meaning of an event. The hypotheses of Sandler and Sandler are substantially borne out by the neuroscientific discoveries concerning *implicit memory*—that is, the entire body of memories that have no access to consciousness. These inaccessible experiences eventually form part of the *unrepressed unconscious*.

It may be postulated that events of which we have no conscious memory, but which nevertheless determine our personality, must have been traumatic in nature. This hypothesis is upheld, among other authors, by Fonagy and co-authors (e.g., 1995, 2003), who assert in their many publications that borderline states have their origins in early traumas incorporated prior to the possibility of representing and understanding them. These traumas then become part of the structure of the personality. For this reason, borderline patients are incapable of mentalizing, so that they cannot understand their own and others' emotional states.

As stated in Chapter Four, my own view is that psychotic disorders affect the functioning of the emotional unconscious, which does not coincide with the dynamic unconscious described by

Freud. In my opinion, "trauma", which acts from the very begin-ning of life, interferes with the functions, of which the subject is unaware, that allow representation of psychic and emotional life, and results in the absence, from infancy on, of a mental structure suitable for understanding psychic reality. A possible metaphor for psychic life might be that of a complex organization that allows a dramatic production to be presented on stage. If the performance is to provide the audience with a comprehensible plot, there must be intense but invisible activity behind the scenes as a coherent support for the action. The actual events on stage are merely the epiphenomenon of a highly complex organization that remains largely anonymous. It is this behind-the-scenes activity that is impaired in psychosis.

Failure of containment

We owe this insight primarily to Bion (1967, 1992), who points out that, in order to develop, a child must have at his disposal a mind in which to project anxieties and needs. Only a mind capable of intuitive reception can give back to the infant the meaning of the projected experience in such a way that it can be understood, and can permit the introjection of an object able to stimulate psychic growth. Bion writes (1967, p. 106): "Projective identification makes it possible for him [the infant] to investigate his own feelings in a personality powerful enough to contain them". Trauma occurs in mother–child communication:

> Denial of the use of this mechanism, *either by refusal of the mother to serve as a repository for the infant's feelings*, or by hatred and envy of the patient who cannot allow the mother to exercise this function, leads to a destruction of the link between infant and breast and consequently to a severe disorder of the impulse to be curious on which all learning depends. The way is therefore prepared for a severe arrest of development. Furthermore, thanks to a denial of the main method open to the infant for dealing with his too-power-ful emotions, the conduct of emotional life, in any case a severe problem, becomes intolerable. Feelings of hatred are thereupon directed against all emotions including hatred itself, and against external reality which stimulates them. It is a short step from hatred of the emotions to hatred of life itself. [*ibid.*, my emphasis]

In his characteristic concise style, Bion condenses into these few lines the description of a process with a complex interlinked structure, which takes place in successive phases during the first years of life: the distortion of the first object relations is followed by later psychopathological processes which progressively alter the subject's perception and awareness of psychic reality. Whereas the ultimate cause lies in the factors that block the development of the functions of which the subject is unaware (the *emotional unconscious*), on which normal emotional functioning depends, one of the later stages in the psychotic development, which is probably always present in the process, is infantile withdrawal. As stated in Chapter Eleven, once mother–child communication breaks down, those destined to become psychotic enter the dissociated world of psychic withdrawal not only as a defence against the anxiety of the void, but also for the pleasure of experiencing an illusory self-sufficiency, an omnipotence that makes anything possible. The destruction of meaning that takes place in withdrawal increasingly distances the child from the possibility of learning from emotional experience, which is facilitated by the maternal presence, and generates a dependence on an omnipotent system based on false constructions.

Psychosis as trauma

Damage

Subsequent waves of devastation occur in the course of the psychotic process after the breakdown: the psychotic crisis has effects similar to those of an unbearable trauma. The massive trauma takes the form of a devastating action that can tear asunder the entity described by Freud as the protective shield against stimuli. The traumatic event exposes the subject to *nameless* terror, and gives rise to a fear of annihilation which, on the biological rather than the psychological level, can destructure the mind. In order for this destabilizing effect to occur, the trauma must be experienced in total solitude and impotence.

In Chapter Eight, discussing the difficulty of working through the psychotic episode analytically, I contended that this episode constitutes a catastrophic event for the mind. The memory of the psychotic breakdown tends to be blotted out as if it had never happened. As a result, the split-off delusional nucleus, like a trauma that cannot be worked through, remains forever active and cannot be "forgotten" or transformed. To avoid being invaded by psychotic anxiety, the patient must sever all direct or indirect psychic links to the psychotic episode; he must limit his capacity to think and to experience emotions, because emotions are likely to give rise to a repetition of the psychotic collapse.

According to Kraepelin's old definition, dementia praecox corresponds to a total incapacity to use thought and to maintain emotional contact owing to the defensive mutilations carried out by the psychotic patient. Benedetti (1980) defines schizophrenia as a *malady of negative existence*, by which he means that existence is reduced to the sensation of non-existence. This author considers that the term "negative existence" is closer to the patient's experience than the concepts of dissociation, fragmentation, or destructuring of the mind, which are commonly used to denote these mental states. After all, the final outcome of the psychotic process coincides with the permanent loss of the perception of personal identity and of the patient's own existence.

Destruction of the self

A surprising analogy exists between the state of non-existence experienced by chronically psychotic patients and that of concentration camp inmates subjected to psychic torture and abuse. It is no coincidence that the term *living dead* has been applied to the victims of the Nazi camps, transformed as they were into dehumanized automata. The psychotherapist Viktor Frankl, himself interned in such a camp, describes the loss of reality resulting from the total lack of hope and of a future in the following terms:

> Anything outside the barbed wire became remote—out of reach and, in a way, unreal. The events and people outside, all the normal life there, had a ghostly aspect for the prisoner. The outside life, that is, as much as he could see of it, appeared to him almost as it might have to a dead man who looked at it from another world. [Frankl, 1964, p. 71]

Sufferers from psychosis are aware that their illness corresponds to psychic death:

> [The others] were dead to me, and I dead to them, and yet with that painful apprehension of a dream, I was cut off from them by a charm, by a riddle I was every moment on the point of guessing. [Podvoll, 1990, p. 43]

These are the words of Perceval, whom I discussed in Chapter Three. Werbart and Linbom-Jakobson (2001), in their study of this analogy, state that both groups, prisoners and psychotic patients, live their lives in a universe of persecution, sadism, and terror. In other words, the analogy between irreparable trauma and the psychotic state is not merely metaphorical: psychosis has the same concrete effect as a prolonged catastrophic trauma. The traumatic anxiety accompanying the psychotic process results in loss of the symbolic universe and destruction of the self, as in extreme traumatic catastrophes.

Trauma and frustration

The bad object

In the eighth chapter of *Second Thoughts*, Bion (1967) states that thought arises out of frustration. A newborn confronted with the momentary unavailability of the breast has two alternatives: he can opt either to avoid the perception of its absence or to modify it. The second solution is possible only if the newborn is endowed with the capacity to endure frustration. In Bion's view, thought is the outcome of the combination of an idea and a negative experience. In the absence of the ability to tolerate frustration, what would have become a thought is transformed into a *bad object* that must be evacuated. The avoidance of reality is mediated by destructive attacks on the consciousness of the data of psychic reality. In the place of a negative realization (the absent breast), omnipotence is affirmed. The result of this operation is a failure to distinguish between true and false.

Bion contends that inability of a psychotic patient to learn from emotional experience has to do with the mother's difficulty in accepting and understanding the child's projective identifications, which operate realistically: that is to say, they transmit emotional realities that await understanding. Their purpose is to induce in the mother precisely the sensation that the newborn is unable to tolerate. In the absence of maternal receptivity, the newborn's rudimentary consciousness must itself assume the impossible task left unperformed by the incapable mother. The psychotic patient is therefore destined to carry with him the same incapacity as that of the maternal object.

According to Bion, in dealing with emotions a psychotic exhibits the same difficulties as he has in formulating the thoughts that ought to modify frustration. In the psyche, the emotions perform the same function as sense impressions do for the objects of external reality. The counterpart in subjective consciousness of consistency between the various sense impressions of objective knowledge is consensual emotional experience, which can be obtained only by the integration of conflicting feelings towards one and the same object. Psychotic patients are unable to achieve such an integration.

Inability to perceive emotions: Fabio

The following brief fragment of an analytic therapy is presented as an example of how the inability to perceive emotions and to understand psychic reality can cause a patient to relapse into psychosis. The victim of the crisis, occurring after three years of analysis, is a thirty-year-old patient whom I shall call Fabio.

Before his treatment began, Fabio had been admitted to hospital on account of a psychotic episode in which he had felt threatened by groups of criminals. The persecution had begun when, after regular visits to a local bar, Fabio had observed that certain individuals, who he said were gangsters, had started openly provoking him. Over the next few days, he had returned to the bar with the aim of challenging them. After this, Fabio's terror had increased exponentially, and he had become so anxious that he could no longer leave his home. Even while at home, he was unable to control the persecutors, who he claimed continued to attack him by chemical means (they had managed to poison the drinking water).

During his therapy, which had commenced six months after his discharge from hospital, the patient had said he had been a fearful child who found it difficult to attend nursery school; he was afraid of meeting other children and was particularly sensitive in relation to the lower-class little boys who lived in his district.

As an infant, Fabio had been cared for by his father, who had given him every privilege and regarded him as special. Fabio had grown up in his father's shadow and identified with him, whereas the personality of the mother, a conventional, dreary woman, had made no impression on him. Together with his father, he had dreamed of "shining" on the stage of life, and, as an adolescent, had enthusiastically engaged in individual sports such as judo and cycling, albeit without much success. What stimulated him most was identifying with his father, and dreaming of outdoing him and beating him in sporting activities. He had always been frightened by "bad" people or criminals, but thought that one day he would be able to take them on and intimidate them.

At the age of about twenty, he had attempted erotic advances to girls, but his encounters had proved disappointing and confused. These girls, who had often declared themselves willing to be with him, had tended to drop him very quickly, preferring the attractions of other men.

It became clear that no one had helped Fabio to overcome the persecutory anxieties that dated back to early infancy, and to acquire an identity of his own. The first two years of therapy had served to free him from the delusional persecutory anxiety that had led to his hospitalization. A substantial improvement had occurred during the treatment, enabling Fabio to relate better to his coevals and to resume the studies he had abandoned long before; in addition, he evidently wanted to overcome the emotional difficulties that had prevented him from having a girlfriend. About a month before the summer holidays at the end of his third year of analysis, Fabio reported that he had met a Greek girl who was studying in Italy. He was very pleased at the fond relationship that had arisen between them. This relationship clearly helped him to believe that he had finally become the equal of his fellows, all of whom had girlfriends.

Of course, even this new relationship was not immune from persecutory suspicion and anxiety. Sometimes, for example, he had thought that his girlfriend was late telephoning him because some envious enemy had persuaded her to leave him. Despite all the uncertainties, however, the relationship had flowered, and Fabio planned a trip to France with her during the holiday break in the analysis. Knowing the patient, I was not at all sure that he would be able to cope with the analytic hiatus without problems, and had therefore parted from him with considerable doubts as to how he would manage. Returning to analysis at the agreed time after the break, he told me that he had broken off the trip with his girlfriend and come home because he had felt ill. He had again felt persecuted: he was certain that there was a conspiracy against him in France and that the Greek girl was an agent of the group of persecutors. He had sensed that she was deceiving him sexually with persons unknown and that she had arranged with a restaurant waiter to poison him. This waiter, a Romanian, had said things that were obviously intended to harm him.

This time, realizing that his psychosis had returned, the patient had phoned home to his father, who had advised him to come back to Italy immediately. We had some difficulty in understanding Fabio's shift from the fond relationship with the girl to the delusional construction concerning her. He was even inclined to believe that she had seduced him before the holiday with the aim of marrying him and seizing his inheritance for herself, but all this was at variance with the girl's dismay on hearing his delusional confessions during the trip.

So what had happened, and why had the patient become delusional again? Fabio said that, before they left for their trip, he had noticed that, one evening when they were together with a friend of his, the friend had approached the girl in a state of obvious erotic excitement. It was clear to the patient that his friend had an erection. Afterwards, Fabio had dissociated this perception; he had not thought about it again, and they had left for their trip. While they were travelling, the vision of the girl turned on by the sight of the erect penis had begun to disturb him. Obsessed by this vision, he had begun to believe that, when she got up at night to go to the lavatory, it was for the purpose of a sexual assignation. When she slept, the position of her hands showed that she wanted to masturbate. Her cheating on him had then assumed a persecutory form: this was proved by the arrangement between his girlfriend and the waiter, who had displayed homicidal intentions towards him. Overcome by psychotic anxiety, Fabio had run away from the restaurant and telephoned his father.

Plainly, this new psychotic episode, which was more contained than its predecessor, had occurred when the patient had become involved in a new emotional experience. What did the conquest of the girl mean for Fabio? Reflecting on what had happened, Fabio said he was pleased with the experience of being in a relationship for the first time, but perhaps the whole thing had caused him to "expand". He remembered that, from a particular point on, the relationship with the girl had no longer felt like a personal experience, but instead like an enterprise that had caused him to "swell up". He mentioned a film in which the hero had arranged with his daughter to commit some fraudulent act, but who then discovered that she was in turn deceiving him, and was in cahoots with his psychiatrist. It now became obvious that Fabio himself was the fraudster, because he had altered his perception of himself along grandiose, narcissistic lines. We realized that the delusion of jealousy and persecution had been facilitated by a misunderstanding: his partner's aloofness had made him suspect that he was being deceived. Fabio recalled that, as his desire for her company became increasingly pressing before their trip, he had sensed that she was not especially happy to be alone with him all the time, but had preferred to see him together with other friends.

Fabio had certainly felt that his demand for intimacy had not been understood; but, equally obviously, this disappointment had wounded his megalomanic self. For this reason, he had thought that the girl was out to humiliate and deceive him. However, although endowed with new insight from his sessions, the patient was by no means prepared to agree with me that his experience had been delusional. Alongside the analytic reconstruction, the former delusional version persisted unaltered; the two versions did not exclude each other, and the delusion continued to be seen as real. And indeed, persisting in his delusional conviction, Fabio avoided seeing the girl again for fear of relapsing into psychosis.

To help him understand why he continued to believe in two incompatible realities, the delusional and the actual reality, I told him that, if he had been able to dream, the delusion of sexual jealousy might have appeared in the dream plot, and we could then have worked on it and thereby made his pre-holiday experience of exclusion meaningful. Instead, unable as he was to "dream" of frustration, Fabio had resorted to the delusion (a vision), which had then colonized him.

From another point of view, his success with the girl might perhaps have gone to his head, causing him to "expand" in such a way as to make him experience the conflicts and jealousy in a dimension of megalomania. All this had caused him to square up once again to the aggressive male figures of whom he had always been afraid. The fresh psychotic episode showed that Fabio had pushed himself too far in relation to the psychic capacity he had acquired. In particular, he had been unable to understand and endure the emotional frustration resulting from his relationship.

It was only after a long period of work that the patient became aware of his lack of insight into his own and his partner's feelings: he had not understood that, although sincerely fond of him, before the holiday she was still hesitating to entrust herself to him completely.

Surprisingly, much later when this situation was already long past, the patient produced a dream that seemed to enlighten him about the circumstances that had triggered the delusion several months earlier. In the dream, Fabio was at the wheel of a car and the Greek girl was sitting beside him. While busy with complex parking manoeuvres, he noticed that the girl was not only not help-ing him, but that her mind was actually elsewhere. In this dream, Fabio had been able to represent his perception of the girl's emotional distance, so that he was no longer compelled to resort to delusion.

On the basis of the analytic reconstruction of the delusional episode, the fresh crisis was manifestly triggered by the patient's wish to emerge from his emotional isolation, that is, by an attempt at progress. However, Fabio did not succeed in moving on, owing to his inability to tolerate and confer meaning on emotional frus-trations. At the time when the delusion was developing, Fabio's mind, in effect, lacked linked-up, differentiated spaces for thought, so that he was unable to keep together the complex emotions involved in the emotional relationship. In other words, he was unable to perform "dream work": that is, to deposit unpleasurable emotions into his unconscious awareness, to recognize conflictual and contradictory feelings, and to contain them. Identification with a megalomanic figure then paved the way for the development of destructive rage and for the transformation of the frustrating object into one that was bad and persecutory.

The traumatic character of an event is inversely proportional to the subject's capacity to tolerate frustration. This capacity varies with the subject's age, personality structure, history, and psychopathological state, that is, with the defences that have developed and are active at the relevant time. A patient in the psychotic state can be said to lack an apparatus for thinking thoughts that is capable of working through emotional frustration; in such a patient, *frustration and trauma coincide*. Whereas frustration is normally something unpleasant that can nevertheless be coped with (indeed, it stimulates learning and mental growth), in the psychotic state it becomes equivalent to trauma, and, as such, gives rise to regression and damage to psychic structures.

CHAPTER FOURTEEN

Some modes of entry into psychosis

"People kept thinking I was regaining my brilliance, but what I was really doing was retreating to simpler and simpler levels of thought"

(The words of Lawrence, a young schizophrenic, quoted in Nasar, 1998, p. 295)

The bat

In a classic paper entitled "What is it like to be a bat?", the philosopher Thomas Nagel (1974) writes that, if we try to imagine how *being a bat* must feel *to a bat*, we notice that our mind's resources are not equal to this task. Since every mental phenomenon is essentially bound up with one's personal point of view, it is not possible to imagine what the consciousness of self of a subject other than ourselves must be like. Nagel is not claiming that we cannot know what it is like to be a bat, but that, in order to *obtain an idea* of what it is like to be a bat, we must *adopt the viewpoint* of the bat. My purpose in citing Nagel is not so much to emphasize the intrinsically subjective character of every mental phenomenon as to draw attention to the distance between our subjective experi-ence and that of a psychotic patient, the "bat".

Attempting to gain insight into the process of transformation that eventually subverts the organization of the mind in the psychotic state is tantamount to trying to understand what it is like to be a bat. The attempt is conditional upon our bearing in mind the silent, sly mode of development of this process. Working with a patient who has been through a psychotic crisis is like venturing into a bombed-out village. Whereas we can observe the catastrophe, we remain in the dark as to its causes. It is only through a know-ledge of the events that led up to the disaster that we can under-stand why it occurred and formulate alternative strategies to prevent any repetition. Since psychotic patients are not usually able to furnish information on the psychotic process, it is only through acquaintance with the nature of this mental state that the therapist can confer meaning on psychic facts that are intrinsically expressed in a manner dissociated from awareness.

A knowledge of the most common pathways into psychosis will facilitate our understanding of the *route that may have been taken by a particular patient*. This will enable us also to predict how he is likely to respond during therapy in the event of similar emotional constellations to those that triggered the crisis.

The modes of entering into psychosis are relatively constant. Some have been described in the clinical cases presented in the previous chapters. I shall now try to illustrate some other typical modes, bearing in mind, as stated in Chapter Eleven, that the clin-ical manifestations of a manifest psychosis are always preceded by a long period of preparation that has accompanied the patient since infancy.

Sexualization

One of the ways in which a patient becomes psychotic is to enter into a sexualized state of mind. This process is also central to perversion. Whereas, in perversion, sexualization is limited to the area of fetishism, paedophilia, exhibitionism, or sadomasochism, in psychosis it invades the perceptual world in such a way that inter-personal relations assume a delusional sexualized dimension. In the psychotic state, sexualization takes the form of an excited entrap-ment of the mind that seduces the patient, who submits to it in total passivity. In such cases, it is important to apprehend the sexualiza-tion promptly when it appears in the clinical material, to prevent it from becoming potentiated and transformed into a delusional state.

The author who has best described the processes of sexualiza-tion in borderline and psychotic patients is Meltzer (1973). I myself have attempted to conceptualize these processes as a fundamental controlling aspect of the world of perversion (De Masi, 1999).

In Chapter Five, I described how Ada, travelling with her father, entered into a delusional sexualized dimension. Looking back on her delusion, this patient said that she had progressively convinced herself that the trip corresponded to an incestuous relationship and that the bedroom in which she slept with her father was a huge, sinful, red vagina. The analyst was consequently equated with a damaged mother and therefore feared.

Fabio (second part)

Fabio, the patient described in the previous chapter, brought dreams with a sexualized content to his analysis on resuming con-tact with his friends after the crisis.

> He dreams that he is watching a pornographic channel on television and masturbating. A childhood friend appears and is also turned on. Sitting beside them is an uncle who wants to watch a football match, and they invite him to view the pornographic film. The uncle refuses. A famous actress appears on the TV screen and strips off in front of the childhood friend, who watches her with an erection.

The dream clearly demonstrates the attraction of the sexualized state for Fabio, who is ultimately projected into the sexual "bubble" (the television screen). However, the part of himself represented by the uncle is unaffected by the power of the pornography. Interestingly, this dream has a very similar atmosphere to that of Ada, reported in Chapter Five, in which she sees her sexual organ opening up to the outside world and a winking alien appears and excites her sexually. It is worth noting that, some months after bringing dreams of this kind to his analysis, where they had been interpreted in detail, Fabio developed a delusion (described in the previous chapter) based on his sexualized state. In this delusional construction, the sexualized world, projected on to his presumed rival and his girlfriend, gradually became transformed into violent persecutory anxiety.

The seduction of madness: Laura

The main determinant of entry into psychosis is often a belief in the existence of a mental condition guaranteeing total pleasure. The patient attempts to achieve this beatific mental state and allows himself to be conquered without putting up any resistance. (An onset of this kind was exhibited by John Perceval [Chapter Three.) Even after "recovery", the patient retains a nostalgic memory of this condition and remains fascinated by the possibility of summoning it up again. As long as this attraction persists, he will be at risk of a fresh crisis. The analyst's work must focus on the nature and manner of operation of this seduction, in order to help the patient to develop an initial awareness of his attraction to psychosis.

I shall now present a fragment of an analytic therapy that illustrates this process. Before her analysis, Laura had had an erotic delusional episode centred on a young man of her age, who had been so horrified by the psychotic explosion that he had left her. (This case was brought in supervision by Dr Loris Zanin.) The session dates from a time when the patient, since improved, has met another man who has shown interest in her. This new relationship seems to her to be much less exciting than its predecessor; the patient often misses the "special sensations" she used to have with her former boyfriend. These "special sensations", however, in fact coincide with the attraction of lapsing once again into the psychotic state. In the session reported below, the fascination of madness is starting to become irresistible.

> Patient: I lent my book to C [the new boyfriend], but it's quite different from two years ago when I gave G [the object of the patient's erotic delusion] *The Little Prince*. That was full of symbols. *He* threw it down on the car's dashboard, but *I* think he understood perfectly what it meant.

Analyst: What did it mean?

Patient: I can't put it into words; it's faded away now . . . that's why I can't put it into words; I was already ill. With C, everything is normal. OK, sometimes we have the same thoughts or like the same things, but that special atmosphere is not there. I really miss those special sensations. I feel that C is always on my back. I can hardly draw breath; I just can't say no to him. He never ever tells me he is tired! He waits for *me* to tell him . . . C and I have been together, but that didn't give me any pleasure, as my mind was elsewhere. Tomorrow I'm going to buy myself a carnival costume and go to a party. It's really lovely. I like dressing up . . .

Analyst: You are attracted by the same sensations as you had when you were ill. Like that feeling [of making love "without touching each other"] you had that evening in the car with G—a state of excitement and fusion. You are swallowed up by this mental state, which makes the emotional contact with me and with C seem dull and colourless to you. You want to go to a party, change your identity, and immerse yourself in a new, exciting carnival.

Patient: But I felt understood by G . . .

Analyst: Maybe you felt you were inside his head for a few moments, putting yourself away in someone else's head. I think that, right now, being understood means going into that ecstatic state . . .

Patient: While you were talking about putting myself away in someone else's head, I remembered the time I felt bad here. Like with G, you told me to "wait"; you restrained me because there was this acceleration, and, lying here on the couch, I felt something: I could see a white light and a wall. If I had continued, I would have got smashed up, and I did get smashed up. It was the end, but I didn't change direction. I didn't know if I could do it in this room.

Analyst: You're telling me about the excitement that leads to psychic death, that was plunging you into a fresh crisis here in the session . . . it seemed like an irresistible force. You seemed to be conscious of it . . . but it was stronger than you were.

Patient: I can't put what I felt into words; perfection can't be put into words. I feel well when I'm ill and I feel ill when I'm well. I felt good because I was ill.

Analyst: You altered your mental state and got more and more turned on—and that was perfect, even though it was devastating.

Patient (very attentively):   Russian roulette is the same thing, it's the same feeling as bungee jumping—it's something where you know you won't die; it's a calculated risk, because your brain knows you're held by the cord. The most extreme thing in life is death: you throw yourself down with your body and your brain reacts as if . . . It's the same feeling as leaping into the void; it's like stopping one step before the extreme; what I felt was no different. It's the same thing with thoughts; I was lying down here and nothing could happen, but it felt like I could have smashed myself up against a wall. Smashing—the same word is used to describe nice things like bungee jumping; that's why I was laughing in the car as we approached N [a village near the town where she lives. She is now referring to a second breakdown, when she felt cold and was wearing a sweater even though it was August, and thought that G was chasing her in a police helicopter]. It was thrilling, and my nerves were all tensed up like the other time. But they didn't take me to A&E as an emergency. This business of thoughts chasing each other was—still is—like having another try at something I've already done that was counter-productive, as you suggested to me, even if it can be entertaining . . .

Analyst: Expensive and destructive entertainment.

Patient: Well, you know some thrills come at a price, but they are after all thrills . . .

In this brief sequence, Laura is obviously aware of the pleasure induced by the psychotic state; even if she senses that the result will be destructive, the allurement seems irresistible. The longing for that state of excitement strips her present life of all its attraction. The idealization of psychosis and the danger of a recurrence of this drugged state will not be easy to transform and will continue to fascinate this patient for a long time to come.

Grandiose persecution: Rino

I shall now present an extended extract from the case history of a patient whose attraction to the psychotic state is very obvious in his communications and "dreams", which for this reason are particularly useful for the purposes of observation and insight. Although this case is very different from Laura's, there are similarities between the two: once again, "bungee jumping"—the exciting plunge into the psychotic state—appears irresistible.

Rino, a male patient aged twenty, came to the analyst about four months after his first admission to hospital for a psychotic decompensation. (This material was presented to me in supervision by Dr Gabriella Giustino.) Before his hospitalization, he had exhibited persecutory delusional ideation accompanied by visual and auditory hallucinations of a persecutory and commanding nature, severe behavioural abnormalities, and fits of smashing everything in sight. The delusion had at first centred on the idea of persecution by members of a "gang" of young drug addicts (which Rino had joined some years earlier), who were subjecting him to terrible threats and physical violence. It had then assumed a more complex form, involving Mafia gangs and Islamic terrorists, until he ended up in the sights of Osama bin Laden.

Rino thought a specific episode had ushered in the actual onset of the delusion: it was a "challenge" thrown down by one of the "gang" members, who was standing outside his house with a girl whom he also fancied, and who had provoked him with a stare. Eventually Rino had in turn given him one of his "fluid-laden" stares, which was so intense that his challenger "had been subdued" and was forced to leave. The persecution had begun immediately after this episode, and Rino had attempted to run away to his uncle and aunt in Rome; they had then managed to bring him back to Milan and have him admitted to hospital.

The auditory hallucinations had initially been characterized both by good, protective voices (priests from his infant school or teachers) and by bad, satanic voices (gangsters, members of the Mafia, or criminals). The voices had become particularly threatening when they had almost convinced him, using Islamic terrorism as their mouthpiece, to kill himself by jumping from the balcony ("If you jump, at least you won't be recruited by the terrorists as a suicide bomber").

The decompensation had in fact been preceded by a period of addiction to drugs (LSD, cocaine, and trichloroethylene); two years earlier, Rino had ended up unconscious in his bedroom after inhaling an overdose of trichloroethylene. He was taken to hospital and treated for severe burns to his mouth and oesophagus. On discharge, he had gone into psychotherapy, but had broken it off almost immediately.

Rino's psychosis had probably begun at the age of about fifteen, when frustrations at school and in relationships had caused him to decide not "to always be the underdog", so that he had entered into the world of boxing and joined a group of "thugs" (drug addicts and petty pushers). After a period in which he had finally felt strong and capable of assuming a place in society, the challenges from various gang members had commenced, and Rino had felt he could not avoid them. At the same time, with a huge effort, he had succeeded in passing his school-leaving examination in classics and enrolled in the IT faculty, leading a kind of double life. By virtue of the difficulty he experienced in continuing his studies, coupled with the increasingly difficult part he had to keep up in the "gang", he had felt more and more lost, isolated, and "lacking a past".

Rino describes himself as an isolated child, often shut up in a feverish imaginary world populated by super-heroes and scenes from science fiction. Sometimes, on returning from school, to impress on his mother that he wanted to be left alone in his room, he would pull his cap down over his face. He would ask to be allowed to eat by himself when he was hungry, and his mother would acquiesce.

He devoured science fiction stories and comics. Particularly telling examples of his reading were Alberto the Wolf running away from Marta the Chicken, and a tale about a monster that emerged from its subterranean lair at night and ate up the village children (who had therefore banded together in a gang so that they could in turn kill the monster).

Rino is an only child. The father is described as good, but a "loser". Of his mother, he says, "She is often impulsive and irritable, but she soon gets over that." Rino is receiving treatment from the public health service, including medication: he is taking a new-generation antipsychotic. He is in the fourth month of therapy at three sessions a week; the persecution feelings are still so intense that he cannot venture outside the house alone. His father accompanies him to his sessions.

The following session dates from this fourth month of his therapy.

Patient: I feel a bit better. I've been out of the house. I went for a stroll to B. with my cousin. I met one of the "gang". I saw him in perspective and was less afraid of him. Actually, handling relations with other people, outside, always frightens me . . . it's the "wild-beast" side of the world.

Analyst: Yet you managed to see one of the gang "in perspective", and we know that the gang was part of the delusion . . . but I think you are telling me how difficult it is for you to handle the "wild-beast side" of life—that is, the cruelty and inhumanity you tend to see in the world . . . Perhaps, if you are less alone (with your cousin), it's less frightening?

Patient: Yes, I think so, but when they say *homo homini lupus*, what does that mean?

Analyst: It refers to a cruel aspect of life where, as you yourself say, "either you are on top or you are underneath"—but that's a limited, inhuman vision that can't fail to terrify you . . .

Patient: Unfortunately the experiences I have had are always like that . . . there came a time when I felt I had no past and I gravitated towards those circles—boxing, drug addicts, the gang. For a while it worked and I felt reasonably good, but then . . . I gradually got so isolated, and without a past, that I thought I was buried under a mountain of shit and that I had to do something . . . and then the delusion came—a vortex, a maelstrom, luring me towards another reality.

Analyst: Experiences of relating to other people, which were probably very frustrating to you although you didn't know why, and the lack of a secure sense of self, seem to have pushed you into joining the gang and the world of boxing, as if you were borrowing the thugs' identity. But the attempt failed, and seems to have caused such a sense of isolation and failure—the mountain of shit—that you were prepared to let yourself be seduced by the delusion if only you could then "be on top". As we know, the delusion held out the promise to you of becoming strong and potent, but then it turned into terrible persecution.

Patient: In the past I had stuck this sort of forceful identity on to myself, but then the challenges started. In the delusion, "being underneath" meant that the others could do what they liked with you and even penetrate inside you and possess you, so then you didn't even have yourself any more. I'm sorry I did that. That way I let myself be seduced by this power . . . I knew what I was doing . . . but I did it even so.

Analyst: I see that you can be sorry and realize that a delusion caused you to destroy your mind's contact with reality . . . and that you have paid a very high price for that.

Patient: Now you're telling me that the world is different from the world of the *Gangs of New York.*

Analyst: There, cruelty and the crushing of the weak reign supreme; people have to kill and massacre each other—it's a completely inhuman world.

Patient: I understand that this more human world you are telling me about exists . . . but I have no experience of it . . . for me, being good is tantamount to being weak and underneath; I too despise weak people.

Analyst: That's right: you don't yet have any experience of a world where it is possible to be both good and strong; that's inconceivable to you. Your idea is that, if you are good, you'll be buried under a mountain of shit. Then along comes the delusion, which promises you that you can do anything you like.

Patient: So in the delusion, I was prepared to do anything I liked with my mind, if only I could be on top. How did I manage to produce the hallucinations as well?

Analyst: The same way—by "being able to do anything with your mind", and altering your relationship with reality. I think that is the real harm you are afraid you have done.

Patient: Yes, the delusion really is very powerful; I must be careful, and do my best to recover the relationship with reality, to withstand the fateful attraction.

Another session, a month later:

Patient: Things are going quite well. During the holidays I went out and met a friend of mine. I even talked to him and managed to tell him something about my absence—along the lines of having had health problems—and he didn't ask too many questions; I managed OK.

Analyst: It's a good sign that you are managing to meet up with other people again to some extent; as we know, one of the things you are afraid of is being stigmatized as mad.

Patient: That's right, you know how it is, people are in a hurry and saddle you with things that you can then never get rid of. In the holidays I had a dream, it was actually a delusion-type dream, as I see it, like those you have when you are half asleep: I had to cross a bridge, and when I was half-way over I had a thrilling sense that I should leap into the void, of a force that was luring me to do so, but I stood up to it and reached the other side.

Analyst: It's a good dream: you resist the thrilling allures of the delusion and reach the other side.

Patient: Yes, but once I got to the other side I also felt tempted to turn back . . .

Analyst: That shows us how strong the attraction of the delusion can be, so that it can return.

Patient: But then I was more or less awake and controlled the whole thing.

Analyst: Maybe the better contact with reality . . .

Patient: Yes, that's how it was, I controlled the whole thing through reality. Then I had another delusion-type dream: someone I knew appeared before me, but then he got all twisted and I moved away.

Analyst: What was the twisting like?

Patient: Nothing . . . Basically, he was spewing out fire and flames.

Analyst: What a scary transformation, quite demon-like . . .

Patient: It was my Greek and philosopher teacher, a rather sly fellow who I tried to get the better of.

Analyst: And if he ends up underneath, as in the delusion, he gets his own back by becoming a terrible demon spewing out fire and flames . . .

Patient: Now I remember that after I met my friend I had another delusion-type dream: there was a kind of evil jousting contest, where people took turns to end up underneath. I was one of them, and if I was defeated I would be beaten to a pulp. The people in charge of the joust were my friend's mother and my doctor, who is also my dentist.

Analyst: How come it was your friend's mother?

Patient: She was a kind of witch, a nervy person; as for my dentist, we've already talked about him.

Analyst: You've said you found him sadistic and sly, and you felt enraged and impotent inside yourself while he was drilling your teeth . . . In the dream, once again we have the evil world of the delusion, the sadistic joust that got the better of you, which you constructed in your fantasy, and were afraid of being dominated by.

Patient: But there's something else: once I got the better of him with a look, one of my fluid-laden stares.

Analyst: So in the delusion he gets his own back and becomes your persecutor.

The above material reveals in outline the association of ideas that underlies the persecutory state. Since childhood the patient has evidently felt weak and ineffective—quite the opposite of the aggressive, bullying nature of the world. To defend against the feared violence, he set about constructing a kind of mental armour based on muscle power and, accepting the logic of the gang—some are underneath and some are on top; some suffer humiliation and others inflict it—he was able to challenge the bullies. This is the logic of *homo homini lupus*, which permeates the patient's persecutory vision: he cannot leave the house; his enemies are cruelty incarnate; and he is alone and unprotected. The psychotic fantasy has progressively eroded his faith in human relations.

Omnipotence, violence, and persecutory ideation

The background to the persecutory delusion is almost always the same. A powerful character, challenged to a conflict which then proves catastrophic, broods vengeance on the patient, who is guilty of an offence and of transgression. (The same scenario features in Arthur Schnitzler's *Dream Story* [1925], in which the protagonist, in the throes of a marital crisis, gets caught up in a tangled web of semi-delusional adventures. Filled with transgressive curiosity, he takes part in a secret organization's orgy and encounters a depraved, violent, and vengeful character who is out to kill him.) Infinite evil and the thirst for domination fuel Rino's persecutory world, so that he imagines he cannot survive the persecution. In this world, the petty local thugs are transformed into emissaries of Osama bin Laden. It all starts because Rino has challenged a member of the group who has "a character disorder" for the possession of a girl.

But the drama really began much earlier, when Rino used to go to the boxing gym to inflate his ego and challenge his enemies. With the collapse of the feeling of omnipotence that served to sedate his perception of weakness, the anxiety of being at the mercy of his enemies' cruelty emerged. The sequence *contest-for-domination* and *collapse-with-persecution* is commonly observed in the development of psychoses involving delusions of persecution. Considered in this light, the persecutor represents a violent part of the patient that is split off and projected into objects suitable for receiving the projection (in Rino's case, the local thugs).

The gaze

The arrogance with which Rino grew up gives rise to the subsequent sense of persecution, in which the human world is transformed into a place inhabited by wolves. The patient himself ends up at the mercy of the cruel system (an eye for an eye, a tooth for a tooth), which he himself has been nourishing for years.

In such cases, the gaze, or stare, plays an important part. Rino challenges and humiliates his rival with his stare. The rival in turn recognizes the aggressive intention and responds in kind. The power attributed to the gaze is a constant in delusions of persecution, as in the delusional experience of Senatspräsident Schreber. Steiner writes,

> Gaze plays an important part in Schreber's Memoirs. The gaze of others, often represented as divine rays in his delusions, was responsible for his humiliation, and his suffering was increased enormously when he felt himself to be observed "fallen so low", and mocked and looked down on. His own gaze was also important in his capacity to challenge authority and defend himself sometimes to triumph over powerful figures like Flechsig and even God. This capacity involved a delusional omnipotence and was strikingly demonstrated, for example in his capacity to out-gaze the sun whose rays went pale as a result. Gaze was also a means by which he was able to project into his objects and through which he believed his objects could project back into him. [2004, p. 276]

After some four months of therapy, Rino seems to be emerging from the psychotic state, which no longer appears to him as a seductive way out, but instead as a perilous risk. Anxiety at the possibility of a relapse into psychosis indicates that the healthy self is operational.

Patient: Last night I had a nightmare and then a vision when I woke up. I was very frightened. Actually I'd had a quarrel with my mother after she showed a lack of respect by bringing up some of the things the psychiatrists had said about me. So I dreamed that I had terrible tachycardia—like what I had in the delusion of persecution, when my heart was also beating like crazy. I touched my father, and he had the same tachycardia. It was very nasty. I woke up and saw a cut-off wolf's head; it then disappeared, but it frightened me. My mother told me that when I trashed the house, I was so mad that I had to be tied up and taken away by force. She provokes me. My father understands that it was something serious; I get on with him better.

Analyst: In the dream, your tachycardia unfortunately seems to infect your father too.

Patient: It was one of those terrible anxieties that I had in the delu-sion—the idea that I could infect other people with madness through the "fluid" . . .

Analyst: Perhaps you are afraid that no one can contain your tachy-cardia—the madness that can invade even your good objects. That fear makes you stay by yourself with your persecutory anxiety, in a cruel world in which the wild-beast image, the image of the wolf, stands out. It's the world where the logic of *homo homini lupus* reigns, and force in the sense of violent oppression rules. You seem to have been afraid in case this world were to invade you again, but you managed to put the madness into the dream. And in the dream, we can also see how it can return.

Patient: Yes, that must have been the meaning of the hallucination. Thank goodness it was quickly over, but it left me feeling disturbed. It was a hallucination, wasn't it?

Analyst: Yes, but let us consider how this mental state arose and where it came from.

Patient: All day long I had been telling myself: "You hold yourself back too much out of fear." Then I felt frustrated, and when my mother came out with this stuff about my being mad, I flew off the handle. Yes, I had felt frustrated all day because of my cowardice. I was also disap-pointed because my friend didn't come. He was connected with the gang, and so the challenge started all over again.

Analyst: Perhaps we can understand that the delusion and the destruction of the human world arise when you experience abandonment as a humiliation and annihilation of yourself. You then plunge into the inhuman world of "some are underneath and some are on top". Only this time, you seem to have had a perfectly rational fear of the cruel world, of the wolf with its head chopped off, which came up as a hallucination.

Patient: Now I feel a bit better. I really do feel very disturbed. The delusion is still so near. In the nightmare I felt somewhere between blood and muscles; I was out of joint—it was a terrible feeling.

Analyst: It certainly is terrible to destroy your own mind and to feel out of joint in your body. Another reason why you feel disturbed is that you are afraid the past might return, and cancel out all the work we have done.

The obvious improvement in this session is that Rino is anxious in case the psychosis returns and aware that rage, too, can impel him in that direction. The fear of the cut-off wolf's head, which tellingly condenses the wild-beast world that used to excite him, demonstrates his need for help. Rino does not want to be swallowed up anew by the pitiless world of psychosis.

Identification with destructive figures

The psychotic experience frequently includes an identification with destructive figures or objects, as is plainly illustrated by the clinical cases described in this book. For instance, Ada (Chapter Five) had identified with Lucifer, who is not only the light-bearing angel but can also challenge the power of God. The identification with an evil figure is often followed by accusations and a sense of guilt so intense as to impel the patient to commit suicide. Ada had been admitted to hospital after a clumsy attempt to suffocate herself, while Alvise (Chapter Six) had jumped off a flyover when he felt "diabolical". The destructive superego first causes the patient to idealize violence and then attacks him, presenting him with suicide as the only way out of persecution and guilt.

We shall now see how such a psychotic identification recurs, again in one of Rino's sessions, and how it can be contained by analytic intervention. As stated earlier, before his therapy Rino had been colonized by voices that told him to take his own life because he had not volunteered as a suicide bomber for Osama bin Laden. The destructive voices were connected with the earlier pathological identification with criminal figures.

> Patient: Things are going quite well, except that I infected my friend with flu. Now I feel a bit better, but yesterday . . . I felt quite a bit of anxiety, because I had got into some arguments. Fortunately I managed to stay calm. It gradually wore off. (He then turned to other, trivial matters.)
>
> Analyst: Was the anxiety about "other kinds" of infection?
>
> Patient: No, no, fortunately my friend didn't know I had flu, and so I managed all right. I don't really know why I got anxious.
>
> Analyst: Let's try and reconstruct it together. So there had been some "arguments"—what were they about? (The patient has difficulty in speaking, or is afraid to speak.) What happened with your friend?
>
> Patient: I remain in his shadow. I let him do things. Then I can stay calm. He behaves in a certain way and I follow him.
>
> Analyst: I think it's simpler for you to imitate a model, otherwise you feel lost.
>
> Patient: My father isn't a model; with him I feel unsure. With my friend, on the other hand . . . he has a very precise style.
>
> Analyst: You sort of "lean" on the identity of someone else who seems to you to be a winner, and secure. Like what happened in the past when you searched for identity in the gang, with strong men, in boxing.
>
> Patient: That's absolutely right. By the way, I heard that this guy—the one with the girl, you know, the challenge—after she left him, he went to her house and went berserk outside; the police came and, basically, he was warned to keep away from me.
>
> Analyst (seeing a kind of triumph in his eyes):   Could it be that the "arguments" you "got into" have to do with him?
>
> Patient: Yes, that's how it was. I started arguing and then I got confused; I was going much too far, but fortunately I stopped.
>
> Analyst: When you say "confused", do you mean that there was a confusion between you and your friend?

Patient: That's exactly it; I had become him—a nasty business, I was starting to get delusional again.

Analyst: But this time you managed to put a stop to the anxiety. You imagine you are getting inside your friend and becoming him. Getting inside another person is something very thrilling: anything is then possible. But then you feel persecuted.

Patient: Yes, because you expand, and then it's all over, because the delusion gets going: anything is possible, but then the other person can also get inside.

Analyst: Exactly, that's what the persecution is about. You lose your identity and your personal space and the other person can do what he likes with you—a terrible punishment for having "expanded".

Patient: And then you lose contact with reality. But does the anxiety warn me?

This session clearly shows that the attempt to improve tends to pass back over the same stages that led the patient into psychosis. Rino admires his friend because, unlike his father, he appears to him secure and dominant; he believes he can absorb his qualities by stealing them from him. By means of projective identification (Klein, 1955), he tries to assume a false identity, which may seem to him to be workable, but which in reality stands in the way of his developing a true identity. After identifying with the admired character, Rino repeats the same operation with the bad, criminal character, his "friend" from the past. Having become him (like Fabien in Julien Green's *If I Were You*), Rino is afraid of infecting others with his destructiveness. That is how we should understand Rino's initial communication to his analyst about the flu he is afraid of giving to his friend.

Destructive narcissism

In identifying with destructive figures, the psychotic nucleus proceeds along the lines described by Rosenfeld (1971) in relation to *destructive narcissism*. For example, when Alvise, the patient described in Chapter Six, hears "voices" telling him to attack me in his session, he has been completely colonized by the destructive nucleus. Once the transformation has taken place, the patient cannot tolerate being wholly bad. Chiara (Chapter Twelve) physically cuts herself or considers throwing herself from a window when she feels trapped in a totally bad or failed identity. In other cases, by contrast, a patient colonized by the destructive part enjoys being bad.

Gerardo, a ten-year-old boy (who was treated by Dr Anna Migliozzi), comes for analytic therapy because he has stopped eating and wants to die. He has difficulty falling asleep because he is afraid that his parents might poison him. In the first few months of sessions, he is terrified of people; he is afraid of being left alone with the analyst, spits, yells, and often masturbates. He eventually confesses that he wants to let himself die because he feels responsible for all kinds of wickedness that he cannot talk openly about. He says he will go to a village for bad children (he mentions places that sound like faecal cavities, where children are shut up and punished for their wickedness), and will then return changed into a good boy.

Gerardo manifestly feels colonized by a destructive superego that wants him dead because of his wickedness. When his grandfather dies, he is afraid of being accused of having killed him. In one session, he acts out a scene in which there are a number of children; he invites the analyst to take him in her arms, and then jumps on her, touching her excitedly and telling her "I love you." In the scene, the analyst is supposed to put the children to bed and then go to sleep with them. When she has fallen asleep, Gerardo will kidnap the little children and enjoy seeing her despair when she wakes up.

This child has totally identified with a bad figure who enjoys destruction, stealing, or making people unhappy. He feels utterly depressed and miserable because he is under the yoke of the destructive narcissistic part, which persecutes him and threatens him with death.

Psychotic transformation of the superego

Nilde is twenty-six years old and married to a teacher; she herself teaches in a secondary school. Lately, the presence in her class of children with severe behavioural disorders—unruly, provocative children who often threaten their fellow pupils or the staff—has made her work particularly difficult. Teaching has always been her dream, but behind this educational aspiration lies concealed the grandiose fantasy of becoming a perfect teacher, a kind of latter-day Maria Montessori.

In her second year at this school, Nilde works with a new colleague, whom she at first sees as resembling herself in his sensitivity and interest in the children and the school. Owing to her problems in the relationship with the difficult pupils (every day violent episodes take place in class and make it impossible to proceed with the syllabus), her new colleague's criticisms and sarcasm, and pressure from the principal, who is concerned about problems of discipline, the patient loses control of her class and feels humiliated at her failure. At this point, she begins to fear that she might be accused and criticized by the whole village. A sadistic superego, projected into the children and her colleagues, and in particular the colleague whom she had initially idealized, observes her implacably, penetrates the walls of her house, and breaches her computer's security systems. She receives constant "concealed messages" from her enemies, threatening and ridiculing her, or from friends who want to help her. She is accused of incompetence as a teacher: she has made mistakes and can be reported to the authorities because she has not completed the syllabuses and has been unable to impose discipline on the pupils. Specifically, one of the pupils, with whom the patient has taken a great deal of trouble (so much so that he almost seems like a sick self of her own), played, and continues to play, an important part in her persecution. Although this pupil at first had a good relationship with her, instead of improving he became an utter thug and was expelled from the school. Nilde feels controlled; she is afraid that bugs have been planted to listen in on what she and her husband say to each other. She fears that she is being observed through the bathroom mirror, and being recorded so that she can be ridiculed; she hears people talking about her and her failure.

The second child in the family, Nilde was an introverted girl who always played by herself. Growing up in the shadow of her brother, an able student ten years her senior, she had taken his place with the mother when he left home to marry. She had become the leading spirit in the family, cast in the role of the person who listens and gives advice, already deemed wise before having had any experience of life. The relationship between Nilde and her mother was described as "marvellous and very trusting". In reality, the therapy was to reveal that her mother exerted great control over her.

She describes her family as having been very strict. The mother was a severe woman who could "turn one to ashes simply with a look" when she wanted to teach her what was right and what was wrong. She and her brother, the patient recalls, had to be aware of the boundaries they must not cross. The mother's severity had perhaps been partly dictated by the need to stand in for an absent father, who was seen as a "scatterbrain, quite unsuited to bringing up children". In her family, the strong ones, able to confront life, had been the women. Her mother had brought up her children by herself; the grandmother had done the same with her children because the grandfather had emigrated; and during the war an aunt had performed heroic deeds to defend the whole family. Nilde passed her university examinations with flying colours, but decided not to pursue an academic life because she wanted to teach.

Nilde's psychotic crisis, in my view, stems from the failure of her grandiose educational project. The superego that seduced her exposed her, after her failure, to derision. This superego results from a pathological identification with the idealized figure of the mother and of the women in the family. The idea of "having to be clever and succeeding" on pain of losing her mother's love and respect seems to have weighed heavily on her growth, to the detriment of her understanding of psychic reality. At the moment of the presumed failure, the ideal superego is transformed into a contemptuous entity, thus exhibiting the other face of narcissism; it is also projected into the external environment, and precisely into the objects that ought to have borne witness to her success (the colleague and the boy she took under her wing).

Putting herself into the minds of others as an ideal object, her mother's and the family's special girl, was the natural preliminary to her subsequent fall. For eventually the superego voices became "sadistic", impelling Nilde to feel attacked. A psychotic mechanism projectively potentiated the exposure to humiliation: her life was now lived in public, she no longer had any intimacy, and her personal space was constantly violated.

One may wonder whether this person ever had a personal space, and whether she had ever constructed an internal world of her own before falling ill. The existence of a narcissistic superego that prevented the development of her identity may be responsible for some of the aspects of Nilde's entry into the psychotic state. She actually wanted not so much to develop relationships with the pupils or to educate them, as to be special, a latter-day Montessori. The superego, which sustained the patient in her ascent towards the state of superiority, has shattered and, projected into tiny, omnipresent, persecutory fragments, is now tormenting her.

CHAPTER FIFTEEN

Concluding remarks

"But there is much we can do in future. It is only by understanding our problems, difficulties, and failures in treating
schizophrenia and other psychotic conditions that we can
gradually achieve greater success"

(Rosenfeld, 1997, p. 23)

I have sought in this book to make clear my conviction that the
difficulties experienced in the treatment of psychotic patients
are due not only to our individual professional limitations,
which in any case emerge in the constant process of comparison
with colleagues, but also to the intrinsic incompatibility of the
psychotic state with the traditional analytic approach. This situation discourages many analysts from taking patients with these
symptoms into therapy.

My own view, however, is that as analysts we are in a privileged
position: that of listening, session after session, to a psychotic
patient who continues to place his trust in our method. No other
clinician has the same opportunity of learning directly from someone, like a patient with this pathology, who has entered the world

of psychosis and can help us to understand it. On commencing the therapy of such patients, we should first and foremost bear in mind the need to forget the route followed by the "average" analysand, and instead prepare ourselves for an unpredictable analytic development, often interspersed with crises that may cause the treatment to be broken off. Sometimes these very crises can prove useful, because they compel us to turn back and try to understand what we have failed to comprehend. When the therapy is broken off, as frequently occurs in such cases, this provides us with an opportunity of gaining further significant knowledge.

The consistent thread that links the chapters of this book is the *specificity of the psychotic state*. It is my conviction that the analytic method, which combines therapy and research (Freud's *Junktim*), is essential to the investigation not only of neurosis but also of the psychotic state, even if the criteria for understanding will differ from those applied to other forms of mental suffering. The laws of unconscious thought discovered by psychoanalysis concern the functioning of *unconscious psychic reality* (with its mechanisms such as repression, unconscious conflict, symbolic transformation, or the phases of infantile sexuality), which is absent in the psychotic state. In my view, the traditional analytic categories of the dynamic unconscious do not enable us to apprehend the specific nature of the illness and its seemingly bizarre and mysterious manner of expression. It is only by forgoing the known as the basis of our approach that we can extend our knowledge and help the patient to find the road to recovery. In other words, we must be able to proceed in the same way as a physicist studying the atom, who does not seek to apply the laws of mechanical physics because he knows that the phenomena he is dealing with belong in a completely different realm.

Just as Freud initially regarded the transference as an obstacle but later saw it as a factor of change, so we must consider the appearance in analysis of psychotic functioning, with its constant transformations and risks, as a *normal event* in the course of therapy and a key to the possible resolution of the therapeutic process.

In Chapter Four, I expressed the view that the psychotic state stems from damage to the functions, of which the subject is unaware, which are necessary for the maintenance of psychic life and which belong to the *emotional unconscious*. These functions, which are structured with the earliest mother–child relations, are essential to the working of the *dynamic unconscious*. Damage to the emotional unconscious constitutes an obstacle to the operation of the dynamic unconscious, preventing the use of repression. For this reason, psychotic disorders are situated on a different level from pathology of the dynamic unconscious, the exploration of which has permitted exhaustive clarification of the origin of neurosis. In the course of therapy, it is quickly found that these patients lack the capacity for intuition and emotion. As a result, they are unable to understand their own mental processes, and their dreams appear bizarre and meaningless.

What, then, are the essential points to which particular attention must be devoted in analytic therapy of the psychotic state? The first, as just stated, is the radical difference between psychotic and neurotic functioning. To avoid misunderstandings, for instance, concerning the notion that we all have moments of psychotic functioning, I have, except where necessary in referring to cited authors, avoided the use in this book of the term *psychotic part* as opposed to the *neurotic part* of the personality. In clinical case descriptions, I have emphasized that the patients in question are either *clinically psychotic* or, if not yet so, already satisfy all the preconditions for entering into that state.

For the purposes of therapy, it is important first of all to identify the *specific structure* that underlies the psychotic state. According to Kleinian theory, psychosis results from an excess of primitive defences and anxieties. Although this hypothesis may be true in general terms, it is, in my view, inadequate on the specific level. Invoking primitive defences does not help us to understand why the patient goes into the psychotic state or why, on the other hand, many patients who resort to primitive defences are not definable as psychotic. A psychotic not only uses primitive defences characteristic of the paranoid–schizoid position, but also forms structures that cause him to deviate from normal development. In my opinion, the term *psychopathological construction* is a better description of the progression towards illness than that of defence. In Chapter Eleven, I considered in depth the dynamic significance of *psychotic withdrawal*, and postulated that this structure facilitates early dissociation from emotional reality and paves the way for illness.

Another hypothesis put forward in this book concerns the origin of anxieties, which are a constant source of terror even after the acute crisis. I contend that persecutory anxiety is preceded by a grandiose state, and that when this collapses, the subjective condition of passivity and persecution arises. Anxiety that the subject's life is in danger now develops quickly by way of associations based on contiguity, assonance, or similarity.

In some respects, the development of anxiety in a psychotic crisis resembles that of a panic attack. In both cases the protective shield against stimuli is broken down, and the danger of death is perceived as real. Psychotic anxiety is truly devastating in character. My own view is that our mental apparatus becomes destructured, sometimes permanently, when it experiences the level of terror attained in the psychotic process. For this reason, psychosis constitutes in itself an emotional trauma that is bound to damage the mental apparatus. Neuroscientific research, which has demonstrated the role of the amygdala and of the primitive (subcortical) fear circuit (LeDoux, 1996, 2002), can perhaps help us to understand the damage wrought by psychotic anxiety. Excessive activation of the amygdala has been shown to interfere with the functions of attention, perception, and memory, as well as with decision-making processes. Another finding is that when the primitive fear circuit (which can be associated only secondarily with the conscious cortical pathways) is overstimulated, a vicious circle arises in which terror is potentiated by the combination of associatively linked stimuli. In the psychotic state, words themselves forfeit their symbolic meaning and become concrete stimuli that reactivate psychotic anxiety even when the crisis is long past. These findings suggest that the frequent past view of psychosis as a form of primitive mental functioning should be seen in a new light. Psychosis is, in fact, not so much the product of regression to a primitive mental state as a catastrophic distortion of emotional experience.

Even if it is for a long time difficult to gain access to a patient's psychotic functioning, it is essential to work on the delusional nucleus. How can the patient help us to get in touch with the madness that constantly threatens or seduces him? In Chapter Five I demonstrated the importance of certain dreams for the understanding of psychotic functioning. I suggested that we must learn to recognize the communicative significance of these dreams because they sometimes reveal how a fresh crisis is being prepared. In Chapter Eight, I proposed that a distinction be drawn between *dreams-as-thought* and *dreams-as-delusion*. The latter type do not lend themselves to symbolic interpretation because they do not carry within them either a latent content or a transference meaning. Interpreting such a dream in this sense would be a serious mistake, replete with negative consequences.

The outbreak of a psychotic crisis leaves behind indelible traces and calls for a difficult process of reconstruction. It must never be forgotten that, once the crisis has occurred, the psychotic nucleus remains like a plant whose stem has been cut off but which retains solid roots in the soil. For this reason, it is desirable to work with patients in infancy or adolescence if signs are already present which, should they go unrecognized, will lead to a much more severe crisis in adulthood.

The therapeutic task is rendered difficult by a large number of factors. *Vis-à-vis* the rest of the personality, the psychotic nucleus acts like a constantly proliferating cancerous metastasis. For this reason, to avoid relapses the psychotic functioning must be analysed in detail; in other words, it is essential to return unremittingly to the manner in which the delusion arose and how it tends secretly to regenerate. Another risk in therapy is that the delusional part of the patient may collude with the healthy part. Reticence is never a good sign, but in fact often proves to be the determinant of further relapses. In Chapter Six, I described a long analysis which was suddenly compromised by a new and devastating psychotic episode.

A patient's resistance to working on his past psychotic crisis can be explained in various ways. Just as it is difficult for the survivor of a catastrophe to relive the terror and senselessness of the violence sustained, so it is for a psychotic patient when he has to turn back in memory and re-experience the catastrophic impact of his mad thoughts. If the analyst wishes to share the psychotic crisis with him, he must exercise caution and sensitivity in approaching areas of suffering that cannot easily be confronted.

The impossibility of remembering is due not only to pain but also to fear. Thinking back over the crisis involves stimulation of the same imagination that gives rise to delusion and could once again invade the patient. Even many years later, when seemingly overcome, the illness takes the form of an invading magma, likely at any time to call into question the equilibrium so laboriously attained. Moreover, it is not only a matter of fear. Perhaps even more tempting is fascination, where the psychotic crisis was experienced as an ecstatic illumination. The patient's acquiescence in the recurrence of the delusion is explained by the attraction of the psychotic nucleus. In Chapter Three, I discussed the case of John Perceval and mentioned the need to adopt an active position to counter the seductive offerings of the "voices". The frequent assertion that delusion manifests itself in the form of an insight presented with great clarity, so that it is immediately accepted by the patient, is false. It does not reflect the actual state of affairs. As explained in Chapter Thirteen, a delusion does not spring ready formed like Minerva from the head of Jove, but is prepared by a series of associative nexuses. These signals are at first disregarded; they are ignored, or rather split off from awareness. It is only at a second stage that they become visible, because they appear in a seemingly coherent sequence. Once a critical point is reached, the microtransformations "suddenly" converge in the delusional enlightenment.

If we really were convinced that analytic change takes place exclusively or predominantly by way of transference interpretation, as first suggested by Freud and subsequently maintained by other authors (in particular, Strachey [1934]), the conclusion would have to be that improvement is not possible for a psychotic patient. Since the development of the transference depends on the possibility of using symbolic thought and on the potential availability of unconscious memories of the past, and since these conditions are not satisfied in the psychotic state, it is illegitimate to use this term to refer to the delusional relationship with the analyst. This is also the position of Margaret Little (1958), who calls this type of transference "delusional" or "psychotic". This author considers that psychotic patients not only do not accept transference interpretations, but also differ *qualitatively* and not quantitatively from other patients.

Each patient has specific *psychotic islands*, which are reactivated by an improving trend. For this reason, the analysis of such patients does not follow a linear path, and every movement towards the recovery of vitality carries the risk of relapse. Excessively fast improvements may prove spurious because the state of well being can rapidly turn into mental excitation. Alternatively, the false step may involve the patient or the analyst falling victim to the illusion that a stable improvement has been attained. Repetition of the crisis, as discussed in Chapter Seven, highlights the dilemma that arouses the anxiety of any analyst grappling with the therapy of the psychotic state: in what way can the therapeutic aim be said to have been achieved? The answer is bound up with the vexed question of whether or not the psychotic structure is amenable to transformation. Emergence from the psychotic state should coincide with the stable acquisition by the patient of an emotional competence that can help him to understand psychic reality and to tolerate the frustrations inherent in his relationship with the world.

A fundamental point emphasized in this book is the relationship between trauma and psychosis. I have contended that the absence of a primary object capable of conferring meaning on emotional communications prevents the child—the patient-to-be—from developing the capacity to understand and confront his own mental states. Obvious as it may be that repeated traumas in infancy, particularly if they stem from attachment figures, pave the way for the psychotic development, configurations—even where not explicitly violent or manifest—that take the form of actual distortions of basic emotional experiences are, in my view, equally pathogenic. Conditions of psychic absence or, conversely, intrusions into the child's mind by parent figures give rise to confusions and falsifications of identity, thus encouraging psychic withdrawal into a retreat structured in effect as an infantile laboratory of omnipotence and destruction of psychic reality. Helping a psychotic patient to develop emotional competence is, however, a complex and prolonged enterprise. We must, therefore, be prepared to work relentlessly in this deficient territory in order to develop the psychic functions that have hitherto lacked the possibility of stable structuring.

It is indeed the case that psychotic patients have never acquired a genuine personality structure. Their precarious identity ultimately collapses with the onset of the psychotic crisis, which sometimes coincides with the breaking off of an idealized link that in effect served as an adhesive. It is not by chance that psychotic crises occur most frequently in the transition from adolescence to maturity, a transition that calls for appropriate emotional competence. Patients who eventually suffer a psychotic crisis function as if they were living in the minds of others or in the world of imagination. When they come to analysis, they expect to re-establish the conditions that prevailed before the psychotic crisis: that is, they expect the recon-struction of the same pseudo-identity whereby they were seemingly able to function. Precisely for this reason, their attempt to adapt to reality deceives their family and friends and sometimes even the analyst; however, this illusion is shattered when a fresh crisis sweeps away the apparent integration. The object of analytic treat-ment must be the construction of a genuine personal identity. Thera-peutic progress must be evaluated in terms of the structuring of this new experience.

Starting with the pioneering work of Abraham and Ferenczi, analytic investigation of the psychotic state has benefited from the original and creative contributions of many authors. The theoretical developments that have periodically broadened the psychoanalytic horizon have extended the field of clinical operationality and rein-vigorated the therapy of psychotic patients. It may be wondered why I have not devoted more space in this book to the clinical con-tributions of analysts such as Fromm-Reichmann, Searles, Rosen-feld, or Benedetti, who grappled bravely and for years on end with the therapy of psychotic patients. The reason is that a review of their contributions would have been relatively unrewarding precisely because of the specificity of their therapeutic approaches, which are based on different clinical theories of the disorder. In other words, although the analytic literature on psychosis bears witness to the valuable heritage of many creative and intelligent analysts, psychoanalysis as a theoretical corpus as yet lacks a robust, overall conception of the psychotic process. The many probes launched into this space have not hitherto succeeded in supplying us with a complete and detailed map of the relevant terrain.

In this book I have attempted to identify certain specific forms of psychotic development and to cast new light on the route whereby the patient, starting in infancy, constructs the prison from which he will not easily emerge. In particular, I have sought to draw attention to the central problems encountered in treatment, on which the outcome of the therapeutic process depends. It is my hope that this book will contribute to clarifying the seemingly mysterious pathways that lead to psychotic illness and help to open up new perspectives for the understanding and therapy of this mental state.

Abraham, K. (1908). The psychosexual differences between hysteria and dementia praecox. In: K. Abraham, *Selected Papers on Psycho-Analysis*. D. Bryan & A. Strachey (Trans.) [reprinted London: Hogarth, 1973, pp. 64–79].

Abraham, K. (1912). Notes on the psychoanalytic investigation and treatment of manic-depressive insanity and allied conditions. In: K. Abraham, *Selected Papers on Psycho-Analysis* (pp. 137–156). D. Bryan & A. Strachey (Trans.). London: Hogarth, 1973.

Abraham, K. (1924). A short study of the development of the libido, viewed in the light of mental disorders. In: K. Abraham, *Selected Papers on Psycho-Analysis* (pp. 418–501). D. Bryan & A. Strachey (Trans.). London: Hogarth, 1973.

Arendt, H. (1943). We refugees. In: R. H. Feldman (Ed.), *The Jew as Pariah: Jewish Identity and Politics in the Modern Age* (pp. 55–66). New York: Grove Press, 1978.

Arieti, S. (1955). *Interpretation of Schizophrenia* (2nd edn). London: Crosby Lockwood Staples, 1974.

Arieti, S. (1963). The psychotherapy of schizophrenia in theory and practice. *Psychiatric Research Report, 17*: 13–29.

Arlow, J.A., & Brenner, C. (1969). The psychopathology of the psychoses: a proposed revision. *International Journal of Psychoanalysis, 50*: 5–14.

Aulagnier, P. (1975). *The Violence of Interpretation*, A. Sheridan (Trans.). Hove: Routledge, 2001.

Aulagnier, P. (1984). *L'apprenti-historien et le maître-sorcier—du discours identifiant au discours délirant*. Paris: Presses Universitaires de France.

Balint, M. (1968). *The Basic Fault: Therapeutic Aspects of Regression*. London: Tavistock.

Baranger, M. (1993). The mind of the analyst: from listening to interpretation. *International Journal of Psychoanalysis, 74*: 15–24.

Bateman, A. (1996). Psychic reality in borderline conditions (panel report). *International Journal of Psychoanalysis, 77*: 43–47.

Bateson, G. (Ed.) (1961). *Perceval's Narrative: A Patient's Account of His Psychosis*. Palo Alto: Stanford University Press.

Baudelaire, C. (1860). Un mangeur d'opium. In: *Les paradis artificiels: Opium et haschisch* (pp. 111–297). Paris: Poulet-Malassis et de Broise.

Benedetti, G. (1980). *Alienazione e personazione nella psicoterapia della malattia mentale*. Turin: Einaudi.

Bertrando, P. (1999). *Vivere la schizofrenia*. Turin: Bollati Boringhieri.

Bion, W. (1957). Differentiation of the psychotic from the non-psychotic personalities. *International Journal of Psychoanalysis, 38*: 266–275 [also in Bion (1967) pp. 43–64].

Bion, W. (1962a). *Learning from Experience*. London: Heinemann.

Bion, W. (1962b). The psycho-analytic study of thinking. *International Journal of Psychoanalysis, 43*: 306–310 [also in Bion (1967) pp. 110–119, as 'A theory of thinking'].

Bion, W. (1965). *Transformations*. London: Heinemann.

Bion, W. (1967). *Second Thoughts. Selected Papers on Psycho-Analysis*. London: Heinemann.

Bion, W. (1970). *Attention and Interpretation. A Scientific Approach to Insight in Psycho-Analysis and Groups*. London: Tavistock.

Bion, W. (1992). *Cogitations*. F. Bion (Ed.). London: Karnac.

Blechner, M. J. (1983). Changes in the dreams of borderline patients. *Contemporary Psychoanalysis, 19*: 485–498.

Blechner, M. J. (2000). Dreams that turn over a page. Letter to the editor. *International Journal of Psychoanalysis, 81*: 174.

Blechner, M. J. (2001). *The Dream Frontier*. London: Analytic Press.

Bleuler, E. (1911). *Dementia Praecox or the Group of Schizophrenias*. New York: International Universities Press, 1950.

Bollas, C. (1987). *The Shadow of the Object. Psychoanalysis of the Unthought Known*. London: Free Association.

Bollas, C. (1992). *Being a Character*. New York: Hill & Wang.

Borges, J. L. (1976). *Libro de sueños*. Buenos Aires: Torres Agüero.

Brenman, E. (1980). The value of reconstruction in adult psychoanalysis. In: E. Brenman, *Recovery of the Lost Good Object* (pp. 11–21). London: Routledge, 2006.

Brenman, E. (1987). Weekend Conference, London, 1986: Concluding remarks. *Psychoanalysis in Europe, 29*: 133–138.

Brenman, E. (2002a). Matters of life and death—real and assumed. In: E. Brenman, *Recovery of the Lost Good Object* (pp. 34–47). London: Routledge, 2006.

Brenman, E. (2002b). *Recovery of the Lost Good Object*. London: Routledge, 2006.

Brentano, F. (1874). *Psychology from an Empirical Standpoint*, O. Kraus (Ed.), A. C. Rancurello, D. B. Terrell & L. L. McAlister (Trans.). London: Routledge & Kegan Paul.

Caper, R. (1998). Psychopathology and primitive mental states. *International Journal of Psychoanalysis, 79*: 539–551.

Capozzi, P., & De Masi, F. (2001). The meaning of dreams in the psychotic state: theoretical considerations and clinical applications. *International Journal of Psychoanalysis, 82*: 933–952.

Cardinal, M. (1975). *The Words to Say It*. P. Goodheart (Trans.). London: Women's Press, 1993.

Carrère, E. (1993). *I Am Alive and You Are Dead: A Journey into the Mind of Philip K. Dick*. T. Bent (Trans.). New York: Metropolitan Books, Henry Holt, 2004.

Chianese, D. (2000). Sogno, visione, modernità (il sogno tra Antico e Moderno). In: *Il Sogno Cent'anni Dopo* (pp. 314–332). Turin: Bollati Boringhieri.

De Masi, F. (1988). Idealizzazione ed erotizzazione della relazione analitica. *Rivista di Psicoanalisi, 34*: 77–120.

De Masi, F. (1996). Strategie psichiche verso l'autoannientamento. *Rivista di Psicoanalisi, 44*: 549–566.

De Masi, F. (1997). Intimidation at the helm: superego and hallucinations in the analytic treatment of a psychosis. *International Journal of Psychoanalysis, 78*: 561–575.

De Masi, F. (1999). *The Sadomasochistic Perversion: The Entity and the Theories*. P. Slotkin (Trans.). London: Karnac, 2003.

De Masi, F. (2000a). The unconscious and psychosis. Some considerations on the psychoanalytic theory of psychosis. *International Journal of Psychoanalysis, 81*: 1–20.

De Masi, F. (2000b). L'inconscio nella psicoanalisi contemporanea. *L'Inconscio. Prospettive attuali, 4*: 85–99.

De Masi, F. (2002). Quale Super-io nella clinica analitica? *Rivista di Psicoanalisi, 48*: 517–535.

De Masi, F. (2003). On the nature of intuitive and delusional thought: its implications in clinical work with psychotic patients. *International Journal of Psychoanalysis, 84*: 1149–1169.

De Masi, F. (2004). The psychodynamics of panic attacks: a useful integration of psychoanalysis and neuroscience. *International Journal of Psychoanalysis, 85*: 311–336.

De Masi, F. (2006). Psychotic withdrawal and the overthrow of psychic reality. *International Journal of Psychoanalysis, 87*: 1–18.

de Nerval, G. (1855). Aurélia. In: *Aurélia and Other Writings*. Berkeley, CA: Exact Change.

Di Caccia, A., & Recalcati, M. (2000). *Jacques Lacan*. Milan: Paravia Bruno Mondadori.

Dick, P. (1981). *Valis*. London: Gollancz, 2001.

Di Francesco, M. (1998). *L'Io e i suoi sé. Identità personale e scienza della mente*. Milan: Raffaello Cortina.

Edelman, G. M. (1992). *Bright Air, Brilliant Fire. On the Matter of the Mind*. London: Allen Lane.

Einstein, A. (1949). *Albert Einstein: Philosopher–Scientist*, P.A. Schilpp (Ed.). Library of Living Philosophers. New York: Tudor, 1951.

Emde, R. N. (1989). The infant's relationship experience: developmental and affective aspects. In: A. J. Sameroff & R. N. Emde (Eds.), *Relationship Disturbances in Early Childhood: The Developmental Approach* (pp. 33–51). New York: Basic Books.

Fairbairn, W. R. D. (1952). *Psychoanalytic Studies of the Personality*. London: Tavistock.

Federn, P. (1952). *Ego Psychology and the Psychoses*. London: Imago, 1953.

Fenichel, O. (1945). *The Psychoanalytic Theory of Neurosis*. London: Routledge & Kegan Paul, 1963.

Ferenczi, S. (1928). The elasticity of psycho-analytical technique. In: M. Balint (Ed.), *Final Contributions to the Problems and Methods of Psycho-Analysis* (pp. 87–101). London: Hogarth, 1955.

Ferenczi, S. (1929). The unwelcome child and his death-instinct. In: M. Balint (Ed.), *Final Contributions to the Problems and Methods of Psycho-Analysis* (pp. 102–107). London: Hogarth, 1955.

Ferenczi, S. (1933). Confusion of tongues between adults and the child. In: M. Balint (Ed.), *Final Contributions to the Problems and Methods of Psycho-Analysis* (pp. 156–167). London: Hogarth, 1955.

Fonagy, P. (1999). Memory and therapeutic action. *International Journal of Psychoanalysis, 80*: 215–223.

Fonagy, P., & Target, M. (1996). Playing with reality: I. Theory of mind and the normal development of psychic reality. *International Journal of Psychoanalysis, 77*: 217–233.

Fonagy, P., Steele, M., Steele, H., Leigh, T., Kennedy, R., Mattoon, G., & Target, M. (1995). Attachment, the reflective self, and borderline states. In: S. Goldberg, R. Muir & J. Kerr (Eds.), *Attachment Theory: Social, Developmental and Clinical Perspectives*. London: Routledge.

Fonagy, P., Target, M., Gergely, G., Allen, J. G., & Bateman, A. W. (2003). The developmental roots of borderline personality disorder in early attachment relationships: a theory and some evidence. *Psychoanalytic Inquiry, 23*: 412–459.

Fornaro, M. (1990). *Psicoanalisi tra scienza e mistica. L'opera di Wilfred R. Bion*. Rome: Studium.

Frankl, V. (1964). *Man's Search for Meaning: An Introduction to Logotherapy*, I. Lasch et al. (Trans.). London: Hodder & Stoughton.

Freeman, T. (2001). Treating and studying schizophrenias. In: P. Williams (Ed.), *A Language for Psychosis. Psychoanalysis of Psychotic States* (pp. 54–69). London: Whurr.

Freud, A. (1967). Comments on psychic trauma. In: *The Writings of Anna Freud: Problems of Psychoanalytic Training, Diagnosis, and the Technique of Therapy* (pp. 221–241), Vol. 5. New York: International Universities Press.

Freud, A. (1968). Difficulties in the path of psychoanalysis: a confrontation of past and present viewpoints. In: *The Writings of Anna Freud: Problems of Psychoanalytic Training, Diagnosis, and the Technique of Therapy* (pp. 124–156), Vol. 7. New York: International Universities Press.

Freud, S. (1900a). *The Interpretation of Dreams. S.E., 4–5*. London: Hogarth.

Freud, S. (1905e). Fragment of an analysis of a case of hysteria. *S.E., 7*: 3–124. London: Hogarth.

Freud, S. (1905d). *Three Essays on the Theory of Sexuality. S.E., 7*: 125–248. London: Hogarth.

Freud, S. (1911c). Psycho-analytic notes on an autobiographical account of a case of paranoia (dementia paranoides). *S.E., 12*: 3–84. London: Hogarth.

Freud, S. (1911)(1911b). Formulations on the two principles of mental functioning. *S.E., 12*: 213–226. London: Hogarth.

Freud, S. (1912a)(1912b). The dynamics of transference. *S.E., 12*: 97–108. London: Hogarth.

Freud, S. (1912e). Recommendations to physicians practising psychoanalysis. *S.E., 12*: 109–120. London: Hogarth.

Freud, S. (1912–1913). *Totem and Taboo*. *S.E.*, *13*: 1–164. London: Hogarth.

Freud, S. (1915e). The unconscious. *S.E.*, *14*: 159–204. London: Hogarth.

Freud, S. (1917d). A metapsychological supplement to the theory of dreams. *S.E.*, *14*: 217–236. London: Hogarth.

Freud, S. (1917e). Mourning and melancholia. *S.E.*, *14*: 237–258. London: Hogarth.

Freud, S. (1920g). *Beyond the Pleasure Principle*. *S.E.*, *18*: 1–64. London: Hogarth.

Freud, S. (1923b). *The Ego and the Id*. *S.E.*, *19*: 3–68. London: Hogarth.

Freud, S. (1923c). Remarks on the theory and practice of dream-interpretation. *S.E.*, *19*: 109–139. London: Hogarth.

Freud, S. (1924b). Neurosis and psychosis. *S.E.*, *19*: 149–156. London: Hogarth.

Freud, S. (1925d). *An Autobiographical Study*. *S.E.*, *20*: 3–76). London: Hogarth.

Freud, S. (1924e). The loss of reality in neurosis and psychosis. *S.E.*, *19*: 183–190. London: Hogarth.

Freud, S. (1924f). A short account of psycho-analysis. *S.E.*, *19*: 191–212. London: Hogarth.

Freud, S. (1927e). Fetishism. *S.E.*, *21*: 152–158. London: Hogarth.

Freud, S. (1930a). *Civilization and Its Discontents*. *S.E.*, *21*: 59–148. London: Hogarth.

Freud, S. (1940e [1938]). Splitting of the ego in the process of defence. *S.E.*, *23*: 271–278). London: Hogarth.

Freud, S. (1940a [1938]). *An Outline of Psycho-Analysis*. *S.E.*, *23*: 141–208. London: Hogarth.

Freud, S. (1985). *The Complete Letters of Sigmund Freud to Wilhelm Fliess 1887–1904*, J. M. Masson (Ed. & Trans.). Cambridge, MA: Belknap Press of Harvard University Press.

Freud, S., & Abraham, K. (1965). *A Psycho-Analytic Dialogue: The Letters of Sigmund Freud and Karl Abraham 1907–1926*. H. C. Abraham & E. L. Freud (Eds.), B. Marsh & H. C. Abraham (Trans.). London: Hogarth [reprinted London: Karnac, 2002].

García Badaracco, J. (1983). Reflexiones sobre sueño y psicosis a la luz de la experiencia clínica. *Revista de Psicoanálisis*, *40*: 693–709.

García Badaracco, J., & Mariotti, P. (2000). Affect and psychosis (Panel report). *International Journal of Psychoanalysis*, *81*: 149–152.

Ghiron, V. (2001). *La teoria dell'immaginazione di Edmund Husserl*. Padua: Marsilio.

Ghent, E. (1990). Masochism, submission, surrender—masochism as a perversion of surrender. *Contemporary Psychoanalysis, 26*: 108–136.

Gilberg, A. (1974). Asceticism and the analysis of a nun. *Journal of the American Psychoanalytic Association, 22*: 381–393.

Goncharov, I. (1858). *Oblomov*. D. Magarshack (Trans.). Harmondsworth: Penguin, 1978.

Green, A. (1977). The borderline concept. In: P. Hartocollis (Ed.), *Borderline Personality Disorders: The Concept, The Syndrome, The Patient* (pp. 15–44). New York: International Universities Press.

Green, J. (1947). *If I Were You*. J. Hellas & F. McEwen (Trans.). New York: Harper, 1949.

Grinberg, L., Sor, D., & De Bianchedi, E. (1974). Bion's concepts of psychosis. *Contemporary Psychoanalysis, 10*: 157–171.

Grotstein, J. (1981). Who is the dreamer who dreams the dream and who is the dreamer who understands it? In: *A Memorial to Wilfred R. Bion* (pp. 1–36). Beverly Hills: Caesura.

Hadamard, J. (1945). *An Essay on the Psychology of Invention in the Mathematical Field*. Princeton, NJ: Princeton University Press, 1996.

Hamilton-Merritt, J. (1976). *A Meditator's Diary: A Western Woman's Unique Experiences in Thailand Monasteries*. London: Souvenir Press.

Henry, M. (1985). *Généalogie de la psychanalyse*. Paris: Presses Universitaires de France.

Hartmann, H. (1953). Contribution to the metapsychology of schizophrenia. In: *Essays on Ego Psychology* (pp. 182–206). New York: International Universities Press, 1964.

Hunter, V. (1994). *Psychoanalysts Talk*. New York: Guilford Press.

Isaacs, S. (1952). The nature and function of phantasy. In: M. Klein, P. Heimann, S. Isaacs, & J. Riviere (Eds.), *Developments in Psycho-Analysis* (pp. 67–121). London: Hogarth [reprinted London: Karnac, 2002].

Katan, M. (1954). The importance of the non-psychotic part of the personality in schizophrenia. *International Journal of Psychoanalysis, 35*: 119–128.

Katan, M. (1960). Dream and psychosis: their relation to hallucinatory processes. *International Journal of Psychoanalysis, 41*: 341–351.

Kernberg, O. (1968). The treatment of patients with borderline personality organization. *International Journal of Psychoanalysis, 49*: 600–619.

Kernberg, O. (1975). *Borderline Conditions and Pathological Narcissism*. New York: Jason Aronson.

Kierkegaard, S. (1849). *The Sickness Unto Death*. A. Hannay (Trans.). Harmondsworth: Penguin, 1989.

Kihlstrom, J. E. (1987). The cognitive unconscious. *Science, 237*: 1445–1452.

Klein, M. (1929). Personification in the play of children. In: *Contributions to Psycho-Analysis 1921–1945* (pp. 215–226). London: Hogarth, 1965.

Klein, M. (1930a). The importance of symbol-formation in the development of the ego. In: *Contributions to Psycho-Analysis 1921–1945* (pp. 236–250). London: Hogarth, 1965.

Klein, M. (1946). Notes on some schizoid mechanisms. In: *Envy and Gratitude and Other Works 1946–1963*. London: Hogarth, 1987.

Klein, M. (1955). On identification. In: *Envy and Gratitude and Other Works 1946–1963*. London: Hogarth, 1987.

Klein, M. (1958). On the development of mental functioning. In: *Envy and Gratitude and Other Works 1946–1963*. London: Hogarth, 1975.

Lacan, J. (1966). *Ecrits*. Paris: Editions du Seuil.

Laplanche, J., & Pontalis, J.-B. (2003). Fantasy and the origin of sexuality. In: R. Steiner (Ed.), *Unconscious Phantasy*. London: Karnac.

LeDoux, J. (1996). *The Emotional Brain. The Mysterious Underpinnings of Emotional Life*. London: Weidenfeld & Nicolson.

LeDoux, J. (2002). *Synaptic Self: How Our Brains Become Who We Are*. New York: Viking.

Little, M. (1958). On delusional transference (transference psychosis). *International Journal of Psychoanalysis, 39*: 134–138.

Loewald, H. W. (1966). Book review: psychoanalytic concepts and the structural theory. *Psychoanalytic Quarterly, 35*: 430–436.

London, N. J. (1973). An essay on psychoanalytic theory: Two theories of schizophrenia. *International Journal of Psychoanalysis, 54*: 169–193.

Mack, J. E. (1969). Dreams and psychosis. *Journal of the American Psychoanalytic Association, 17*: 206–221.

McGrath, P. (1990). *Spider*. London: Viking.

Meltzer, D. (1973). *Sexual States of Mind*. Strath Tay, Perthshire: Clunie Press.

Meltzer, D. (1984). *Dream Life*. Strath Tay, Perthshire: Clunie Press.

Money-Kyrle, R. (1971). The aim of psychoanalysis. *International Journal of Psychoanalysis, 52*: 103–106.

Nacht, S., & Racamier, P. C. (1958). La théorie psychanalytique du délire. *Revue Française de Psychanalyse, 22*: 418–508.

Nagel, T. (1974). What is it like to be a bat? In: N. Warburton (Ed.), *Philosophy: Basic Readings* (pp. 422–433) (2nd edn). London: Routledge, 2004.

Nasar, S. (1998). *A Beautiful Mind*. London: Faber & Faber.

Nissim Momigliano, L., & Robutti, A. (Eds.) (1992). *Shared Experience: The Psychoanalytic Dialogue*. London: Karnac.

Ogden, T. (1982). *Projective Identification and Psychotherapeutic Technique*. Northvale, NJ: Jason Aronson.

O'Shaughnessy, E. (1981). A clinical study of a defensive organization. *International Journal of Psychoanalysis, 62*: 359–369.

Pally, R. (1997). Memory: brain systems that link past, present and future. *International Journal of Psychoanalysis, 78*: 1223–1234.

Pao, P.-N. (1979). *Schizophrenic Disorders*. New York: International Universities Press.

Podvoll, E. M. (1990). *The Seduction of Madness: Revolutionary Insights into the World of Psychosis and a Compassionate Approach to Recovery at Home*. New York: HarperCollins.

Poincaré, H. (1908). *Science et méthode*. Paris: Flammarion, 1968.

Pontalis, J.-B. (1977). *Frontiers in Psychoanalysis: Between the Dream and Psychic Pain*. London: Hogarth, 1981.

Quinodoz, J.-M. (1999). Dreams that turn over a page: integration dreams with paradoxical regressive content. *International Journal of Psychoanalysis, 80*: 225–238.

Quinodoz, J.-M. (2000). Response (to M. J. Blechner). *International Journal of Psychoanalysis, 81*: 175.

Quinodoz, J.-M. (2001). *Dreams That Turn Over a Page: Paradoxical Dreams in Psychoanalysis*. P. Slotkin (Trans.). Hove: Brunner-Routledge, 2002.

Racamier, P. C. (1976). Rêve et psychose: rêve ou psychose. *Revue Française de Psychanalyse, 40*: 173–193.

Racamier, P. C. (1994). Interview with Giuseppe Marini. *Interazioni, 1*: 103–110.

Racamier, P. C. (2000). Un espace pour délirer. *Revue Française de Psychanalyse, 64*: 823–829.

Rinaldi, L. (Ed.) (2003). *Stati caotici della mente*. Milan: Raffaello Cortina.

Riolo, F. (1983). Sogno e teoria della conoscenza in psicoanalisi. *Rivista di Psicoanalisi, 29*: 279–295.

Roberts, D. C. (2000). Discussion review: The unconscious and psychosis: some considerations on the psychoanalytic theory of psychosis by Franco De Masi. *International Journal of Psychoanalysis, 81*: 625–635.

Rosenfeld, H. (1952). Notes on the psycho-analysis of the super-ego conflict in an acute catatonic patient. *International Journal of Psychoanalysis, 33*: 111–131.

Rosenfeld, H. (1965). *Psychotic States*. London: Hogarth.

Rosenfeld, H. (1969). On the treatment of psychotic states by psychoanalysis: an historical approach. *International Journal of Psychoanalysis, 50*: 615–631.

Rosenfeld, H. (1971). A clinical approach to the psychoanalytic theory of the life and death instincts. An investigation into the aggressive aspects of narcissism. *International Journal of Psychoanalysis, 52*: 169–178.

Rosenfeld, H. (1978). Notes on the psychopathology and psychoanalytic treatment of some borderline patients. *International Journal of Psychoanalysis, 59*: 215–221.

Rosenfeld, H. (1979). Transference psychosis. In: J. LeBoit & A. Capponi (Eds.), *Advances in Psychotherapy of the Borderline Patient* (pp. 187–206). New York: Jason Aronson.

Rosenfeld, H. (1997). *Herbert Rosenfeld at Work. The Italian Seminars*. F. De Masi (Ed.), A. Victor (Trans.). London: Karnac.

Roussillon, R. (2001). *Le plaisir et la répétition. Théorie du processus psychique*. Paris: Dunod.

Sandler, J., & Sandler, A. M. (1987). The past unconscious, the present unconscious and the vicissitudes of guilt. *International Journal of Psychoanalysis, 68*: 331–341.

Schnitzler, A. (1925). *Dream Story*. J. M. Q. Davies (Trans.). Harmondsworth: Penguin, 1999.

Schreber, D. P. (1903). *Memoirs of My Nervous Illness*. I. Macalpine & R. Hunter (Ed. & Trans.). London: Dawson, 1955.

Searles, H. (1965). *Collected Papers on Schizophrenia and Related Subjects*. New York: International Universities Press.

Searles, H. (1979). The schizophrenic's individual experience of his world. In: *Countertransference and Related Subjects: Selected Papers*. New York: International Universities Press.

Segal, H. (1954). A note on schizoid mechanisms underlying phobia formation. *International Journal of Psychoanalysis, 35*: 238–241.

Segal, H. (1956). Depression in the schizophrenic. *International Journal of Psychoanalysis, 37*: 339–343.

Segal, H. (1991). *Dream, Phantasy, and Art*. London: Routledge.

Shevrin, H. (1986). Subliminal perception and dreaming. *The Journal of Mind and Behavior, 7*(2–3): 379–396.

Sohn, L. (1995). Unprovoked assaults—making sense of apparently random violence. *International Journal of Psychoanalysis, 76*: 565–575.

Sparti, D. (2000). *Identità e coscienza*. Bologna: Il Mulino.

Steiner, J. (1982). Relationships between parts of the self: a clinical illustration. *International Journal of Psychoanalysis, 63*: 241–251.

Steiner, J. (1991). A psychotic organization of the personality. *International Journal of Psychoanalysis, 72*: 201–207.

Steiner, J. (1993). *Psychic Retreats: Pathological Organisations of the Personality in Psychotic, Neurotic, and Borderline Patients.* London: Routledge.

Stolorow, R. D., & Atwood, G. E. (1992). *Contexts of Being: The Intersubjective Foundations of Psychological Life.* Hillsdale, NJ: Analytic Press.

Strachey, J. (1934). The nature of the therapeutic action of psychoanalysis. *International Journal of Psychoanalysis, 15*: 127–159.

Sutin, L. (1989). *Divine Invasions: A Life of Philip K. Dick.* London: Paladin, 1991.

Tarizzo, D. (2003). *Introduzione a Lacan.* Rome: Laterza.

Werbart, A., & Levander, S. (2005). Understanding the incomprehensible: private theories of first-episode psychotic patients and their therapists. *Bulletin of the Menninger Clinic, 69*: 103–136.

Werbart, A., & Linbom-Jakobson, M. (2001). The "living dead" survivors of torture and psychosis. In: Williams, P. (Ed.), *A Language for Psychosis. Psychoanalysis of Psychotic States.* London: Whurr.

Werbart A. (2002). Discussion review: The meaning of dreams in the psychotic state: theoretical considerations and clinical applications: Paola Capozzi and Franco De Masi. *International Journal of Psychoanalysis, 83*: 551–563.

Wexler, M. (1971). Schizophrenia: conflict and deficiency. *Psychoanalytic Quarterly, 40*: 83–99.

Williams, P. (1998). Discussion review: "Psychopathology and primitive mental states" by Robert Caper. *International Journal of Psychoanalysis, 79*: 1055–1064.

Winnicott, D. (1952). Psychoses and child care. In: *Collected Papers: Through Paediatrics to Psycho-Analysis* (pp. 219–228). New York: Basic Books, 1958.

Winnicott, D. (1954). Metapsychological and clinical aspects of regression within the psycho-analytic set-up. In: *Collected Papers: Through Paediatrics to Psycho-Analysis* (pp. 278–294). New York: Basic Books, 1958.

Winnicott, D. (1965). *The Family and Individual Development.* London: Tavistock.

Winnicott, D. (1971). Dreaming, fantasying, and living: a case-history describing a primary dissociation. In: *Playing and Reality* (pp. 26–37). London: Tavistock.

Winnicott, D. (1987). *The Spontaneous Gesture: Selected Letters of D. W. Winnicott*. F. R. Rodman (Ed.). London: Karnac.

INDEX

model(s)
continuity-based, 3–4, 11
discontinuity-based, 3–4
Money-Kyrle, R., 28–29, 216, 300
mother *see also*: depression, violence
–child relationship, 19, 21–22, 24,
251–253, 287
grand-, 139, 282
step-, 128, 179

Nacht, S., 227, 300
Nagel, T., 263, 300
Name-of-the-Father, 21–22
narcissism, xxi, 7, 117, 120, 122, 136,
165, 197, 259, 280, 282–283
see also: neurosis
destructive, 32–33, 122, 175, 279
primary, 2, 9, 22
Nasar, S., 142, 263, 301
Nash, J., 142
neuroscience, xxix–xxx, 54–55,
58–59, 153, 239, 251, 288
neurosis, xx, 4–6, 9–10, 13, 15, 39,
46, 60–61, 97, 190, 219, 249,
286–287
narcissistic, 189
transference, 175, 190
neurotic
dream(s), 82
patient(s), xxiv, xxviii, 4, 10, 19,
21, 29, 67, 72, 130, 190, 194, 219
transference, 192–193
Nissim Momigliano, L., 58, 171, 301

object, xx, xxviii, 5–14, 16, 19–21,
48–50, 59, 61–62, 67, 72, 81–83,
93, 95, 98, 100, 108, 111, 116,
122–124, 139, 152, 157, 160, 164,
175, 178, 182, 184–186, 191, 193,
200, 204, 210, 214, 216–219, 224,
226–228, 239, 241–242, 250, 252,
256, 261, 275, 277, 282
bad, 19, 50, 84, 175, 203, 255
external, 8–10, 12, 19, 33, 42, 116,
182, 215
good, 10, 33, 50, 175, 203, 276

internal, 16, 21, 33, 49, 81, 122,
190, 209
love, 10
new, 186–187
primary, 16, 21, 62, 172, 220, 233,
250, 291
relationship, 10, 27, 49, 51, 62, 73,
175, 190, 218, 226, 228, 253
Ogden, T., xix, 58, 119, 301
omnipotence, xix, 10, 18, 21, 26–28,
30–31, 35, 39, 43–44, 53, 62,
65–67, 71–72, 87, 95–96, 102,
122–124, 149, 151–152, 157–158,
163–166, 185, 200, 207, 217,
223–224, 226–228, 230, 241–242,
247, 253, 255, 274–275, 291
see also: fantasy
O'Shaughnessy, E., 33, 301

Pally, R., 54, 301
Pao, P.-N., xix, xxi, xxiii, 15–16, 38,
118–119, 301
paranoid-schizoid position, 10–11,
16–17, 24, 26, 30, 33, 51, 185,
287
pathological
identification, 150, 243, 278, 282
organization, 15, 62, 226–227, 232
structure, xxi, xxix, 31, 33–34,
132–133, 137, 186, 210, 226, 232,
239, 250
patient(s) *see* neurotic, psychotic
Perceval, J., 39–44, 255, 266, 290
personal identity, xxvii, 13, 18, 24,
60, 62, 65, 67, 72, 97, 118, 159,
163, 166, 215–216, 232, 237,
239–240, 247, 254, 292
pleasure, 23, 32, 34, 40, 43–44,
85–87, 125, 143, 145, 193,
223–225, 228–230, 242, 253,
266–268
principle, 48, 166–167
sensual, 38, 39, 113, 125
Podvoll, E. M., 40, 255, 301
Poincaré , H., 144–145, 301
Pontalis, J.-B., 82, 218, 300–301